Globalex Workshop on Linked Lexicography (GWLL 2022)

Held at LREC 2022

Marseille, France
20 – 25 June 2022

Editors:

Ilan Kernerman
Simon Krek

ISBN: 978-1-7138-6122-5

Printed from e-media with permission by:

Curran Associates, Inc.
57 Morehouse Lane
Red Hook, NY 12571

Some format issues inherent in the e-media version may also appear in this print version.

Association for Computational Linguistics
209 N. Eighth Street
Stroudsburg, Pennsylvania 18360

Phone: 1-570-476-8006
Fax: 1-570-476-0860

acl@aclweb.org

Additional copies of this publication are available from:

Curran Associates, Inc.
57 Morehouse Lane
Red Hook, NY 12571 USA
Phone: 845-758-0400
Fax: 845-758-2633
Email: curran@proceedings.com
Web: www.proceedings.com

LREC 2022 Workshop
Language Resources and Evaluation Conference
20-25 June 2022

Proceedings of Globalex Workshop on Linked Lexicography (GWLL)

PROCEEDINGS

Editors: Ilan Kernerman, Simon Krek

globaLex

Proceedings of the LREC 2022 workshop Globalex Workshop on Linked Lexicography (GWLL 2022)

Edited by: Ilan Kernerman and Simon Krek

For more information:
European Language Resources Association (ELRA)
9 rue des Cordelières
75013, Paris
France
http://www.elra.info
Email: lrec@elda.org

Preface to the Proceedings of

Globalex Workshop on Linked Lexicography

Globalex Workshop on Linked Lexicography (GWLL 2022) is the fourth iteration of the GLOBALEX full-day workshop series held in conjunction with LREC. It pursues and expands the topic of linking data across lexicographic resources and with other lexical resources – in the aim of enhancing language data methodologies and applications – which was the focus of our third workshop at LREC 2020 that was cancelled due to the COVID-19 pandemic. Earlier on, the second workshop at LREC 2018 had the main theme of Lexicography and WordNets, and it followed on the first workshop at LREC 2016, on Lexicographic Resources and Human Language Technology.

These proceedings feature 11 papers (including one extended abstract) highlighting lexicographic issues related to linguistic linked data, wordnets, dictionary generation, sign language, collocations, senses, and word formation and morphology, as well as two papers stemming from the fifth edition of TIAD shared task on Translation Inference Across Dictionaries.

We would like to thank all the authors, our colleagues in TIAD and the Review Committee, namely Thierry Declerck, Jorge Gracia, Besim Kabashi, Iztok Kosem, Nikola Ljubešić, and John McCrae, as well as Teja Goli, ELRA, ELEXIS and GLOBALEX, for their contribution to GWLL @ LREC 2022.

Ilan Kernerman and Simon Krek

Organizers

Ilan Kernerman – K Dictionaries – Lexicala
Simon Krek – Institut Jožef Stefan

TIAD 2022 Organizers:

Jorge Gracia – University of Zaragoza, Aragon Institute of Engineering Research (I3A)
Besim Kabashi – University of Erlangen-Nurenberg, Corpus and Computational Linguistics
Ilan Kernerman – K Dictionaries – Lexicala

Review Committee:

Thierry Declerck, DFKI (GERMANY)
Jorge Gracia, University of Zaragoza (SPAIN)
Besim Kabashi, University of Erlangen-Nurenberg (GERMANY)
Ilan Kernerman, K Dictionaries – Lexicala (ISRAEL)
Iztok Kosem, Institut Jožef Stefan (SLOVENIA)
Simon Krek, Institut Jožef Stefan (SLOVENIA)
Nikola Ljubešić, Institut Jožef Stefan (SLOVENIA)
John McCrae, National University of Ireland, Galway (IRELAND)

Table of Contents

Workshop Program

Monday, June 20, 2022

9:00–9:05	*Welcome*
9:05–9:35	*Towards the Profiling of Linked Lexicographic Resources* Lenka Bajcetic, Seung-bin Yim and Thierry Declerck
9:35–10:05	*Towards the Linking of a Sign Language Ontology with Lexical Data* Thierry Declerck
10:05–10:35	*Modelling Collocations in OntoLex-FrAC* Christian Chiarcos, Katerina Gkirtzou, Maxim Ionov, Besim Kabashi, Fahad Khan and Ciprian-Octavian Truică
10:35–11:05	*Coffee Break*
11:05–11:20	**GLOBALEX – Overview and Update** Ilan Kernerman
11:20–11:50	*Creating Bilingual Dictionaries from Existing Ones by Means of Pivot-Oriented Translation Inference and Logistic Regression* Yves Bestgen
11:50–12:20	*Compiling a Highly Accurate Bilingual Lexicon by Combining Different Approaches* Steinþór Steingrímsson, Luke O'Brien, Finnur Ingimundarson, Hrafn Loftsson and Andy Way
12:20–12:50	*A Category Theory Framework for Sense Systems* David Strohmaier and Gladys Tyen
12:50–14:00	*Lunch Break*
14:00–14:30	**ELEXIS – Overview and Update** Simon Krek

Monday, June 20, 2022 (continued)

14:30–15:00 *Converting a Database of Complex German Word Formation for Linked Data*
Petra Steiner

15:00–15:30 *Resolving Inflectional Ambiguity of Macedonian Adjectives*
Katerina Zdravkova

15:30–16:00 *Morpholex Turkish: A Morphological Lexicon for Turkish*
Bilge Arican, Aslı Kuzgun, Büşra Marşan, Deniz Baran Aslan, Ezgi Saniyar, Neslihan Cesur, Neslihan Kara, Oguzhan Kuyrukcu, Merve Ozcelik, Arife Betul Yenice, Merve Dogan, Ceren Oksal, Gökhan Ercan and Olcay Taner Yıldız

16:00–16:30 *Coffee Break*

16:30–17:00 *Time Travel in Turkish: WordNets for Modern Turkish*
Ceren Oksal, Hikmet N. Oguz, Mert Catal, Nurkay Erbay, Ozgecan Yuzer, Ipek B. Unsal, Oguzhan Kuyrukcu, Arife B. Yenice, Aslı Kuzgun, Büşra Marşan, Ezgi Sanıyar, Bilge Arican, Merve Dogan, Özge Bakay and Olcay Taner Yıldız

17:00–17:30 *WordNet and Wikipedia Connection in Turkish WordNet KeNet*
Merve Doğan, Ceren Oksal, Arife Betül Yenice, Fatih Beyhan, Reyyan Yeniterzi and Olcay Taner Yıldız

17:30–18:00 *Homonymy Information for English WordNet*
Rowan Hall Maudslay and Simone Teufel

18:00–18:05 *Closing*

Proceedings of the Globalex Workshop on Linked Lexicography @LREC2022, pages 1–5
Marseille, 20 June 2022

Towards the Profiling of Linked Lexicographic Resources

Lenka Bajčetić[1], Seung-Bin Yim[1], Thierry Declerck[2]
[1] Austrian Centre for Digital Humanities and Cultural Heritage, Austrian Academy of Sciences, Vienna, Austria
[2] DFKI GmbH, Multilinguality and Language Technology Lab, Saarland University Campus D3 2, Germany
[1]Lenka.Bajcetic@oeaw.ac.at, Seung-Bin.Yim@oeaw.ac.at, declerck@dfki.de

Abstract

This paper presents Edie: ELEXIS Dictionary Evaluator. Edie is designed to create profiles for lexicographic resources accessible through the ELEXIS platform. These profiles can be used to evaluate and compare lexicographic resources, and in particular they can be used to identify potential data that could be linked.

Keywords: ELEXIS, Lexicographic Profiling, Dictionary evaluation

1. Introduction

The work described in this paper is done in the context of the ELEXIS project,[1] which is dealing with the building of a large European lexicographic infrastructure. It pursues this goal by providing the lexicographic infrastructure with interactions with Natural Language Processing (NLP) tools and resources, for both access to and creation of linked lexical data. The resulting multilingual infrastructure is intended to be used by academics, students, researchers, programmers, dictionary creators, etc.

At the core of ELEXIS is the so-called dictionary matrix, a universal repository of linked senses, meaning descriptions, etymological data, collocations, phraseology, translation equivalents, examples of usage and all other types of lexical information found in all types of existing lexicographic resources, multilingual, monolingual, modern, historical etc. Data from the dictionary matrix is available through a RESTful Web service, which also make the data available for consumption through tools to Sketch Engine and Lexonomy.[2] Edie is situated at this access interface. Figure 1 shows the overall architecture of ELEXIS and the place the dictionary matrix has in this infrastructure.

ELEXIS offers a well-defined interface (McCrae et al., 2019) that supports the access to the data sets hosted by the ELEXIS infrastructure, but it also guides users by the creation, modification, and publication of dictionaries with the ELEXIS infrastructure. Figure 2 sketches the access procedure to (linked) lexical data included in the dictionary matrix, where we can see that the data is serialized in three different formats: TEI,[3] OntoLex-Lemon,[4] or JSON.[5] This is the lexical data which EDIE is accessing and profiling. Edie can retrieve this data via the Lexonomy interface as a dictionary, a lexical entry or a lemma, and generate profiles based on this information, both at the level of metadata and data.
Table 1shows the kind of information Edie is accessing, when querying for a dictionary within the ELEXIS infrastructure.
and the Table 2 shows the type of information that is accessed by Edie when querying for an individual entry of a dictionary.
Edie can also access lemma information.
Since there are numerous possible use-cases, as well as different types of end users, we needed to create a generic dictionary assessment tool which would work best under these ambiguous circumstances. Since we cannot make any definitive assumptions regarding the goal of the end users and their priorities regarding dictionary quality, we have decided to create a tool which would leave the final evaluation to the end users, while providing them with a profile with enough information to make their own estimate. The tool is described in the next section.

2. Edie

EDIE is an acronym for the ELEXIS DIctionary Assessment tool[6]. This tool is aimed to assist users with context-dependent qualitative assessment of linguistic resources by creating lexicographic profiles which can be easily compared and evaluated by the end user.

2.1. Implementation

The EDIE infrastructure consists of three main components:

- the main evaluator which consists of three evaluator modules

[1]See `https://elex.is/` and (Woldrich et al., 2021) for more details.

[2]See `https://www.sketchengine.eu/` and `https://www.lexonomy.eu/` repsectively

[3]See `https://dariah-eric.github.io/lexicalresources/pages/TEILex0/TEILex0.html`

[4]See `https://www.w3.org/2016/05/ontolex/`

[5]See `https://www.json.org/json-en.html`

[6]The code is available here: https://github.com/ELEXIS-eu/edie and the service will be deployed shortly on the ELEXIS platform

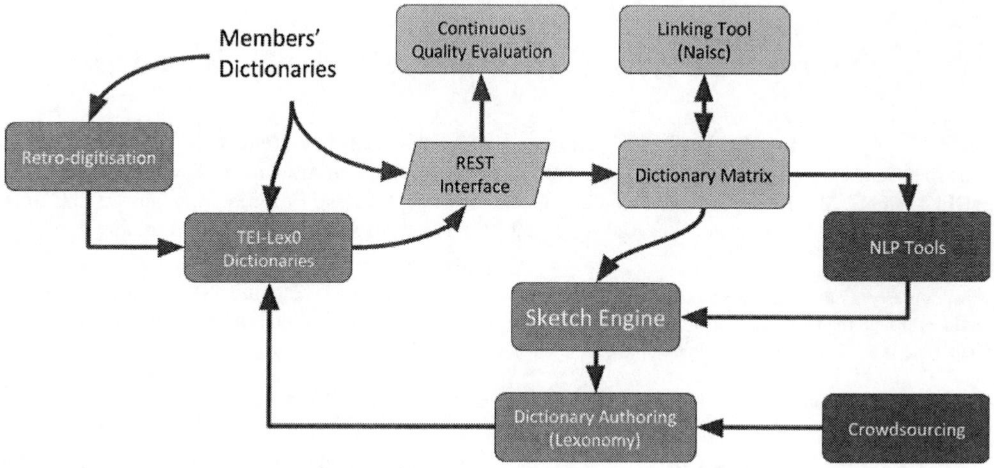

Figure 1: The interface for accessing lexical data in the dictionary matrix, taken from (McCrae et al., 2019)

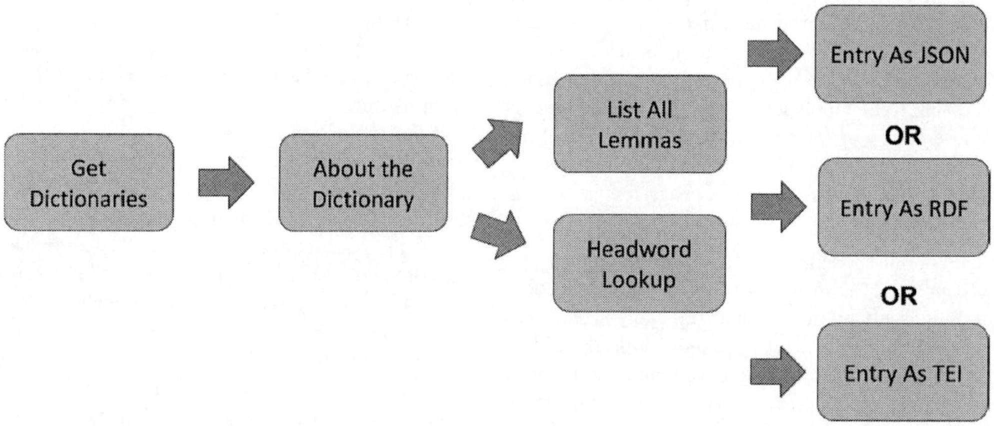

Figure 2: Overall Architecture of ELEXIS, taken from (McCrae et al., 2019)

- API client which retrieves necessary data
- helper functions

The three evaluator modules are designed to assess different aspects of the resources, and in combination they create the resource's profile. The content of a lexical resource is represented on entry level by a model which has all the fields an entry could have, e.g. lemma, senses, examples, part of speech, etc. Iterating through the entries of a lexical resource, EDIE creates a statistical overview of a 'typical' entry, defining the average structure and type of information which can be found in such a dictionary and providing the user a quick insight into the dictionary structure, sense granularity, and the type of information they can expect to encounter.

Besides the content of a dictionary, EDIE also takes into account the resource's metadata. The metadata information which can be found in the Elexis infrastructure is represented by the metadata model which has all fields defined by Dublin Core, and those used by the whole Elexis infrastructure. Since an automatic verification of the accuracy or quality of the metadata is too advanced, the metadata evaluation only takes into account the completeness of the data. This means the final profile of the resource will consist of a summary of the existing metadata, accompanied with a list of any missing information.

Finally, the provided metadata is also used to perform context-specific profiling and resource comparison. We call this "aggregated" profiling because it aims to contextualize a particular resource by comparing it to others, thus providing a more comprehensive resource profile. The language and type of a resource are used so that the output of our assessment would provide the user information within a sensible context. If a dictionary is categorized as a terminological dictionary of French, we can compare its properties to other terminological dictionaries of French. This way, we make sure that the comparisons we make are useful and reasonable. For instance, if a user wants to make sure that

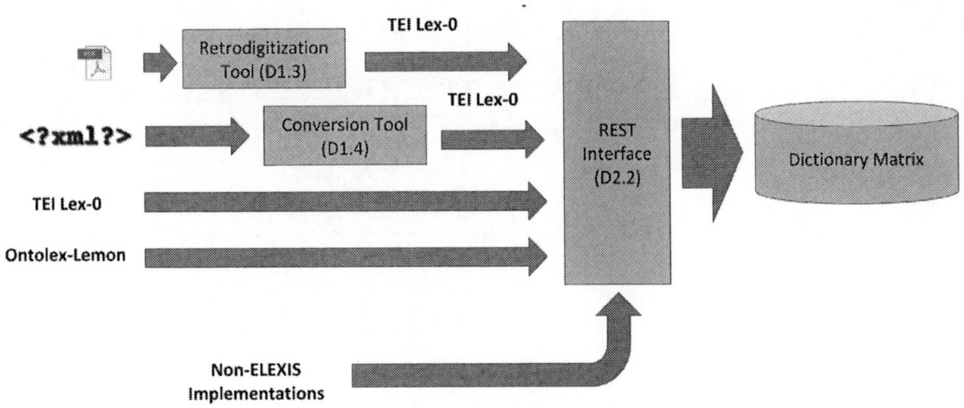

Figure 3: How to upload lexical resources to the dictionary matrix, taken from (McCrae et al., 2019)

Method Name:	/about
Parameters:	The dictionary ID
Returns:	An object describing the dictionary
Example Request:	http://www.example.com/about/example-dictionary

Example Response:	{
	"release": "PUBLIC",
	"sourceLanguage": "en",
	"targetLanguage": ["en", "de"],
	"genre": ["gen"],
	"license": "creativecommons.org/licenses/by/4.0/",
	"title": "The Human-Readable Name of this resource",
	"creator": [{
	    "name": "Institute of This Resource",
	    "email": "contact@institute.com"
	    }],
	"publisher": [{
	    "name": "Publishing Company"
	    }
	]}

Table 1: Type of information returned by querying for a dictionary within the ELEXIS infrastructure

they are using the largest available resource in a particular category, they can easily see how the resource compares in size with the other resources in that category.

2.2. Usage

As previously mentioned, EDIE is situated at the access interface for the dictionary matrix, and it can be accessed through a RESTful Web service. Since there are many dictionaries with several thousands of entries, creating their profiles can take time. Additionally, we can assume that the data will not be changed frequently. In order to save time, a resource is profiled as soon as it is added to the dictionary matrix, and this profile is later accessed on user demand. If the resource content or metadata is altered in any way, the profile is created anew. Since aggregated evaluation takes into account several dictionaries depending on the categorization created by the user, this cannot be done in advance. However, aggregating does not take too long because the system works with the existing profiles.

Once a user selects the resource they are interested in, or the category they wish to compare using aggregated profiling, they can send a parameterized request to EDIE using the REST API, and quickly get a response in JSON format. The response is EDIE's end report which consists of the resource's content statistics, metadata with the missing data pointed out, formatting errors, and the aggregation profile if requested. A sample of the end report can be seen in Figure 4.

3. Related work

Evaluation of dictionaries and linguistic resources relies on the accuracy and thoroughness of the metadata which accompanies them. Without relevant information regarding the resource, the user cannot create a

Method Name:	`/list/`*dictionary*
Parameters:	A limit and an offset
Returns:	A list of lexical entry descriptions
Example Request:	`http://www.example.com/list/example-dictionary?limit=2`

Example Response:	[
	{
	"release": "PUBLIC",
	"lemma": "work",
	"language": "en",
	"id": "work-n",
	"partOfSpeech": ["NOUN"],
	"formats": ["tei"]
	}, {
	"release": "PUBLIC",
	"lemma": "work",
	"language": "en",
	"id": "work-v",
	"partOfSpeech": ["VERB"],
	"formats": ["tei"]
	}
	]

Table 2: Type of information returned by querying for an individual entry of a dictionary within the ELEXIS infrastructure


```
{
  "endpoint": "http://lexonomy.elex.is/",
  "available": true,
  "dictionaries": {
    "elexis-dsl-moth": {
      "entry_report": {
        "errors": [
          "Part of speech value was invalid: ['sb.']",
          "Part of speech value was invalid: ['adv.']",
          "Part of speech value was invalid: ['pr\u00e6p.']",
          "Part of speech value was invalid: ['sb.']",
          "Part of speech value was invalid: ['udr\u00e5bsord']",
        ]
      },
      "metadata_report": {
        "errors": [
          "License not specified"
        ],
        "metric count": 18,
        "total metrics": 112,
        "sizeOfDictionary": 93832
      }
    },
    "elexis-oeaw-jakob": {
      "entry_report": {
        "errors": [
          "No type of entry",
          "No type of entry",
```


Figure 4: A sample of EDIE's end report

verdict about the quality or the usability of a particular resource for their purpose. The assessment of metadata provided with a lexicographic resource is also called *metalexicography* (Swanepoel, 2008).

One example of metadata schema used to evaluate and connect language resources is given by the META-SHARE ontology, which is described in (Gavrilidou et al., 2012).[7] While the META-SHARE ontology is a very important resource for our work, we are not aware of any initiative using it for (automatic) usability assessment of lexical resources.

Another initiative related to this topic of accessing metadata of linguistic resources is "LingHub" ((McCrae and Cimiano, 2015))[8], which is combining metadata from different schemes, like LRE-MAP, META-SHARE, CLARIN and more. This integration is resulting in an RDF-based set of metadata that are greatly improving the discovery of language resources. But

[7]The latest version of the META-SHARE ontology is available at `http://www.meta-share.org/ontologies/meta-share/meta-share-ontology.owl/documentation/index-en.html`.

[8]See also `https://linghub.org/`.

LingHub is not dealing directly with the data itself, and the quality issues dealt with by the developers of LingHub are primarily concerning the encoding of the metadata.
In the field of profiling Knowledge Graphs (KG) We are aware of work pursued within the COST Action "NexusLinguarum"[9] and dealing with data profiling in the Linguistic Linked Open Data (LLOD)[10], using for this the ABSTAT tool ((Spahiu et al., 2018) ; (Principe et al., 2018))[11] This work is dealing primarily with the establishment of specific metrics to describe the structural features, or schema-level patterns, of knowledge graphs encoding linguistic data – basically the data sets included in the LLOD cloud. But it doesn't address directly the linguistic features included in those data, and their compliance to a standardized vocabulary.
As it has been noticed by (Rabby et al.,), sets of schema-level patterns delivered by profiling tools such as ABSTAT ((Principe et al., 2018)), may be huge, and might deal with very generic features. Therefore our approach in Edie is focusing directly on the content of the RDF-based lexical data sets included in the dictionary matrix.

4. Conclusions and Future work

We have presented EDIE, the tool designed for profiling lexicographic resources within the ELEXIS infrastructure. EDIE is designed to allow users to assess different aspects of dictionaries based on their metadata and entries. Furthermore, users can utilize aggregated profiling to compare relevant dictionaries for their specific use cases. The current implementation of EDIE does not have any graphical user interface for interactive exploration of the lexicographic resources. Such an user interface in combination with different statistics and comparative visualizations based on different criteria selected by users (dictionary types, genres, languages, etc.) would help the users to assess different dictionaries in a more user-friendly manner.

5. Acknowledgements

This paper is based upon work from the COST Action NexusLinguarum – European network for Web-centered linguistic data science (CA18209), supported by COST (European Cooperation in Science and Technology). It is also supported by the Horizon 2020 research and innovation programme with the projects Prêt-à-LLOD (grant agreement no. 825182) and ELEXIS (grant agreement no. 731015).

[9]nexuslinguarum.eu/.

[10]See https://linguistic\protect\discretionary{\char\hyphenchar\font}{}{}lod.org/ for more details on the LLOD cloud.

[11]See the "Intermediate Activity Report Working Group 1 'Linked data-based language resources'" of the NexusLinguarum COST Action at https://nexuslinguarum.eu/wp-content/uploads/2021/11/D1.3_IntermediateActivityReport.pdf.

6. Bibliographical References

Gavrilidou, M., Labropoulou, P., Desipri, E., Piperidis, S., Papageorgiou, H., Monachini, M., Frontini, F., Declerck, T., Francopoulo, G., Arranz, V., and Mapelli, V. (2012). The METASHARE metadata schema for the description of language resources. In *Proceedings of the Eighth International Conference on Language Resources and Evaluation (LREC'12)*, pages 1090–1097, Istanbul, Turkey, May. European Language Resources Association (ELRA).

McCrae, J. P. and Cimiano, P. (2015). Linghub: a linked data based portal supporting the discovery of language resources. In Agata Filipowska, et al., editors, *Joint Proceedings of the Posters and Demos Track of 11th International Conference on Semantic Systems - SEMANTiCS 2015 and 1st Workshop on Data Science: Methods, Technology and Applications (DSci15) 11th International Conference on Semantic Systems - SEMANTiCS 2015, Vienna, Austria, September 15-17, 2015*, volume 1481 of *CEUR Workshop Proceedings*, pages 88–91. CEUR-WS.org.

McCrae, J. P., Tiberius, C., Khan, A. F., Kernerman, I., Declerck, T., Krek, S., Monachini, M., and Ahmadi, S. (2019). The ELEXIS interface for interoperable lexical resources. In *Proceedings of the sixth biennial conference on electronic lexicography (eLex)*, pages 642–659, Sintra, Portugal, 10.

Principe, R. A. A., Spahiu, B., Palmonari, M., Rula, A., Paoli, F. D., and Maurino, A. (2018). ABSTAT 1.0: Compute, manage and share semantic profiles of RDF knowledge graphs. In Aldo Gangemi, et al., editors, *The Semantic Web: ESWC 2018 Satellite Events - ESWC 2018 Satellite Events, Heraklion, Crete, Greece, June 3-7, 2018, Revised Selected Papers*, volume 11155 of *Lecture Notes in Computer Science*, pages 170–175. Springer.

Rabby, G., Keya, F., Svátek, V., and Principe2, R. A. P. (). Effect of heuristic post-processing on knowledge graph profile patterns: cross-domain study. unpublished.

Spahiu, B., Maurino, A., and Palmonari, M. (2018). Towards improving the quality of knowledge graphs with data-driven ontology patterns and SHACL. In Martin G. Skjæveland, et al., editors, *Proceedings of the 9th Workshop on Ontology Design and Patterns (WOP 2018) co-located with 17th International Semantic Web Conference (ISWC 2018), Monterey, USA, October 9th, 2018*, volume 2195 of *CEUR Workshop Proceedings*, pages 52–66. CEUR-WS.org.

Swanepoel, P. H. (2008). Towards a framework for the description and evaluation of dictionary evaluation criteria. *Lexikos*, 18:207–231.

Woldrich, A., Goli, T., Kosem, I., Matuška, O., and Wissik, T. (2021). ELEXIS: Technical and social infrastructure for lexicography, July. Published in K Lexical News (28), pp. 45-52.

Proceedings of the Globalex Workshop on Linked Lexicography @LREC2022, pages 6–9
Marseille, 20 June 2022

Towards the Linking of a Sign Language Ontology with Lexical Data

Thierry Declerck
German Research Center for Artificial Intelligence (DFKI)
Saarland Informatics Campus D3 2
66123 Saarbrücken, Germany
declerck@dfki.de

Abstract

We describe our current work for linking a new ontology for representing constitutive elements of Sign Languages with lexical data encoded within the OntoLex-Lemon framework. We first present very briefly the current state of the ontology, and show how transcriptions of signs can be represented in OntoLex-Lemon, in a minimalist manner, before addressing the challenges of linking the elements of the ontology to full lexical descriptions of the spoken languages

Keywords: Linked Data, Sign Languages, OntoLex-Lemon

1. Extended Abstract

The final goal of our work is to provide for a multimodal extension to the OntoLex-Lemon framework (Cimiano et al., 2016), which was originally conceived for covering the written and phonetic representation of lexical data, as can be seen in the relation existing between the `ontolex:LexicalEntry` and `ontolex:Form` classes, which are displayed with the core module of OntoLex-Lemon in Figure 1.

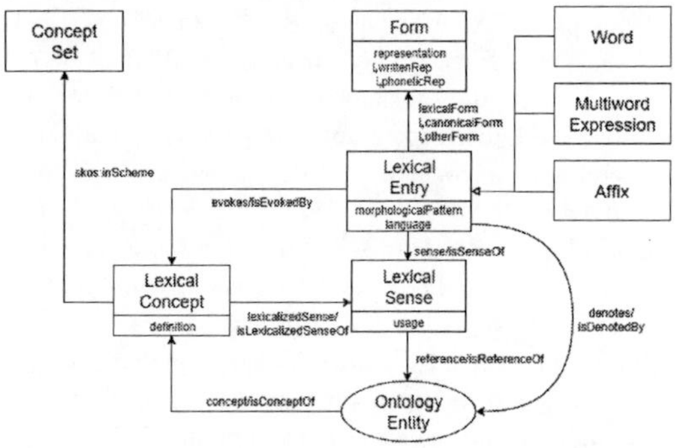

Figure 1: The core module of OntoLex-Lemon, taken from `https://www.w3.org/2016/05/ontolex/`

Thereby, we aim at supporting the same type of semantic interoperability between Sign Language(s) (SL) lexical data as this is achieved in OntoLex-Lemon for the written or phonetic representations of lexical data.

Sign Language is a type of natural language with distinctive properties.[1] It poses a challenge for its integration in OntoLex-Lemon, as SL descriptions and interpretations involve a huge number of descriptors (or data categories), including information about "physical" (body parts) and spatial (orientation, movements, etc.) elements, which are not playing any role when it comes to represent the "classical" lexical data in the spoken or written language. This complexity of the SL lexical data and the challenges it poses for its full formal representation in the OntoLex-Lemon lexical framework might lead to the design of a specific module extension, in which we can also address the issue on how to represent cross-modal relations, as this was not needed in the case of the values of only the `ontolex:writtenRep` and `ontolex:phoneticRep` properties (see Figure 1).

One aspect of our work was to design and implement an ontology of the data categories used for describing Sign Languages, including the already mentioned "physical" (body parts) and spatial (orientation, movements, etc.) elements, but also classifications of different types of sign languages, the phonological properties of SL, etc. The current status of this ontology is presented in a paper ("Towards a new Ontology for Sign Language") to be presented at the LREC conference, and which we briefly summarise in this extended abstract.

We built the ontology on the basis of a number of available SL resources, like the CLARIN concept repository (`https://www.clarin.eu/content/clarin-concept-registry`), the American Sign Language lexicon (`https://asl-lex.org/visualization/`), the British Sign Language dictionary (`https://www.british-sign.co.uk/british-sign-language/dictionary/`) or the Institute for German Sign Language and Communication of the Deaf at the University of Hamburg (`https://www.idgs.uni-hamburg.de/`), and the "SignGram Blueprint. A Guide to Sign Language Grammar Writing" publication, resulting from the SignGram COST Action: `https://parles.upf.edu/llocs/cost-signgram/node/18`.

Our approach consisted mainly in proposing an har-

[1] Specifics of Sign Languages and the challenges for defining a corresponding writing system are described in depth in (Bianchini, 2021)

monisation of all the features (or data categories) introduced and explained in those different highly relevant sources, and to organise this harmonised set of descriptors into an ontology, while conserving the information on the origin of the data. We have for now more than 260 harmonised ontology elements, organised in a (tentative) hierarchy. Figure 2 is displaying aspects of the current state of the SL ontology.

Parallel to this work, we started to investigate the encoding of transcriptions of Sign Language data in OntoLex-Lemon. For this purpose, we studied the type of transcription offered by the HamNoSys notational system (Hanke, 2004).[2] Figure 3 displays the sign labelled with the German word "Busch".

As HamNoSys per se is not machine-readable, we are making use of a conversion of it into an XML format called SiGML, which is very often used as the input to avatar generation software, as described in (Jennings et al., 2010). There exists a python implementation that transforms HamNoSys in SiGML, which is described in (Neves et al., 2020). The resulting notational code, an example of which is displayed in Figure 4, is the one we use to be included in OntoLex-Lemon, and from which we can link to elements of the ontology, or to a pose or video streaming object.

We tentatively represent this SiGML code as a value of the OntoLex-Lemon "writtenRep" property, with a special tag "sigml", as can be seen in Figure 5. We need to stress here that the string "Busch" associated with the HamNoSys notation of the sign is to be considered as a label, and not as a lexical entry. In our suggested representation, we can see how three encodings for "Busch" are representing three different modalities, with different types of information. But other options are under discussion within the Ontolex community.

An alternative solution could consist in introducing a specific lexical entry for the "word" used for labelling the sign, and to "loosely" relate it to the lexical entry that is encoding the word "Busch" as used in the spoken language. Another option would be to consider the label "Busch" rather as a conceptual entity, which can be linked to a number of lexical entries that could be a lexical realisation of this conceptual "tagging", as we can think that the annotators of SL corpora are rather using concepts instead of specific lexical entries of the spoken language. In this we would orient ourselves towards a WordNet like representation of the semantics of signs.

2. Current Work

While the solution presented in the former section for encoding transcriptions of SL data in OntoLex-Lemon seems to be relatively straightforward, it does ignore many aspects of Sign Languages, which are encoded in our ontology. Our current work, to be made soon available in a first version, consists in implementing a strategy for linking the descriptors included in the SL Ontology with the OntoLex-Lemon representation of HamNosys/SiGML encodings, maybe also including videos sequences as external references.

We need for this to take into account a variety of descriptor types, some of which we summarise in this section.

The ASL-LEX (`https://asl-lex.org/visualization/`) resource uses for describing a sign ca 95 features distributed over 7 main classes: Frequency Properties, Iconicity Properties, Lexical Properties, Sign Duration, Phonology, Phonological Calculations, and Acquisition Information. As we can see, some of those data categories are not included in the HamNoSys/SiGML set of features. We will need to include the "Acquisition Information" within the Metadata Module for OntoLex (LIME), which might need to be extended. This high number of descriptors is challenging, as it makes it difficult to link them in a consistent way to the HamNoSys/SiGML representation in OntoLex-Lemon, also with the question if all the 95 features are equally relevant for this linking task.

The British Sign Language dictionary (`https://www.british-sign.co.uk/british-sign-language/dictionary/`) has an interesting approach, as it offers textual descriptions of the sign used for a concept. For example for "aeroplane", the site is providing this information: " **Description**: Thumb and little finger of primary hand extended with palm facing downwards. Hand starts in front of body and moves up at an angle across body. **Definition**: A machine that can fly. It has wings and engines. **Also Means**: plane, flight". The text included in the "Description" section is very interesting and very specific to Sign Language (or for describing gestures in general), and for which we have no field in OntoLex-Lemon. It will be challenging to link this kind of information to an HamNoSys/SiGML representation in OntoLex-Lemon, as the text has to correspond to the features used in the XML code. Also interesting in the "Aeroplane" example is the fat that various meanings are given to the sign. This calls also for a WordNet like representation in OntoLex-Lemon, and linking thus the set of features used for describing the sign to an ontolex:LexicalConcept instance.

We also need to handle multilingual aspects. The Dicta-Sign project is offering a list of 1000 concepts realised in 4 languages (German, Greek, English and French), with videos and HamNoSys transcriptions. As the "words" used to label the concepts (like "abandon") can not be considered as lexical entries, we will integrate those labels as instances of the ontolex:LexicalConcept. It remains unclear to how many lexical entries those concepts can be linked.

As a consequence of this preliminary study, we see that

[2]See also `https://www.sign-lang.uni-hamburg.de/dgs-korpus/files/inhalt_pdf/HamNoSys_2018.pdf` for a detailed graphical representation of HamNoSys

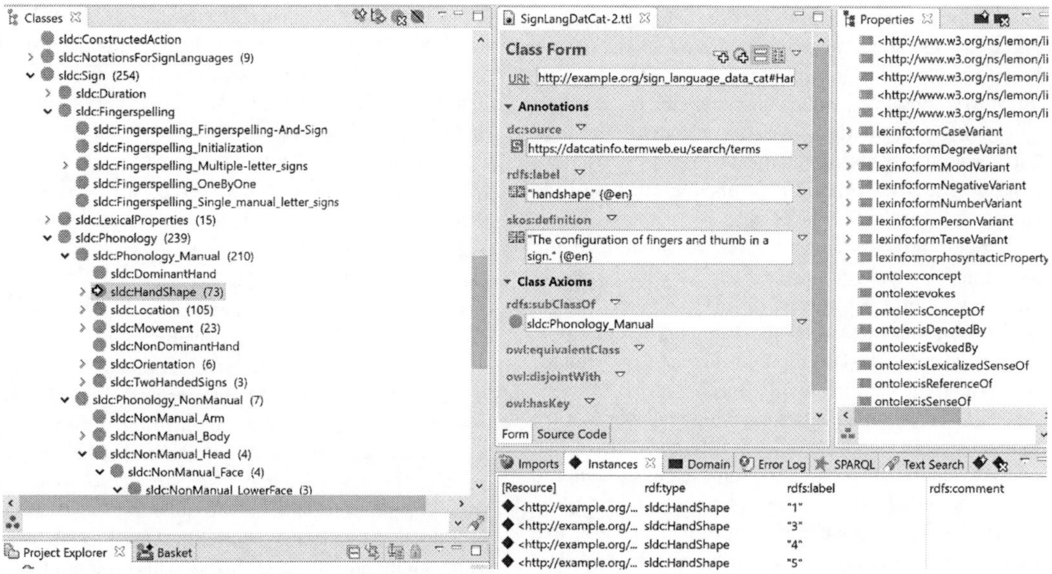

Figure 2: A screenshot of the ontology, displaying parts of its tentative hierarchy of classes

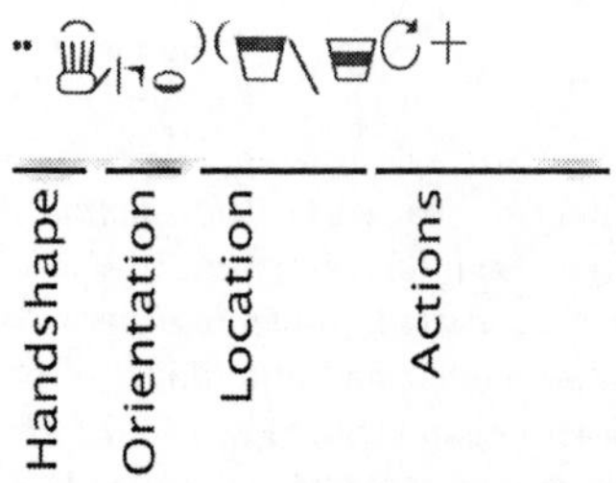

Figure 3: The sign labelled with the German Word "Busch" in HamNoSys notation, using the four features: Handshape, Orientation, Location and Actions.

Figure 4: The Transformation of an HamNoSys notation for the German label "Busch" in SiGML code

linking a set of features describing signs to a lexical entry of the spoken language might not always be possi-

```
SignLangDatCat-2.ttl

ontolex:Busch_Sg
  rdf:type ontolex:Form ;
  lexinfo:gender lexinfo:masculine ;
  lexinfo:number lexinfo:singular ;
  rdfs:label "\"Busch\""@de ;
  ontolex:phoneticRep "\"bʊʃ\""@IPA ;
  ontolex:writtenRep "\"Busch\""@de ;
  ontolex:writtenRep "\"hamsymmlr
          hamfinger2345
          hamfingerbendmod
          hamthumboutmod
          hamextfingeruo
          hampalmd
          hamclose
          hamshoulders
          hambetween
          hamchest
          hamcircleo
          hamrepeatfromstart\""@de-DE-sigml ;
.
```

Figure 5: Inclusion of the SiGML code as an instance of the `ontolex:Form` class

ble, but rather to instances of ontolex:LexicalConcept. An other consequence seems to be that we might need a specific module for describing dictionaries or lexicons of sign languages.

3. Acknowledgements

This paper is based upon work from the COST Action NexusLinguarum – European network for Web-centered linguistic data science (CA18209), supported by COST (European Cooperation in Science and Technology). The article is also supported by the Hori-

zon 2020 research and innovation programme with the projects Prêt-à-LLOD (grant agreement no. 825182) and ELEXIS (grant agreeement no. 731015).
We thank the members of the W3C Ontolex Community Group for their contributions to the discussions on this extension work.

4. Bibliographical References

Bianchini, C. S. (2021). How to improve metalinguistic awareness by writing a language without writing: Sign Languages and SignWriting. In Y. Haralambous, editor, *Proceedings of Grapholinguistics in the 21st Century, 2020*, volume 5 of *Grapholinguistics and Its Applications*, pages 1037–1063. Fluxus Editions.

Cimiano, P., McCrae, J. P., and Buitelaar, P. (2016). Lexicon Model for Ontologies: Community Report. W3C community group final report, World Wide Web Consortium.

Hanke, T. (2004). HamNoSys – representing sign language data in language resources and language processing contexts. In Oliver Streiter et al., editors, *Proceedings of the LREC2004 Workshop on the Representation and Processing of Sign Languages: From SignWriting to Image Processing. Information techniques and their implications for teaching, documentation and communication*, pages 1–6, Lisbon, Portugal, May. European Language Resources Association (ELRA).

Jennings, V., Elliott, R., Kennaway, R., and Glauert, J. (2010). Requirements for a signing avatar. In Philippe Dreuw, et al., editors, *Proceedings of the LREC2010 4th Workshop on the Representation and Processing of Sign Languages: Corpora and Sign Language Technologies*, pages 133–136, Valletta, Malta, May. European Language Resources Association (ELRA).

Neves, C., Coheur, L., and Nicolau, H. (2020). HamNoSyS2SiGML: Translating HamNoSys into SiGML. In *Proceedings of the 12th Language Resources and Evaluation Conference*, pages 6035–6039, Marseille, France, May. European Language Resources Association.

Proceedings of the Globalex Workshop on Linked Lexicography @LREC2022, pages 10–18
Marseille, 20 June 2022

Modelling Collocations in OntoLex-FrAC

Christian Chiarcos[1,2], Katerina Gkirtzou[3], Maxim Ionov[1,2], Besim Kabashi[4], Anas Fahad Khan[5], Ciprian-Octavian Truică[6]
[1]Applied Computational Linguistics, Goethe University Frankfurt, Frankfurt am Main, Germany
[2]Institute for Digital Humanities, University of Cologne, Germany
[3] Institute of Language and Speech Processing, Athena Research Center, Athens, Greece
[4]Computational and Corpus Linguistics, Friedrich-Alexander University of Erlangen-Nuremberg, Germany
[5]Istituto di Linguistica Computazionale A. Zampolli, Consiglio Nazionale delle Ricerche, Italy
[6]Department of Information Technology, Uppsala University, Sweden
[1]{chiarcos,ionov}@cs.uni-frankfurt.de, [3]katerina.gkirtzou@athenarc.gr, [4]besim.kabashi@fau.de,
[5]fahad.khan@ilc.cnr.it, [6]ciprian-octavian.truica@it.uu.se

Abstract

Following presentations of frequency and attestations, and embeddings and distributional similarity, this paper introduces the third cornerstone of the emerging OntoLex module for Frequency, Attestation and Corpus-based Information, OntoLex-FrAC. We provide an RDF vocabulary for collocations, established as a consensus over contributions from five different institutions and numerous data sets, with the goal of eliciting feedback from reviewers, workshop audience and the scientific community in preparation of the final consolidation of the OntoLex-FrAC module, whose publication as a W3C community report is foreseen for the end of this year. The novel collocation component of OntoLex-FrAC is described in application to a lexicographic resource and corpus-based collocation scores available from the web, and finally, we demonstrate the capability and genericity of the model by showing how to retrieve and aggregate collocation information by means of SPARQL, and its export to a tabular format, so that it can be easily processed in downstream applications.

Keywords: lexical resources, standards, OntoLex, collocation analysis

1. Background

Since its publication in 2016, the OntoLex-Lemon vocabulary (McCrae et al., 2017) has become the dominant vocabulary for modelling machine-readable dictionaries on the Semantic Web. OntoLex-FrAC, the OntoLex module for *Frequency, Attestation and Corpus information*, is an emerging vocabulary for enriching machine-readable lexicons with corpus information. Since 2018, OntoLex-FrAC has been under development as a companion vocabulary for (and a module of) OntoLex-Lemon in the context of the W3C community group Ontology-Lexica (OntoLex). The module is targeted at complementing dictionaries and other linguistic resources containing lexicographic data with a vocabulary to express the lexical information found in or derived from corpora, i.e., (collections of) text, written or spoken.

The current OntoLex-FrAC vocabulary is illustrated in Fig. 1. Previous publications discussing OntoLex-FrAC centered on attestations and frequency (Chiarcos et al., 2020) and corpus-based information such as embeddings and distributional similarity (Chiarcos et al., 2021). Here, we describe the extension of OntoLex-FrAC for collocation analysis.

In linguistics, the term *collocation* is used to describe the analysis of word combinations. Many groups of words can be freely combined with each other, whereas others have a strong tendency to co-occur, while others can only be combined with a limited number of other words, or are even part of fixed idioms. For example, English *heavy rain* is a common phrase, whereas *strong rain* is not. But this is language-specific: German *starker Regen* ("strong rain") is common while *schwerer Regen* ("heavy rain") is not.

The analysis of collocations and their automated retrieval from corpora is a key technique in modern digital lexicography: It supports lexicographers in identifying context-dependent patterns of use of a particular lexeme, which can then stimulate and direct further lexicographic analysis. A number of tools for this purpose have been developed, e.g., SketchEngine (Kilgarriff et al., 2014) and Corpus WorkBench (Hardie, 2012), and although they currently lack machine-readable interface specifications, their APIs represent a de facto standard in digital lexicography. OntoLex-FrAC is dedicated to addressing this gap and closely follows the requirements of these tools. At the same time, collocation dictionaries are also lexicographic resources in their own right, e.g., as tools to support learners and second language speakers in finding contextually appropriate expressions, and they have characteristics that set them apart from both general-purpose machine-readable dictionaries (covered by OntoLex-Lemon) and traditional dictionaries as used and created in lexicographic research (covered by OntoLex-Lexicog, Bosque-Gil and Gracia, 2019). OntoLex-FrAC covers both use cases: collocation dictionaries and automated collocation analysis.

Within OntoLex, collocations have been modeled for the first time as part of **OntoLex-FrAC**, and to the

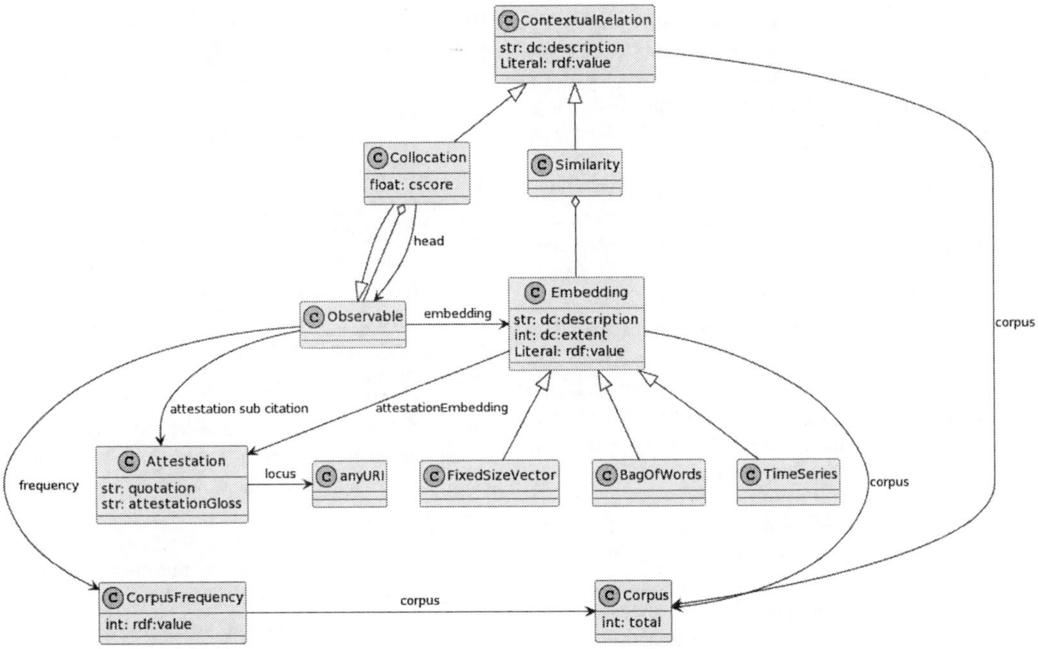

Figure 1: OntoLex-FrAC, draft version of March 2022 as UML class diagram, cf. Suchánek and Pergl (2020) for notational conventions

best of our knowledge, no machine-readable vocabulary for collocation dictionaries and related resources on the basis of RDF technologies has been suggested before. Some precedent may be seen in the collocation vocabulary for lexical entries as described in the XML-based Text Encoding Initiative (TEI) guidelines (Initiative, 2022). Although TEI is not Linked Data based, it does give us a useful point of reference for seeing how collocations can be representing as structured data in computational lexicons.

In fact, there are at least three different ways of representing collocations in TEI lexicons, using different vocabulary elements, one being `colloc` ('sequence of words that co-occur with the headword with significant frequency')[1]. Secondly, collocations can also be specified using the `gram` element (as part of the grammatical description of a lexical entry), as is seen in the example given of the preposition *de* collocate of the French word *médire* given in Section 9.3.2 of the TEI guidelines. Thirdly, collocations can be described using the usage element `usg` by specifying the `@type` attribute of the element as "colloc". The important insights to be drawn from the TEI guidelines is that (a) there is a demand for modelling collocations in the context of dictionaries (hence multiple, incompatible ways to model it, driven by different use cases and requirements), but that (b) at the moment, the support for modelling collocation scores in this context is severely limited. From the options mentioned above only `colloc` allows to specify collocation scores by adding a `certainty` element and *ab*using its `@cert` attribute, which, however, is only used with human-readable labels in the guidelines,[2] but neither with numerical scores nor with a systematic means of defining the type of collocation score.

2. Collocations in OntoLex-FrAC

The base element of OntoLex-FrAC is `frac:Observable`, i.e., any element that observations can be made about *in a corpus*. This corpus-based focus also defines our understanding of collocations not as lexical units, but as being characterized by certain association scores (for which high values may hint at a lexicalized collocation, but which can be calculated and returned for *any* combination of words). Typical observables are words (`ontolex:Form`) or lexemes (`ontolex:LexicalEntry`), but also lexical concepts or general ontological concepts can be observed – if annotated in a corpus. This definition of observables – motivated from other aspects of corpus-based information before – is organically applicable to collocation analysis: collocations are usually defined on surface-oriented criteria, i.e., as a relation between forms or lemmas (lexical entries), not between senses, but they can be analyzed on the level of word senses (the sense that gave rise to the idiom or collocation).

Collocations are not constrained to pairs of words, longer collocations are also possible. Accordingly, we

[1] `https://tei-c.org/release/doc/tei-p5-doc/en/html/ref-colloc.html`

[2] `https://tei-c.org/release/doc/tei-p5-doc/en/html/ref-certainty.html`

model collocations as an aggregate of observables, not as a relation between words. Moreover, collocations *are* observables in their own right. In particular, they can have attestations (i.e., corpus examples that show the words under consideration in context, frequencies, similarity scores, etc.).
Collocations obtained by quantitative methods are :

Def. 2.1 (`frac:Collocation`). An RDF container (`rdfs:Container`, i.e., `rdf:Seq` or `rdf:Bag`) that contains two or more `frac: Observables` based on their co-occurrence within the same context window and that can be characterized by their method of creation (`dct: description`), their collocation score (weight, collocation strength) (`frac:cscore`), and the corpus used to create them (`frac:corpus`).

Collocations may have fixed or variable word order. Where fixed word order is required, the collocation must be defined as a sequence (`rdf:Seq`), otherwise, the default interpretation is as an unordered set (`rdf:Bag`). The elements of any collocation can be accessed by `rdfs:member`. Optionally, the elements of an ordered collocation can be accessed by numerical indices (`rdf:_1`, `rdf:_2`, etc.).
Additional parameters such as the size of the context window used for collocation analysis can be provided in human-readable form in `dct:description`.
Note that FrAC collocations can be used to represent collocations both in the lexicographic sense (as complex units of meaning) and in the quantative sense (as determined by collocation metrics over a particular corpus), but that the quantitative interpretation is the preferred one in the context of FrAC. To mark collocations in the lexicographic sense as such, they can be assigned a corresponding `lexinfo:termType`, e.g., by means of `lexinfo:idiom`, `lexinfo: phraseologicalUnit` or `lexinfo:set Phrase`. If explicit sense information is being provided, the recommended modelling is by means of `ontolex:MultiWordExpression`; it can be defined as `frac:Collocation` (`rdfs:member` can be left implicit).
In automated collocation analysis, collocations can be described in terms of various collocation scores:

Def. 2.2 (`frac:cscore`). Collocation score is a subproperty of `rdf:value` that provides the value for one specific type of collocation score for a particular collocation in its respective corpus.

We define popular collocation metrics as sub-properties of `frac:cscore` (Sect. 3). For those that are asymmetric (e.g., `frac:relFreq`), we distinguish the lexical element they are about (the head) from its collocate(s). If such metrics are provided, a collocation should identify the element that it conveys information about, modelled here with the property `frac:head`:

Def. 2.3 (`frac:head`). Identifies the `rdfs: member` of a collocation that its scores are about. A collocation must not have more than one head.

3. Collocation Scores

OntoLex-FrAC defines popular collocation scores as sub-properties of `frac:cscore`, and users are encouraged to define their own subproperties if different scores are being used. In case only one kind of score is provided by a source, users can also use `rdf:value` along with a `dct:description` explaining the metric. We present selected sub-properties along with their mathematical definition.

Def. 3.1 (`frac:relFreq`). Relative frequency indicates how often a specific word y in the collocation occurs together with the head word x: $\texttt{relFreq}_x = \frac{p(x,y)}{p(x)}$.

Def. 3.2 (`frac:pmi`). Pointwise Mutual Information (PMI) measures the extent to which the words in a collocation occur more frequently than by chance. If two words appear together more than expected under independence there must be some kind of semantic relationship between them (Role and Nadif, 2011). Thus, PMI is the log of the ratio of the observed co-occurrence frequency to the frequency expected under independence: $\text{PMI}(x,y) = \log \frac{p(x,y)}{p(x)p(y)}$

PMI variants, such as normalized PMI, cf. (Role and Nadif, 2011), are provided as well, i.e. `frac:npmi`, `frac:pmi2` and `frac:pmi3`.

Def. 3.3 (`frac:dice`). Dice coefficient is a statistic used to gauge the collocation of two words x and y (Manning and Schutze, 1999): $\texttt{dice}(x,y) = \frac{2p(x,y)}{p(x)+p(y)}$

Def. 3.4 (`frac:minSensitivity`). Minimum sensitivity is computed as the minimum between the relative sensitivity of word x and of word y (Pedersen, 1998): $\texttt{minSensitivity}(x,y) = \min(\frac{p(x,y)}{p(y)}, \frac{p(x,y)}{p(x)})$

In addition to collocation scores, statistical independence tests are employed as collocation scores, including `frac:tScore` (Student's t test), `frac:chi2` (Pearson's χ^2), `frac:likelihood_ratio` (Log Likelihood Ratio test) (Manning and Schutze, 1999).
Furthermore, related metrics from disciplines other than computational lexicography and corpus linguistics are also provided as `frac:cscore` subproperties. In association rule mining, for example, an association rule $x \rightarrow y$ corresponds to a collocation in that the existence of word x implies the existence of word y.

Def. 3.5 (`frac:support`). indicates how frequently the rule appears in the dataset (Larose and Larose, 2014): $\texttt{support}(x \rightarrow y) = p(x,y)$

Def. 3.6 (`frac:confidence`). indicates how often the rule has been found to be true (Larose and Larose, 2014): $\texttt{confidence}(x \rightarrow y) = \frac{p(x,y)}{p(x)}$

Def. 3.7 (`frac:lift`). (or interest of a rule) measures how many times more often x and y occur together than expected if they are statistically independent (Larose and Larose, 2014): $\texttt{lift}(x \rightarrow y) = \frac{p(x,y)}{p(x)p(y)}$

Def. 3.8 (`frac:conviction`). (conviction of a rule) is the ratio of the expected frequency that x occurs without y, i.e., the frequency that the rule makes an incorrect prediction, if x and y are independent divided by the observed frequency of incorrect predictions (Brin et al., 1997): $\text{conviction}(x \rightarrow y) = \frac{p(x)p(\neg y)}{p(x,\neg y)}$

Where:

- x, y - the (head) of the word and its collocate
- $p(x)$, $p(y)$ the probabilities of word x and y
- $p(\neg x) = 1 - p(x)$
- $p(x, y)$ the probability of the co-occurrence of x and y

4. Case Studies

We illustrate the application of OntoLex-FrAC to (a) the conversion of an existing collocation dictionary to a machine-readable format, and (b) its enrichment with collocation scores obtained from an external corpus. It is to be noted, however, that OntoLex-FrAC is not an independent vocabulary, but that it builds on OntoLex (and can thus complement existing OntoLex data). It can also be applied in conjunction with other OntoLex modules. We illustrate the conjoined application of OntoLex-FrAC and OntoLex-Lexicog to the Oxford Collocation Dictionary for Students.

4.1. The Oxford Collocations Dictionary

We show an example of the application of Ontolex-FrAC by looking at an example encoding of the entry for the word *point* from *the Oxford Collocations Dictionary for Students of English* (OCDS) (OUP, 2002). Figure 2 shows how the OCDS groups together the entry with individual collocations for better accessibility and readability.

For instance *point*-collocations are first grouped together on the sense level, then on the basis of the part of speech of the collocated word and/or whether the collocation constitutes a phrase, and finally at the level of similarity of meaning of the collocation (note that there is also a division of examples for the same meaning grouping). In the OCDS the separation of groupings on the basis of meaning is visually effected by the | symbol. We refer to these (potentially nested) groupings of collocation information as *collocation patterns*

point *noun*

1 thing said as part of a discussion

• ADJ. **good, interesting, valid | important | minor | subtle | moot | central, crucial, key, major, salient | controversial | talking** *The possibility of an interest rate cut is a major talking point in the City.*

• VERB + POINT **have** *She's got a point.* | **see, take** *I see your point.* ◇ *Point taken.* | **concede | cover, make, raise** *She made some interesting points.* | **argue, discuss** *They argued the point for hours.* | **illustrate | get across, make, prove** *He had trouble getting his point across.* ◇ *That proves my point.* | **drive/hammer home, emphasize, labour, press, stress** *I understand what you're saying—there's no need to labour the point.*

• PHRASES **a case in point** (= an example relevant to the matter being discussed), **the point at issue, a point of agreement/disagreement, a point of law**

⇨ Special page at MEETING

Figure 2: Entry for *point* in the Oxford Collocations Dictionary

in what follows. The *point* example is interesting for showing how OntoLex-FrAC can be used together with the OntoLex-Lexicographic model.

Note that in our RDF modelling we represent the collocations themselves using the FrAC vocabulary and the domain-specific segmentation of the entry into collocation patterns using OntoLex-Lexicog. Indeed we use the class `lexicog:LexicographicComponent` to represent this organisation that is so typical of collocation dictionaries.

We start by looking at the modelling of the lexical content of the entry and introduce the `:point` lexical entry, giving part of speech information about the word and about its lemma form. We also introduce `:ls_point_1`, the first sense of the word corresponding to the first sense listed in the dictionary entry in Figure 2 (we only look at this first sense in the following example).

```
:point a ontolex:LexicalEntry ;
  lexinfo:partOfSpeech lexinfo:noun ;
  ontolex:sense :ls_point_1 ;
  ontolex:canonicalForm
    [ ontolex:writtenRep "point"] .

:ls_point_1 a ontolex:LexicalSense ;
    # p_s
    skos:definition "thing said as part
        of a discussion" .
```

The following lexical entries represent the collocates of the word *point*. We will refer to these entries in the descriptions of the collocations below:

```
:have a ontolex:LexicalEntry ;
  lexinfo:partOfSpeech lexinfo:verb ;
  ontolex:canonicalForm
    [ ontolex:writtenRep "have"] .

:see a ontolex:LexicalEntry ;
  lexinfo:partOfSpeech lexinfo:verb ;
```

```
  ontolex:canonicalForm
    [ ontolex:writtenRep "see" ] .

:take a ontolex:LexicalEntry ;
  lexinfo:partOfSpeech lexinfo:verb ;
  ontolex:canonicalForm
    [ ontolex:writtenRep "take" ] .
```

The collocations of *point*, or to be more accurate the collocations of the first sense of the word *point*, are represented using the FrAC classes which we introduce as follows.

```
:col_have_point a frac:Collocation ,
    rdf:Seq ;
  lexinfo:example "She's got a point" ;
  frac:head :ls_point_1 ;
  rdf:_1 :have ;
  rdf:_2 :ls_point_1 .

:col_see_point a frac:Collocation ,
    rdf:Seq ;
  lexinfo:example "I see your point" ;
  frac:head :ls_point_1 ;
  rdf:_1 :see ;
  rdf:_2 :ls_point_1 .

:col_take_point a frac:Collocation ,
    rdf:Seq ;
  lexinfo:example "Point taken" ;
  frac:head :ls_point_1 ;
  rdf:_1 :take ;
  rdf:_2 :ls_point_1 .
```

Note the use of the property `head` to specify the head of the collocation in each case, as well as that of the lexinfo property `example` to give the example presented in the original entry. Note in addition the use of `rdf:_1` and `rdf:_2` to represent the order of the collocates.

Next we represent the arrangement of this information as it is found in the dictionary itself using lexicog classes and `lexicog:LexicographicComponent` in particular. The dictionary entry (as opposed to the lexical entry) for *point* is represented by `:e_point` an individual of type `lexicog:Entry`. As we can see below, `:e_point` is linked to the lexical entry `:point` via the `lexicog:describes` property.

```
:e_point a lexicog:Entry ;
  lexicog:describes :point ;
  lexicog:subComponent
  [ a lexicog:LexicographicComponent ;
    lexicog:describes :ls_point_1 ;
    lexicog:subComponent
      :lc_point_pattern_1 ,
      :lc_point_pattern_2 ] .
```

For reasons of space we only (partially) model two of the collocation patterns in the entry in our RDF encoding: those pertaining to the collocation of the word *point* with an adjective and those pertaining to its collocation with a proceeding verb. These are `:lc_point_pattern_1` and `:lc_point_pattern_2` respectively. Both of these are lexicog lexicographic components. The text associated with each in the original entry is specified using the property `dct: description`.

```
:lc_point_pattern_1
  a lexicog:LexicographicComponent ;
  dct:description "ADJ" .

:lc_point_pattern_2
  a lexicog:LexicographicComponent ;
  dct:description "VERB + POINT" ;
  lexicog:subComponent :lc_have_point ,
    :lc_see_take_point .
```

Note that `:lc_point_pattern_2` is broken up into two further collocation patterns; the first, `:lc_have_point`, describes the word's collocates with *have*, and the second, `:lc_see_take_point`, its collocates with *see* and *take*. These are described below.

```
:lc_have_point
  a lexicog:LexicographicComponent ;
  lexicog:describes :col_have_point .
:lc_see_take_point
  a lexicog:LexicographicComponent ;
  lexicog:describes :col_see_point ,
        :col_take_point .
```

4.2. Enrichment with Collocation Scores

Aside from lexicographic expertise, the ODCS builds on (but does not provide) collocation scores. However, these can be added from other sources. One example here is the Leipzig Corpora Collection / Deutscher Wortschatz, a project of Leipzig University, the Saxon Academy of Sciences and Humanities in Leipzig and the Institute for Applied Informatics (Goldhahn et al., 2012).

Considering the word *point* in the English News (2020) corpus at the Wortschatz portal,[3] we find that *see* co-occurs with *point* 544 times (co-occurrence in the same sentence), while *point* occurs 183,306 times. In OntoLex-FrAC, the absolute frequencies can be modelled as follows:

```
:N2020_Frequency
  rdfs:subClassOf frac:CorpusFrequency,
    [ a owl:Restriction ;
      owl:onProperty frac:corpus ;
      owl:hasValue
        <https://corpora.uni-leipzig.de/en/
            res?corpusId=eng_news_2020>
    ] .

:col_see_point
  frac:frequency
```

[3]https://corpora.uni-leipzig.de/en/res?corpusId=eng_news_2020&word=point

```
    [ a :N2020_Frequency ;
      rdf:value "544" ] .

:point
  frac:frequency
    [ a :N2020_Frequency ;
      rdf:value "183,306" ] .
```

We introduce the class `:N2020_Frequency` for frequencies from the News 2020 corpus, so that frequency declarations are compactly represented with three triples only.

The Wortschatz Portal does not provide relative frequencies, but these can be calculated, and accordingly, we can extend the original OCDS data with information such as:

```
:col_have_point
  frac:relfreq "0.002967715186628";
  frac:corpus
    <https://corpora.uni-leipzig.de/en/
    res?corpusId=eng_news_2020> .
```

It is important to note here that these scores also require to provide the original corpus URI.

5. Applications

5.1. Querying OntoLex-FrAC Data

For any downstream application of OntoLex-FrAC, queriability is the most elementary required for a user. Indeed, a key benefit of modelling lexical resources in OntoLex is that they can be processed by standard RDF tools and Linguistic Linked Open Data (LLOD) technology. Using HTTP-resolvable URIs for shared vocabularies allows to operate on consistent, well-defined and machine-readable data models, so that data can be more easily re-used. Using HTTP-resolvable URIs for the data itself allows to establish links between resources hosted by different providers, and thus to develop a decentralized ecosystem for language technology and lexical resources on the web. Over such data, the application of SPARQL includes the possibility to query across data sets hosted by different providers (SPARQL federation) and across heterogeneous data, i.e., data stored in different kinds of technical backends, be it exposed as plain files (SPARQL LOAD), via a web service (SPARQL SERVICE, e.g., an endpoint) or by means of a wrapper technology created around another kind of data source (e.g., a relational data base, using R2RML technology,[4] over XML data with GRDDL[5] or over JSON data with JSON-LD[6] context definitions).

To demonstrate the viability of our modelling for collocations, we demonstrate the application of SPARQL to retrieve data from OntoLex-FrAC from the data described in Sect. 4.1 in three different scenarios.[7]

With the first query, we retrieve all collocates per collocation:

```
SELECT DISTINCT ?collocation ?member ?order
WHERE {
  ?collocation a frac:Collocation ;
  ?prop ?member .
  FILTER(?prop=rdfs:member ||
    regex(str(?prop),".*#_[0-9]+$"))
  OPTIONAL {
    ?collocation ?nrel ?member .
    FILTER(regex(str(?nrel),".*#_[0-9]+$"))
    BIND(replace(str(?nrel),".*#_([0-9]+)$","$1")
    AS ?order )
  }
} ORDER BY ?collocation ?order ?member
```

This query evaluates two kinds of membership queries, either via `rdfs:member` (unordered) or (filter `||`) in their sequential order (if defined with `rdf:_1`, `rdf:_2`, ...). Note that with RDFS reasoning enabled at the query engine, `rdfs:member` would also be inferred from `rdf:_1`, etc.

For the ODCS sample data above, a query with Apache Jena arq retrieves the following table:

collocation	member	order
<col_have_point>	<have>	"1"
<col_have_point>	<ls_point_1>	"2"
<col_see_point>	<see>	"1"
<col_see_point>	<ls_point_1>	"2"
<col_take_point>	<take>	"1"
<col_take_point>	<ls_point_1>	"2"

The second query retrieves all collocations for a given lexical entry:

```
SELECT DISTINCT ?form ?pos
                ?collocation ?isHead
WHERE {
  ?collocation a frac:Collocation.
  ?collocation ?prop ?observable.
  FILTER(?prop=rdfs:member   ||
    regex(str(?prop),".*#_[0-9]+$"))
  ?entry
    (ontolex:sense|ontolex:lexicalForm)?
      ?observable.
  ?entry
    ontolex:canonicalForm/
    ontolex:writtenRep    ?form .
  OPTIONAL {
    ?collocation frac:head ?observable.
  BIND("true" as ?isHead)
  }
  OPTIONAL {
    ?entry lexinfo:partOfSpeech ?pos
  }
} ORDER BY ?form ?pos
    ?collocation ?isHead
```

[4] `https://www.w3.org/TR/r2rml/`
[5] `https://www.w3.org/TR/grddl/`
[6] `https://www.w3.org/TR/json-ld/`

[7] Queries were tested with Apache Jena 4.2.0, using the arq command line tool. For reasons of brevity, we skip prefix declarations. The following non-standard prefixes have been used:
`ontolex:` `http://www.w3.org/ns/lemon/ontolex#`, `skos:` `http://www.w3.org/2004/02/skos/core#`, `frac:` `http://www.w3.org/ns/lemon/frac#`, and `lexinfo:` `http://www.lexinfo.net/ontology/3.0/lexinfo#`.

This query exploits SPARQL property paths to return collocates of any kind of observables, so the `?observable` could be identical to (lexical) `?entry` (no `ontolex:sense` or `ontolex:lexicalForm` relation; it could be the `ontolex: sense` or it could be a `ontolex: lexicalForm`. If defined in the data, it returns the `frac:head` status or the `lexinfo: partOfSpeech`:

```
| form     | pos           | collocation        | isHead |
===========================================================
| "have"   | lexinfo:verb  | <col_have_point>   |        |
| "point"  | lexinfo:noun  | <col_have_point>   | "true" |
| "point"  | lexinfo:noun  | <col_see_point>    | "true" |
| "point"  | lexinfo:noun  | <col_take_point>   | "true" |
| "see"    | lexinfo:verb  | <col_see_point>    |        |
| "take"   | lexinfo:verb  | <col_take_point>   |        |
```

With the third query, we retrieve and aggregate (generate) string representations for collocations:

```
SELECT DISTINCT ?collocation ?string
WHERE {
  { SELECT ?collocation
    (GROUP_CONCAT(?wrep; separator=" ")
     AS ?string)
    WHERE {
      { SELECT ?collocation ?member
            ?wrep ?order
        WHERE {
          ?collocation a frac:Collocation ;
            ?prop ?member .
          FILTER(?prop=rdfs:member ||
            regex(str(?prop),".*#_[0-9]+$"))
          ?member ((^ontolex:sense)?/
                   ontolex:canonicalForm)?/
                   ontolex:writtenRep ?wrep.
          OPTIONAL {
            ?collocation ?nrel ?member .
            FILTER(regex(str(?nrel),".*#_[0-9]+$"))
            BIND(replace(str(?nrel),".*#_([0-9]+)$",
              "$1")
            AS ?order)
          }
        } GROUP BY ?collocation ?member ?wrep ?order
          ORDER BY ?collocation ?order ?member
      }
    } GROUP BY ?collocation
  }
}
```

The challenge in this query is that the ordering information retrieved above is to be used in an aggregation (in the embedded `SELECT` statement) by means of `GROUP_CONCAT`:

```
| collocation        | string        |
=====================================
| <col_have_point>   | "have point"  |
| <col_take_point>   | "take point"  |
| <col_see_point>    | "see point"   |
```

These surface strings are, indeed, not literally identical to contextualized versions of the corresponding collocations, but they are true to the lexical data in that they implement the `VERB + POINT` pattern specified in the original dictionary.

5.2. Information Integration for Downstream Applications

Collocations have been used successfully in information integration for downstream applications. One application of collocation is in creating recommendation systems.

To enhance the user experience when using e-commerce platforms, in (Wang and Qiu, 2021) the authors propose a novel fashion collocation recommendation model. The solution uses textual descriptions, purchase data, and category information of items to 1) build a a knowledge graph for modeling the purchase data and category information of items, 2) create knowledge embeddings from the graph, and 3) design a fashion collocation recommendation model that computes the probability of fashion collocation between items to recommend to users. In (Mao et al., 2018), an expert system is designed for costume recommendations which provides customers clothing collocation as recommendations. The system inference engine employs designed rules and user related facts (i.e., physical characteristics) to match customers preferences and generates a clothing recommendation list. @Collocation are also used in recommending news articles to users.

In (Kompan and Bieliková, 2011), the authors include collocations into the preprocessing steps used in text mining to create a fast news articles recommendation system. The system relies on collocations extracted from the articles' characteristics, e.g., title, content, topics, etc., to recommend news content to users.

In (Chu and Wang, 2018), the authors build a collocation corpus for academic writing in engineering and science fields which is used for establishing a sentence-wide collocation recommendation and error detection system for academic writing. After extracting the collocations from sentences, they are classified to create the collocation corpus. The corpus is then used to create a recommendation system for collocations that is also able to detect collocation errors at sentence level.

6. Summary and Discussion

With the collocation extensions for OntoLex-FrAC introduced in this paper, we provide an RDF vocabulary for collocation dictionaries and automated methods of collocation analysis, established as a consensus over contributions from five different institutions and numerous data sets, with the goal of eliciting feedback from reviewers, workshop audience and the scientific community in preparation of the final consolidation of the OntoLex-FrAC module, publication of which as a W3C community report is foreseen for the end of this year.

The key benefit of modelling lexical resources in OntoLex is two-fold:

- It allows us to provide data in a form that can be easily re-used by clients and applications. They can be processed by standard RDF tools and Linguistic Linked Open Data (LLOD) technology. This includes the application of SPARQL for querying distributed lexical data sets.

- It allows to integrate and link such data from distributed and remote sources on the web. Again, this functionality is also integrated in SPARQL (with keywords such as `SERVICE`, `FROM`, or `LOAD`).

With the collocation vocabulary of OntoLex-FrAC, an important contribution has been made in that, now, machine-readable (editions of) traditional collocation dictionaries and collocation scores (automatically generated, either on a fly by a web service, or, as illustrated here, from an existing web portal) can be modelled in the same vocabulary, and can be seamlessly integrated with each other. In comparison to the current capabilities of both TEI (addressing the requirements for collocation *dictionaries* as emerging from traditional lexicographic research) and collocation scores (as generated by tools like SketchEngine or provided by portals such as the Leipzig Wortschatz portal), OntoLex-FrAC covers *both* the needs of developers and APIs (collocation scores, lacking in TEI) and the needs of the lexicographer (modelling dictionaries and their lexicographic structure by means of OntoLex and OntoLex-Lexicog – lacking in Wortschatz or SketchEngine).

Although these additions to OntoLex-FrAC appear to be minimal (one new class for collocations, one new object property to identify their head, one new datatype property to represent collocations cores – and its large and extensible set of subproperties), they have been shown to be sufficient and to be sufficiently generic to model both collocation dictionaries and API/collocation score requirements.

Acknowledgments

The research described in this paper was conducted in the context of the Cost Action CA18209 *Nexus Linguarum. European network for Web-centred linguistic data science* and innovation programme via the project Prêt-à-LLOD (2019-2022, grant agreement no. 825182, Maxim Ionov). Moreover, the authors would like to thank Julia Bosque-Gil for contributing to the development of OntoLex-FrAc as well as to all OntoLex-FrAC contributors.

7. Bibliographical References

Bosque-Gil, J. and Gracia, J. (2019). The OntoLex Lemon Lexicography Module. Final Community Group Report. Technical report, W3C.

Brin, S., Motwani, R., Ullman, J. D., and Tsur, S. (1997). Dynamic Itemset Counting and Implication Rules for Market Basket Data. In Joan Peckham, editor, *SIGMOD 1997, Proceedings ACM SIGMOD International Conference on Management of Data, May 13-15, 1997, Tucson, Arizona, USA*, pages 255–264. ACM Press.

Chiarcos, C., Ionov, M., de Does, J., Depuydt, K., Khan, F., Stolk, S., Declerck, T., and McCrae, J. P. (2020). Modelling frequency and attestations for ontolex-lemon. In *Proceedings of the 2020 Globalex Workshop on Linked Lexicography*, pages 1–9.

Chiarcos, C., Declerck, T., and Ionov, M. (2021). Embeddings for the Lexicon: Modelling and Representation. In *Proceedings of the 6th Workshop on Semantic Deep Learning (SemDeep-6)*, pages 13–19.

Chu, Y.-L. and Wang, T.-I. (2018). A Sentence-Wide Collocation Recommendation System with Error Detection for Academic Writing. In *Lecture Notes in Computer Science*, pages 307–316. Springer International Publishing.

Goldhahn, D., Eckart, T., and Quasthoff, U. (2012). Building large monolingual dictionaries at the leipzig corpora collection: From 100 to 200 languages. In *Proceedings of the Eighth International Conference on Language Resources and Evaluation (LREC'12)*, pages 759–765.

Hardie, A. (2012). CQPweb. Combining power, flexibility and usability in a corpus analysis tool. *International journal of corpus linguistics*, 17(3):380–409.

Initiative, T. E. (2022). P5: Guidelines for electronic text encoding and interchange, chap. 9 dictionaries. Technical report. Version 4.4.0. Last updated on 19th April 2022, revision ff9cc28b0.

Kilgarriff, A., Baisa, V., Bušta, J., Jakubíček, M., Kovář, V., Michelfeit, J., Rychlý, P., and Suchomel, V. (2014). The Sketch Engine: ten years on. *Lexicography*, 1(1):7–36.

Kompan, M. and Bieliková, M. (2011). News Article Classification Based on a Vector Representation Including Words' Collocations. In *Advances in Intelligent and Soft Computing*, pages 1–8. Springer Berlin Heidelberg.

Larose, D. T. and Larose, C. D., (2014). *Association Rules*, chapter 12, pages 247–265. John Wiley and Sons, Ltd.

Manning, C. and Schutze, H. (1999). *Foundations of Statistical Natural Language Processing*. MIT Press Ltd, May.

Mao, Q., Dong, A., Miao, Q., and Pan, L. (2018). Intelligent Costume Recommendation System Based on Expert System. *Journal of Shanghai Jiaotong University (Science)*, 23(2):227–234, apr.

McCrae, J. P., Bosque-Gil, J., Gracia, J., Buitelaar, P., and Cimiano, P. (2017). The Ontolex-Lemon model: development and applications. In *Proceedings of eLex 2017 conference*, pages 19–21.

OUP. (2002). *Oxford Collocations Dictionary for Students of English*. Oxford University Press, USA.

Pedersen, T. (1998). Dependent bigram identification. *AAAI/IAAI*, 1197.

Role, F. and Nadif, M. (2011). Handling The Impact of Low Frequency Events on Co-Occurrence Based Measures of Word Similarity - A Case Study of Pointwise Mutual Information. In *Proceedings of the International Conference on Knowledge Discovery and Information Retrieval - Volume 1: KDIR, (IC3K 2011)*, pages 218–223. INSTICC, SciTePress.

Suchánek, M. and Pergl, R. (2020). Case-study-based review of approaches for transforming UML class diagrams to OWL and vice versa. In *2020 IEEE 22nd Conference on Business Informatics (CBI)*, volume 1, pages 270–279. IEEE.

Wang, S. and Qiu, J. (2021). A deep neural network model for fashion collocation recommendation using side information in e-commerce. *Applied Soft Computing*, 110:107753, oct.

Proceedings of the Globalex Workshop on Linked Lexicography @LREC2022, pages 19–25
Marseille, 20 June 2022

TIAD 2022
The Fifth Translation Inference Across Dictionaries Shared Task

Jorge Gracia[1], Besim Kabashi[2], Ilan Kernerman[3]
[1] Aragon Institute of Engineering Research (I3A), University of Zaragoza, Spain, jogracia@unizar.es
[2] Corpus and Computational Linguistics, University of Erlangen-Nuremberg, Germany, besim.kabashi@fau.de
[3] K Dictionaries - Lexicala, Tel Aviv, Israel, ilan@kdictionaries.com

Abstract

The objective of the Translation Inference Across Dictionaries (TIAD) series of shared tasks is to explore and compare methods and techniques that infer translations indirectly between language pairs, based on other bilingual/multilingual lexicographic resources. In this fifth edition, the participating systems were asked to generate new translations automatically among three languages - English, French, Portuguese - based on known indirect translations contained in the Apertium RDF graph. Such evaluation pairs have been the same during the four last TIAD editions. Since the fourth edition, however, a larger graph is used as a basis to produce the translations, namely Apertium RDF v2. The evaluation of the results was carried out by the organisers against manually compiled language pairs of K Dictionaries. For the second time in the TIAD series, some systems beat the proposed baselines. This paper gives an overall description of the shard task, the evaluation data and methodology, and the systems' results

Keywords: TIAD, translation inference, lexicographic data, dictionary, Apertium RDF

1. Introduction

A number of methods and techniques have been explored in the past with the aim of automatically generating new bilingual and multilingual dictionaries based on existing ones. For instance, given a bilingual dictionary containing translations from one language L1 to another language L2, and another dictionary with translations from L2 to L3, a new set of translations from L1 to L3 is produced. The intermediate language (L2 in this example) is called pivot language, and it is possible to use multiple pivots for this purpose. When using intermediate languages, it is necessary to discriminate wrong inferred translations caused by translation ambiguities. The method proposed by Tanaka and Umemura (Tanaka and Umemura, 1994) in 1994, called One Time Inverse Consultation (OTIC), identified incorrect translations when constructing bilingual dictionaries intermediated by a third language. This was a pioneering work and it still constitutes a baseline that is hard to beat, as the previous TIAD editions demonstrated. The OTIC method has been further adapted and evolved in the literature, for instance by Lim et al. (Lim et al., 2011), who grounded on it for their method for multilingual lexicon creation. From a different perspective, other works were proposed that relied on cycles and graph exploration to validate indirectly inferred translations, such as the SenseUniformPaths algorithm by Mousam et al. (Mausam et al., 2009), the CQC algorithm by Flati et al. (Flati and Navigli, 2013) or the exploration based on cycle density by Villegas et al. (Villegas et al., 2016).

However, previous work on the topic of automatic bilingual/multilingual dictionary generation was usually conducted on different types of datasets and evaluated in different ways, applying various algorithms that are often not comparable. In this context, the objective of the Translation Inference Across Dictionaries (TIAD) shared task is to support a coherent experiment framework that enables reliable validation of results and solid comparison of the processes used. In addition, this initiative aims to enhance further research on the topic of inferring translations across languages.

The TIAD first edition[1] took place in Galway (Ireland) in 2017, co-located with the LDK'17 conference. The second edition[2] in 2019 was co-located with LDK'19 in Leipzig (Germany), and the third one was planned at LREC'20 in Marseille (France) as part of the Globalex Workshop on Linked Lexicography[3]. Although the workshop of the third edition did not take place because of the COVID-19 crisis, the evaluation was run and the results published[4]. Participants in the 3rd edition had the opportunity to present their systems jointly with the contributors to the 4th TIAD edition[5], during the whorkshop that took place in Zaragoza (Spain) at LDK'21. The fifth edition of TIAD was held in conjunction to the GLOBALEX 2022 – Linked Lexicography workshop[6] at the 13th Language Resources and Evaluation Conference (LREC 2022)[7] in Marseille (France) on June 20, 2022. In this paper, we give an overall description of the shard task, the evaluation data and methodology, and the system results of TIAD 2022.

---

[1] `https://tiad2017.wordpress.com/`
[2] `https://tiad2019.unizar.es`
[3] `https://globalex2020.globalex.link/globalex-workshop-lrec2020-about-globalex-lrec2020/`
[4] `https://tiad2020.unizar.es`
[5] `https://tiad2021.unizar.es`
[6] `https://globalex2022.globalex.link/lrec2022/`
[7] `https://lrec2022.lrec-conf.org/en/`

The remainder of this paper is organised as follows. In Section 2, an overall description of the shared task is given. Section 3 describes the evaluation data and Section 4 explains the evaluation process. In Section 5 the system results are reported, and conclusions are summarised in Section 6.

2. Shared task description

The objective of TIAD shared task is to explore and compare methods and techniques that infer translations indirectly between language pairs, based on other bilingual resources. Such techniques would help in auto-generating new bilingual and multilingual dictionaries based on existing ones.

In this fifth edition, the participating systems were asked to generate new translations automatically among three languages: English, French, and Portuguese, based on known translations contained in the Apertium RDF v2.0 graph[8]. As these languages (EN, FR, PT) are not directly connected in this graph, no translations can be obtained directly among them there. Based on the available RDF data, the participants had to apply their methodologies to derive translations, mediated by any other language in the graph, between the pairs EN/FR, FR/PT and PT/EN.

Participants could also make use of other freely available sources of background knowledge (e.g. lexical linked open data and parallel corpora) to improve performance, as long as no direct translation among the studied language pairs were available. Beyond performance, participants were encouraged to consider also the following issues in particular:

1. The role of the language family with respect to the newly generated pairs
2. The asymmetry of pairs, and how translation direction affects the results
3. The behavior of different parts of speech among different languages
4. The role that the number of pivots plays in the process

The evaluation of the results was carried out by the organisers against manually compiled pairs of K Dictionaries (KD), extracted from its Global Series[9], which were not accessible to the participants. A validation data set was made available to participants, upon request, in particular a 5% of randomly selected translations for each language pair. The goal of this validation data is to allow participants to analyse the nature of the data, to run some validation tests, and to analyse negative results.

[8] https://tiad2021.unizar.es/images/ApertiumRDFv2.0_graph.png

[9] https://www.lexicala.com/

3. Evaluation data

In this section we briefly describe the input data source that has been proposed in the shared task as a source of known translations, i.e., Apertium RDF, as well as the Global series data used as golden standard, from KD.

3.1. Source data

As mentioned above, the shared task relies on known translations contained in Apertium RDF, which were used to infer new ones. Apertium RDF is the linked data counterpart of the Apertium dictionary data. Apertium (Forcada et al., 2011) is a free open-source machine translation platform. The system was initially created by Universitat d'Alacant and is released under the terms of the GNU General Public License. In its core, Apertium relies on a set of bilingual dictionaries, developed by a community of contributors, which covers more than 40 languages pairs.

Apertium RDF (Gracia et al., 2018) is the result of publishing the Apertium bilingual dictionaries as linked data on the Web. The result groups the data of the (originally disparate) Apertium bilingual dictionaries in the same graph, interconnected through the common lexical entries of the monolingual lexicons that they share. An initial version of 22 language pairs was developed by Universidad Politécnica de Madrid and Universitat Pompeu Fabra[10]. A later conversion of the Apertium data into RDF, which we call Apertium RDF v2 in the following, was made by Goethe University Frankfurt and University of Zaragoza (Gracia et al., 2020). It contains 44 languages and 53 language pairs, with a total number of 1,540,996 translations between 1,750,917 lexical entries. In the second and third TIAD editions, the first version of Apertium RDF was used, while in the fourth and fifth editions we moved to the larger and richer Apertium RDF v2 graph.

In its first version, Apertium RDF was modeled using the *lemon* model (McCrae et al., 2012) jointly with its translation module (Montiel-Ponsoda et al., 2011), while Apertium RDF v2 uses the Ontolex lemon core model to represent the data (McCrae et al., 2017), jointly with the lemon vartrans module[11].

Each original Apertium bilingual dictionary was converted into three different objects in RDF: source lexicon, target lexicon, and translation set. As a result, two independent monolingual lexicons per dictionary were published as linked data on the Web, along with a set of translations that connects them. Note that the naming rule used to build the identifiers (URIs) of the lexical entries allows to reuse the same URI per lexical entry across all the dictionaries, thus explicitly connecting them. For instance the same URI is used for

[10] http://linguistic.linkeddata.es/apertium/

[11] https://www.w3.org/2016/05/ontolex/#variation-translation-vartrans

the English word *bench* as a noun[12]: throughout the Apertium RDF graph, no matter if it comes from, e.g., the EN-ES dictionary or the CA-EN one. More details about the generation of Apertium RDF based on the Apertium data can be found at (Gracia et al., 2018).

Figure 1: The Apertium RDF v2 graph. The nodes in the figure represent the monolingual lexicons and the edges are the translation sets between them. The darker the colour, the more connections a node has. We have highlighted the three languages of this evaluation campaign: PT, FR, and EN.

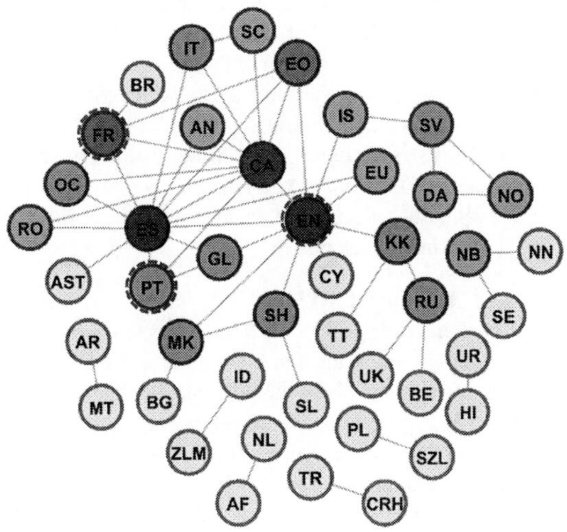

Figure 1 illustrates the Apertium RDF v2 unified graph. The nodes in the figure are the languages and the edges are the translation sets between them. All the datasets are available in Zenodo[13]. There is a plan to store the data in a permanent triplestore and expose it through a SPARQL endpoint in the near future, as part to the Prêt-à-LLOD project[14].

There were several ways in which the evaluation data was available to the participants: (i) through the data dumps available in Zenodo, which need to be loaded in a local triplestore, e.g., Apache Fuseki, and queried locally; (ii) through a testing SPARQL endpoint[15], and (iii) in a ZIP file in comma separated values (CSV) format[16], for those not acquainted with semantic web technologies. More details on how to access the data are available in the TIAD 2022 website[17].

3.2. Gold standard

The evaluation of the results was carried out by the organisers against manually compiled language pairs of K Dictionaries, extracted from its Global series, particularly the following pairs: BR-EN, EN-BR, FR-EN, EN-FR, FR-PT, PT-FR. The translation pairs extracted from these dictionaries served as a golden standard and remained blind to the participants. Notice that the Brazilian Portuguese variant was used for the translations to/from English (whereas the European Portuguese variant was used with French), which might introduce a bias; however its influence should be equivalent to every participant system thus still allowing for a valid comparison.

Given the fact that the coverage of KD is not the same as Apertium, we took the subset of KD that is covered by Apertium to build the gold standard and allow comparisons, i.e., those KD translations for which the source and target terms are present in both Apertium RDF source and target lexicons.

Table 1 shows the size (in number of translations) of the different language pairs in the gold standard. This number might differ from previous TIAD editions because since TIAD'20 the golden standard data have been curated with respect to the initial version in several aspects (see (Kernerman et al., 2020)) and, further, the use of a larger Apertium graph since TIAD'21 might have slightly changed the overlap degree between Apertium lexica and KD data.

Table 1: Number of translations per language pair in the gold standard.

Language pair	Size
EN-FR	12,453
EN-PT	10,151
FR-EN	16,103
FR-PT	7,982
PT-EN	12,219
PT-FR	6,589

4. Evaluation methodology

The participants run their systems locally, using the Apertium RDF data as known translations, to infer new translations among the three studied languages: FR, EN, PT. Once the output data (inferred translations) were obtained, they loaded the results into a file per

[12] http://linguistic.linkeddata.es/id/apertium/lexiconEN/bench-n-en

[13] https://tinyurl.com/apertiumrdfv2

[14] https://pret-a-llod.eu/

[15] Hosted by the University of Frankfurt at http://dbserver.acoli.cs.uni-frankfurt.de:5005/dataset.html. The queries should be restricted to this graph: http://linguistic.linkeddata.es/id/apertium-ud. Since this is for testing purposes, there is no guarantee of a quick and efficient response, and the link may not be persistent long after the evaluation campaign. See an example query at https://ndownloader.figshare.com/files/26321950

[16] https://tiad2021.unizar.es/data/TransSets_ApertiumRDFv2_1_CSV.zip

[17] See the "how to get the data source" section at https://tiad2022.unizar.es/task.html

language pair in TSV format, containing the following information per row (tab separated):

"source written representation"
"target written representation"
"part of speech"
"confidence score"

The confidence score takes float values between 0 and 1 and is a measure of the confidence that the translation holds between the source and target written representations. If a system does not compute confidence scores, this value had to be put to 1.

4.1. Evaluation process

The organisers compared the obtained results with the gold standard automatically. This process was followed for each system results file and per language pair:

1. Remove duplicated translations (if any).
2. Filter out translations for which the source entry or the target entry are not present in the golden standard (otherwise we cannot assess whether the translation is correct or not). We call *systemGS* the subset of translations that passed this filter, and *GS* the whole set of gold standard translations, in the given language pair.
3. Translations with confidence degree under a given threshold were removed from $systemGS$. In principle, the used threshold is the one reported by participants as the optimal one during the training/preparation phase.
4. Compute the coverage of the system with respect to the gold standard, i.e., how many gold standard entries in the source language were effectively translated by the system (no matter if they were correct or wrong ones).
5. Compute precision as P = (#correct translations in systemGS) / |systemGS|
6. Compute recall as R = (#correct translations in systemGS) / |GS|
7. Compute F-measure as $F = 2 * P * R / (P + R)$

The precision/recall metrics calculated after applying steps 1 to 3 correspond to what in (Goel et al., 2021) is defined as *both-word precision* and *both-word recall.* The idea is to reduce the penalization to a system for inferring correct translations that are missing in the golden standard dictionary because human editors might have overlooked them when elaborating the dictionary. Note that in TIAD editions previous to TIAD'21 we only filtered out translations for which the source entry was not present in the translation (step 2), which led to computing the so-called one-word precision/recall, thus only partially covering such a goal.

4.2. Baselines

We have run the above evaluation process with results obtained with two baselines, to be compared with the participating systems' results:

4.2.1. Baseline 1 - Word2Vec

The method uses Word2Vec (Mikolov et al., 2013) to transform the graph into a vector space. A graph edge is interpreted as a sentence and the nodes are word forms with their POS tag. Word2Vec iterates multiple times over the graph and learns multilingual embeddings (without additional data). We used the Gensim[18] Word2Vec implementation. For a given input word, we calculated a distance based on the cosine similarity of a word to every other word with the target-POS tag in the target language. The square of the distance from source to target word is interpreted as the confidence degree. For the first word the minimum distance is 0.6^2, for the others it is 0.8^2. Therefore multiple results are only in the output if the confidence is not extremely weak. In our evaluation, we applied an arbitrary threshold of 0.5 to the confidence degree[19].

4.2.2. Baseline 2 - OTIC

In short, the idea of the One Time Inverse Consultation (OTIC) method (Tanaka and Umemura, 1994) is to explore, for a given word, the possible candidate translations that can be obtained through intermediate translations in the pivot language. Then, a score is assigned to each candidate translation based on the degree of overlap between the pivot translations shared by both the source and target words[20]. In our evaluation, we applied the OTIC method using Spanish as pivot language, and using an arbitrary threshold of 0.5.
Note that since the TIAD'21 edition, the Word2Vec baseline, although based on the same principles, was re-implemented and re-trained to be adapted to the new Apertium RDF v2 dataset, thus leading to different (generally better) results than in the previous TIAD editions. The OTIC baseline, although it does not need retraining, was also re-run for TIAD'21 to be adapted to the new Apertium RDF v2 dataset (the new baseline results remain valid for TIAD'22). The results are generally worse than in TIAD'20 (with the smaller Apertium RDF v1 graph).
Strictly speaking, these are not baselines as they are conceived in other shared tasks, meaning naive approaches with a straightforward implementation, but state-of-the-art methods to solve the task.

5. Results

In this section we review the participating systems in TIAD 2022 and their evaluation results.

[18] https://radimrehurek.com/gensim/
[19] The code can be found at https://github.com/kabashi/TIAD2022_word2vec
[20] You can find the code at https://gitlab.com/sid_unizar/otic

5.1. Participating systems

Two teams participated in this edition of the shared task, contributing with four systems or system variants. Table 2 lists the participant teams and systems.

The first team, L. Dranca from Centro Universitario de la Defensa (CUD), Spain, developed three variants of a system that was based on the use of FastRP (Chen et al., 2019). The algorithm, generates embeddings form a graph node (in this case words) based on the neighbourhood information, in this case translations into other languages. Thus, words with similar translations will have similar FastRP embeddings. They use ES as a pivot language, or both ES and CA. Note that we cannot refer to a detailed description of the system because the author decided not to publish their system description paper, nor to participate in the workshop. We still include their result here for completeness.

The second team, Y. Bestgen (Bestgen, 2022) from Universite catholique de Louvain, Belgium, presented a system that combines a classical machine learning technique such as logistic regression with the use of pivot languages to obtain inferred translations.

5.2. Evaluation results

The complete evaluation results per system and per language pair are accessible in the TIAD 2022 website[21]. In order to give an overview of the results, we include here Table 3, which shows the averaged results, evaluated by using the confidence threshold that every participant reported as optimal according to their internal tests. Since the evaluation setup was identical as in TIAD 2021, we combine in the table the results of both evaluation campaigns.

5.3. Discussion

As can be seen in Table 3, two of the four systems obtained better results than both baselines in terms of F-measure. This continues a trend started in TIAD 2021 when some systems were able to beat both baselines, since in previous TIAD editions there was no system beating both baselines. Interestingly, the OTIC method, based on purely graph exploration and dated back to 1994, systematically outperformed more contemporary methods based on word embeddings and distributional semantics, which gives an idea of the difficulty of the task. The last two years' results confirm our intuition that OTIC was not an upper bound and that there were still much room for improvement for more methods.

Note that the precision values shown in Table 3 are conservative since there is a small but undefined number of false negatives (correct translations that are not present in the gold standard) that can be found in the results. For example, from the EN→FR set of translations are as follows: "wizard"→"sorcier" (noun), "abandon"→"quitter" (verb) and the "dump"→"vider" (verb).

[21]Cf. `https://tiad2022.unizar.es/results.html` under the section "Evaluation results".

6. Conclusions

In this paper we have given an overview of the 5th Translation Inference Across Dictionaries (TIAD) shared task, and a description of the results obtained by the four participating systems and two baselines, compared also with the results of the previous campaign. In this edition, the participating systems were asked to generate new translations automatically among English, French, Portuguese, based on known indirect translations contained in the Apertium RDF graph. Same as in the previous edition, a new larger version of the data graph was used, that is Apertium RDF v2. The evaluation of the results was carried out by the organisers against manually compiled pairs of K Dictionaries. The results are good (two systems beat the baselines), are along the lines of the previous edition, and illustrate improvement in the area of translation inference across dictionaries despite the difficulty of the task. However, we consider that the task is far from being solved, with much room for improvement and other aspects and languages to be explored.

7. Acknowledgements

We would like to thank Miguel López-Otal (University of Zaragoza) for his assistance with the baselines and evaluation process. This work has been supported by the European Union's Horizon 2020 research and innovation programme through the projects Prêt-à-LLOD (grant agreement No 825182) and Elexis (grant agreement No 731015). This work is also based upon work from COST Action CA18209 – NexusLinguarum "European network for Web-centred linguistic data science", supported by COST (European Cooperation in Science and Technology). It has been also partially supported by the Spanish project PID2020-113903RB-I00 (AEI/FEDER, UE), by DGA/FEDER, and by the *Agencia Estatal de Investigación* of the Spanish Ministry of Economy and Competitiveness and the European Social Fund through the "Ramón y Cajal" program (RYC2019-028112-I).

8. Bibliographical References

Bestgen, Yves. (2022). Creating bilingual dictionaries from existing ones by means of pivot-oriented translation inference and logistic regression. In *Proc. of Globalex 2022*.

Chen, Haochen and Sultan, Syed Fahad and Tian, Yingtao and Chen, Muhao and Skiena, Steven. (2019). Fast and accurate network embeddings via very sparse random projection. In *Proc. of International Conference on Information and Knowledge Management*, pages 399–408. Association for Computing Machinery, nov.

Flati, Tiziano and Navigli, Roberto. (2013). The CQC Algorithm: Cycling in Graphs to Semantically Enrich and Enhance a Bilingual Dictionary (Extended Abstract). In *Proce. of the 23th International Joint*

Table 2: Participant systems.

Team	System
Lacramiora Dranca (Centro Universitario de la Defensa, Spain)	FastRP_ES FastRP_fasttext_ES FastRP_fasttext_ES_CA
Yves Bestgen (Université catholique de Louvain, Belgium)	SATLab

Table 3: Averaged system results, ordered by F-measure in descending order. In **bold** the baselines, and in *italics* you can find the participants of TIAD 2022 (the rest are participants of TIAD 2021)

System	Precision	Recall	F-measure	Coverage
PivotAlign-R	0.71	0.58	0.64	0.77
PivotAlign-F	0.81	0.51	0.62	0.68
SATLab	0.86	0.48	0.62	0.70
ACDcat	0.75	0.53	0.61	0.75
TUANWEsg	0.81	0.47	0.59	0.76
TUANWEcb	0.81	0.47	0.59	0.76
ULD_graphSVR	0.70	0.49	0.57	0.69
fastRP_fastText_ES_CA	0.85	0.28	0.42	0.43
PivotAlign-P	0.86	0.24	0.37	0.33
baseline-Word2Vec	0.69	0.23	0.33	0.40
ULD_MUSE	0.29	0.41	0.33	0.65
baseline-OTIC	0.78	0.18	0.29	0.28
fastRP_fastText_ES	0.83	0.15	0.25	0.25
fastRP_ES	0.83	0.15	0.25	0.25
ULD_onetaSVR	0.76	0.10	0.17	0.14
TUANMUSEca	0.86	0.10	0.16	0.16
TUANMUSEes	0.87	0.08	0.13	0.14
ULD_oneta2	0.64	0.07	0.13	0.11
ULD_vecmap	0.36	0.01	0.01	0.02
ULD_mbert	0.00	0.00	0.00	0.11

Conference on Artificial Intelligence, IJCAI '13, pages 3151–3155. AAAI Press.

Forcada, Mikel L. and Ginestí-Rosell, Mireia and Nordfalk, Jacob and O'Regan, Jim and Ortiz-Rojas, Sergio and Pérez-Ortiz, Juan Antonio and Sánchez-Martínez, Felipe and Ramírez-Sánchez, Gema and Tyers, FrancisM. (2011). Apertium: a free/open-source platform for rule-based machine translation. *Machine Translation*, 25(2):127–144.

Goel, Shashwat and Gracia, Jorge and Forcada, Mikel Lorenzo. (2021). Bilingual dictionary generation and enrichment via graph exploration. *Semantic Web Journal*.

Gracia, Jorge and Villegas, Marta and Gómez-Pérez, Asunción and Bel, Núria. (2018). The apertium bilingual dictionaries on the web of data. *Semantic Web*, 9(2):231–240.

Gracia, Jorge and Fäth, Christian and Hartung, Matthias and Ionov, Max and Bosque-Gil, Julia and Veríssimo, Susana and Chiarcos, Christian and Orlikowski, Matthias. (2020). Leveraging Linguistic Linked Data for Cross-Lingual Model Transfer in the Pharmaceutical Domain. In Bo Fu et al., editors, *Proc. of 19th International Semantic Web Conference (ISWC 2020)*, pages 499–514. Springer.

Kernerman, Ilan and Krek, Simon and McCrae, John P. and Gracia, Jorge and Ahmadi, Sina and Kabashi, Besim. (2020). Introduction to the proceedings of globalex 2020 workshop on linked lexicography. In *Proc. of Globalex 2020 Workshop on Linked Lexicography – Twelfth International Conference on Language Resources and Evaluation (LREC 2020), Marseílle, France*. European Language Resources Association (ELRA).

Lim, Lian T and Ranaivo-Malançon, Bali and Tang, Enya K. (2011). Low Cost Construction of a Multilingual Lexicon from Bilingual Lists. *Polibits*, 43:45–51.

Mausam and Soderland, Stephen and Etzioni, Oren and Weld, Daniel S and Skinner, Michael and Bilmes, Jeff. (2009). Compiling a Massive, Multilingual Dictionary via Probabilistic Inference. In *Proc. of the Joint Conference of the 47th Annual Meeting of the ACL and the 4th International Joint Conference on Natural Language Processing of the AFNLP: Volume 1 - Volume 1*, ACL '09, pages 262–270, Stroudsburg, PA, USA. Association for Computational Linguistics.

McCrae, John and Aguado-de-Cea, Guadalupe and Buitelaar, Paul and Cimiano, Philipp and Declerck, Thierry and Gómez-Pérez, Asunción and Gracia, Jorge and Hollink, Laura and Montiel-Ponsoda, Elena and Spohr, Dennis and Wunner, Tobias. (2012). Interchanging lexical resources on the Semantic Web. *Language Resources and Evaluation*, 46:701–719.

McCrae, John P and Bosque-Gil, Julia and Gracia, Jorge and Buitelaar, Paul and Cimiano, Philipp. (2017). The OntoLex-Lemon Model: Development and Applications. In *Electronic lexicography in the 21st century. Proc. of eLex 2017 conference, in Leiden, Netherlands*, pages 587–597. Lexical Computing CZ s.r.o., sep.

Mikolov, Tomas and Chen, Kai and Corrado, Greg and Dean, Jeffrey. (2013). Efficient Estimation of Word Representations in Vector Space. In *Proc. of International Conference on Learning Representations (ICLR)*.

Montiel-Ponsoda, E. and Gracia, J. and Aguado-De-Cea, G. and Gómez-Pérez, A. (2011). Representing translations on the semantic Web. In *Proc. of the 2nd International Workshop on the Multilingual Semantic Web (MSW) at ISWC '11*, volume 775. CEUR Press.

Tanaka, Kumiko and Umemura, Kyoji. (1994). Construction of a Bilingual Dictionary Intermediated by a Third Language. In *COLING*, pages 297–303.

Villegas, Marta and Melero, Maite and Bel, Núria and Gracia, Jorge and Bel, Núria. (2016). Leveraging RDF Graphs for Crossing Multiple Bilingual Dictionaries. In *Proc. of 10th Language Resources and Evaluation Conference (LREC'16) Portorož (Slovenia)*, pages 868–876, Paris, France, may. European Language Resources Association (ELRA).

Proceedings of the Globalex Workshop on Linked Lexicography @LREC2022, pages 26–31
Marseille, 20 June 2022

Creating Bilingual Dictionaries from Existing ones by Means of Pivot-Oriented Translation Inference and Logistic Regression

Yves Bestgen
Laboratoire d'analyse statistique des textes
Université catholique de Louvain
Place Cardinal Mercier, 10 1348 Louvain-la-Neuve, Belgium
yves.bestgen@uclouvain.be

Abstract

To produce new bilingual dictionaries from existing ones, an important task in the field of translation, a system based on a very classical supervised learning technique, with no other knowledge than the available bilingual dictionaries, is proposed. It performed very well in the Translation Inference Across Dictionaries (TIAD) shared task on the combined 2021 and 2022 editions. An analysis of the pros and cons suggests a series of avenues to further improve its effectiveness.

Keywords: Apertium RDF graph, transitivity, supervised learning

1. Introduction

Despite recent advances in neural machine translation, bilingual dictionaries remain useful resources for both language learning and human post-editing of automatic translation as well as for language technologies (Goel et al., 2022). Unfortunately, such dictionaries are never completely up-to-date because languages evolve and speakers create new words. Moreover, some languages have far fewer bilingual dictionaries than others. Being able to automatically produce new bilingual dictionaries from existing ones has thus been an active area of research for the last 30 years (Tanaka-Ishii and Umemura, 1994; Mausam et al., 2009; Goel et al., 2022).

It is in this context that the Translation Inference Across Dictionaries (TIAD) shared task was created (Alper, 2017; Gracia et al., 2019; Gracia et al., 2021). In its 2021 and 2022 editions, it proposes to the participating teams to create automatically bilingual dictionaries between English, French and Portuguese, based on the many other bilingual dictionaries connected in the Apertium RDF graph (Gracia et al., 2018). This report presents the participation of SATLab to the fifth edition of this task proposed as part of the GLOBALEX 2022 workshop at LREC 2022.

This task has several characteristics that make it particularly complex. First of all, if the Apertium RDF graph is large since it contains 51 bilingual dictionaries[1] covering 42 languages, only three languages are present in many bilingual dictionaries (twelve for Spanish and ten for Catalan and English) whereas twenty languages are present in only one dictionary. Moreover, Apertium is largely focused on Spanish languages (Aragonese, Asturian, Basque, Catalan, Galician and Spanish) and even more on Catalan and Spanish since these languages are present in 21 dictionaries out of 51.

Secondly and most importantly, the evaluation of the effectiveness of the systems is not carried out on materials similar to that of the learning phase, but on the basis of manually compiled pairs of *K Dictionaries* (`https://lexicala.com/lexical-data/#dictionaries`) and other resources. The organizers provide a sample of this gold standard, but its use for optimizing systems is not easy as it is small (only 80 instances for one of the pairs of languages). On the other hand, it is far from clear that optimizing the system by means of a cross-validation procedure on the learning materials could be useful for the test materials. Consequently, the goal of the SATLab was to develop without optimization a system that potentially works and see what result it gets. If they are good, it will be interesting to look for an evaluation situation in which an optimization is easy to achieve.

To try to reach this goal, I chose to convert the problem into a supervised learning task, handled without external resources or complex learning procedures, an approach I have already used, sometimes successfully, to solve other NLP problems (Bestgen, 2021a; Bestgen, 2021b). The chance of success was not a priori zero since an approach of this type has already been recently used in this context (McCrae and Arcan, 2020; Ahmadi et al., 2021) and has produced interesting results, even if they were outperformed by more complex systems. The approach developed by these authors was graph-based and was a step towards more complex techniques such as Neural Machine Translation and cross-lingual word embedding mapping techniques. For my part, and even if the two approaches are similar, I started without preconceived ideas by considering the problem as a statistical data mining situation, based on computational procedures that rely on the sole notion of transitivity.

[1] The numbers given here refer to the CSV version of Apertium, provided by the task organizers, which was used in this study and contains two less dictionaries than the RDF version.

2. Approach

The objective is to arrive at potential translations of words for each of which a series of features will be used to decide whether these translations are assumed to be correct or not. These lists of translations or inferred dictionaries were obtained for all language pairs for which the gold standard is available in Apertium and for the six test language pairs. The approach developed is based on the following steps.

2.1. Data Processing

Reading the data. All CSV files were read and only the following three variables were kept: the word in the source language and in the target language and the grammatical category. These files were duplicated by reversing the source and target languages. All the dictionaries where one of the two languages is present in only one dictionary were deleted recursively.

Path search. For each dictionary, all paths, however long, from the source language to the target language through the bilingual dictionaries available in Apertium were identified. The only limiting condition applied is that the path cannot include the same language twice. As an example, 241 paths were found to go from FR[2] to PT and vice versa, and 146 to go from EN to PT. For a large number of language pairs, only 40 paths, including the direct path, were found (e.g., AN>ES, CA>ES or IT>SC). Some paths between the source and target languages pass through eight intermediate languages such as this one from EN to PT via EO>FR>OC>CA>SC>IT>ES>GL.

Producing bilingual dictionaries by inference. The paths identified in the previous step are used to produce bilingual dictionaries by inference, i.e. on the basis of at least one intermediate language, using transitivity. A more formal description of this approach under the name of *pivot-oriented translation inference* is given in Torregrosa et al. (2019). Starting from the source dictionary, the procedure is to use each intermediate dictionary as a pivot to the next one until the target dictionary is reached. At the end of the procedure, we obtain *for each path* an inferred bilingual dictionary which contains the source and target words, the grammatical category and the number of intermediate languages used. For each of these quadruplets, the following numerical data are computed in the dictionary in question:

- #Source: the number of occurrences of the source word.
- #Target: the number of occurrences of the target word.
- #Pair: the number of occurrences of the pair of words. It is indeed possible to reach the same pair by passing through different intermediate words.
- #SourceInPair: the number of different pairs containing the source word.
- #TargetInPair: the number of different pairs containing the target word.
- Source Ratio: #Pair divided by #Source.
- Target Ratio: #Pair divided by #Target.

Pooling of all bilingual dictionaries for a language pair. The average values of all the indices from the previous step is computed for each quadruplet. Two new indices are added: N, the frequency of each quadruplet, as well as the Total N, the frequency of the triplet composed of the source word, the target word, and the grammatical class. The first of these two values is therefore the number of paths of a given length that led to this triplet and the second is the total number of "paths" that led to this triplet. These two values are divided by the total number of paths that go from the source language to the target one. Finally, it is added whether the translation is correct or not according to the Apertium dictionary for this language pair. All these operations were also performed on the six test language pairs, but of course the gold standard, according to the Apertium dictionaries, is not added since it is unknown.

Preparing the data for supervised learning procedure. For each number of intermediate languages, ten features are encoded for each pair of translated words: the nine already described and the number of intermediate languages. So there can be from 10 to 80 features for each pair of words. To these, the size of the smallest path found that leads to this translation is added.

The values of each feature are then normalized by a MinMax transformation slightly modified compared to the classical formula:

$$MinMax = \frac{Feature_i\_score - min}{max - min} + 0.01 \quad (1)$$

The value of 0.01 is added to distinguish the minimum value of a feature with the value of 0, which codes the absence of a feature.

2.2. Supervised Learning Procedure

The supervised learning procedure used is the L1-regularized logistic regression as implemented in the LIBLinear package (Fan et al., 2008), The two parameters to optimize are the regularization parameter C and -wi which allows to adjust this parameter C for the two categories. After a few trials, the regularization parameter C was set to 80 and w1 to 2. The bias (B) was set to 1.

2.3. First Evaluation

In order to determine if the proposed approach had a chance to be sufficiently efficient, it was applied to the prediction of the EN to ES pair by means of a cross-validation procedure with 80% of the instances for training and the rest for testing. To also have an

[2] The languages are indicated by means of ISO 639-1 codes (see `https://en.wikipedia.org/wiki/List_of_ISO_639-1_codes`)

Type	Max Nbr	P	R	F1
L	5	0.8223	0.7139	0.7643
T	5	0.8184	0.7115	0.7612
L	4	0.8213	0.7157	0.7649
T	4	0.8176	0.7121	0.7612
L	3	0.8218	0.7114	0.7626
T	3	0.8166	0.7133	0.7614
L	2	0.8251	0.7094	0.7629
T	2	0.8205	0.7104	0.7615
L	1	0.8085	0.6808	0.7391
T	1	0.8105	0.6819	0.7406

Table 1: Results for the cross-validation analyses on EN to ES translations

Type	Max Nbr	P	R	F1
L	5	0.8225	0.7137	0.7643
T	5	0.8425	0.6224	0.7159
L	4	0.8213	0.7125	0.7631
T	4	0.8384	0.6223	0.7144
L	3	0.8209	0.7120	0.7626
T	3	0.8519	0.6118	0.7122
L	2	0.8242	0.7095	0.7626
T	2	0.8572	0.6210	0.7202
L	1	0.8086	0.6810	0.7393
T	1	0.8620	0.6120	0.7158

Table 2: Results by learning using EN to ES translations and predicting for FR to ES translations

evaluation situation that resembles the test situation in which it is not possible to learn and test on the same pair of languages, the system was also evaluated using a semi-external validation procedure, by learning on the EN to ES pair and testing on the FR to ES pair. The measures of effectiveness were precision (P), recall (R) and F1-score (F1) for the predicted translations according to whether they are present in the gold standard or not. In other words, the translations inferred but rejected by the logistic regression were not included in the calculation of the system's efficiency. In this evaluation, the maximum path size was manipulated. The results are presented in Tables 1 and 2.

These tables suggest that the performances are not too bad, but they do not seem exceptional either. They also indicate a total absence of overfit in CV and a relatively limited loss in semi-external validation. The impact of the number of intermediate languages is very small in both cross- and semi-external validation, except when the prediction is based on a single intermediate language. It was therefore decided to use this approach for the shared task by setting the number of intermediate languages at maximum three.

D1	D2	C	D1	D2	C	D1	D2	C
0	1	.18	4	0	.71	2	3	.89
1	0	.18	1	2	.81	3	2	.89
0	2	.36	2	1	.81	2	4	.90
1	1	.36	1	3	.82	4	2	.90
2	0	.36	3	1	.82	3	3	.93
0	3	.54	1	4	.83	3	4	.96
3	0	.54	4	1	.83	4	3	.96
0	4	.71	2	2	.83	4	4	1.0

Table 3: Computation of the Confidence score (C) according to the number of semi-external learning sets which lead to the translation for each direction (D1 and D2).

System	P	R	F1
PivotAlign-R	0.71	0.58	0.64
PivotAlign-F	0.81	0.51	0.62
SATLab	0.86	0.48	0.62
ACDcat	0.75	0.53	0.61
TUANWEsg	0.81	0.47	0.59
TUANWEcb	0.81	0.47	0.59
ULD_graphSVR	0.70	0.49	0.57
fastRP	0.85	0.28	0.42
PivotAlign-P	0.86	0.24	0.37
Baseline W2V	0.69	0.23	0.33

Table 4: Official results for 2021 et 2022 editions

2.4. System Submitted for the Shared Task

The system used for the official task has some specificities compared to the one described above. It should be noted that no further evaluation attempts were made since, as explained in the introduction, there is no guarantee that an Apertium-based optimization would be informative for the official test set.

First, several semi-external learning sets were arbitrarily selected for each target language:

- For FR>EN and PT>EN: CA>EN, ES>EN, EU>EN and EO>EN
- For EN>FR and PT>FR: CA>FR, ES>FR, OC>FR and EO>FR
- For EN>PT and FR>PT: CA>PT, ES>PT and GL>PT

Then the predictions in both directions for the same pair of test languages were combined to obtain the same inferred bilingual dictionary. Finally, the final decision for each pair was based on the number of models that predict this translation for each of the two directions as shown in Table 3. The threshold used for the official submission was set to 0.80.

3. Results

3.1. Results on the Official Test Set

The SATLab submitted only one system, as the official challenge website (https://tiad2022.unizar.es) did not indicate that more than one system could be submitted.

As the 2022 edition of the TIAD challenge is identical to the 2021 edition, the organizers have released, in addition to the results for 2022, the combined results for these two editions. Table 4 presents the results of the ten best submissions in this combined ranking. The official measure of the challenge is the F1-score.

The SATLab ranked third, close to the top two submissions of the first team in 2021 (Steingrimsson et al., 2021). Compared to the system also based on pivot-oriented translation inference and supervised learning (ULD_graphSVR in Ahmadi et al., 2021), the SATLab gets 5 more F1-points.

Since the systems submitted a confidence score for each proposed translation, the results reported in Table 4 were obtained by dichotomizing the scores, using the threshold value proposed by the teams. The organizers also provided an analysis of the performance of the systems when varying this threshold. As shown in Table 5, the SATLab scores best for the majority of thresholds, but the differences between the best systems are small and it is unlikely that an analysis using confidence intervals (Bestgen, 2022), unfortunately not possible here because the complete data are not available, would report important or statistically significant differences.

Finally, Table 6, provided by the organizers, presents the SATLab results separately for the six test language pairs. One can observe very strong variations according to the pair and the direction since the maximum difference between two F1-scores is 0.22. It would be really interesting to try to understand the origin of such differences, but it seems impossible without having access to the test set.

3.2. Additional Evaluation on the Learning Materials

As the test materials is not available, it is interesting to evaluate the proposed system in different (semi-) external learning configurations using Apertium. Table 7 presents the main results of these analyses.

The first section answers the question whether the same pair of languages used for learning (here, EN>ES) produces equivalent results for different test materials. The answer is very clearly negative, the difference between the test on AN>ES and on EO>ES being almost 0.40 of F1-score.

In the second section, the same semi-external evaluation procedure is used, but the language to be predicted is no longer ES. The results are overall worse than with ES, suggesting that this language is probably easier to predict.

In the last section, a completely external evaluation procedure is used since the four languages are different from each other. In two out of three cases, very poor performance is observed. These results suggest that it is desirable to learn by the semi-external procedure and therefore that one language should be the same for learning and testing.

4. Conclusion

The proposed system for the TIAD 2022 task scored well above my expectations, but it is important to note that many systems get very close scores. This system employs no knowledge other than the training set and is based on a very classical supervised learning technique. This submission has only scratched the surface of this interesting task. Indeed, there are still a number of options to try which are as many possibilities for future work. The main avenues seem to be the following:

- Optimizing features. It is very likely that some features are not very useful, but it is also far from obvious that all the features are computed in an optimal way. For example, it is questionable whether calculating the mean of #Pair is really preferable to taking the sum, since the values of this variable are almost always equal to 1.

- Reducing the number of paths. The results presented in Tables 2 and 3, as well as other analyses not reported here, suggest that limiting the number of intermediate languages to two might be beneficial.

- Evaluating other cases of semi-external validation. The proposed system relies on the presence of the same target language in the learning sets and in the test sets (e.g., ES>**EN** and FR>**EN**). It would be desirable to also evaluate models in which the source language is identical (e.g., **FR**>ES and **FR**>EN). It would also be interesting to see if using more than 7 or 8 models would improve the results.

- Finally, it would be interesting to compare the models of the logistic regression for different pairs of test languages to determine if the features are used in a similar way.

However, it is far from obvious that optimizing on the learning materials is relevant for the test materials, which is understandably not available. In this regard it would be interesting to find out if it is possible to put the task on a competition site by evaluating on one part of the data during development and on another part during the official test phase, possibly even on different test language pairs. I think this would make the task more attractive, but more importantly it would allow the development of better systems.

5. Acknowledgements

The author is a Research Associate of the Fonds de la Recherche Scientifique (FRS-FNRS).

Threshold	SATLab	PivotAlign-R	PivotAlign-F	ACDcat	TUANWEcb	ULD Gr SVR
0.0	**0.65**	0.64	0.62	0.61	0.59	0.60
0.1	**0.65**	0.64	0.62	0.61	0.59	0.59
0.2	0.63	**0.64**	0.62	0.61	0.59	0.59
0.3	0.62	**0.63**	0.62	0.61	0.59	0.58
0.4	**0.62**	0.61	0.60	0.61	0.59	0.57
0.5	**0.62**	0.58	0.58	0.61	0.59	0.57
0.6	**0.62**	0.54	0.53	**0.62**	0.60	0.57
0.7	**0.62**	0.49	0.47	**0.62**	0.60	0.55
0.8	**0.62**	0.41	0.38	**0.62**	0.59	0.54
0.9	0.47	0.30	0.25	**0.61**	0.57	0.51
1.0	0.31	0.12	0.07	**0.59**	0.14	0.25

Table 5: Results for the threshold analysis (best F1-scores are bolded)

Test	P	R	F1
EN>PT	0.85	0.41	0.55
EN>FR	0.82	0.40	0.54
FR>EN	0.83	0.47	0.60
FR>PT	0.89	0.53	0.67
PT>EN	0.86	0.42	0.57
PT>FR	0.90	0.66	0.76

Table 6: SATLab results for the six test language pairs

Learn	Test	P	R	F1
EN>ES	RO>ES	0.8818	0.7155	0.7900
EN>ES	AN>ES	0.9487	0.8332	0.8872
EN>ES	EO>ES	0.6346	0.4007	0.4912
SC>CA	EN>CA	0.7042	0.5427	0.6130
FR>CA	EN>CA	0.7823	0.5795	0.6658
ES>EU	EN>EU	0.8186	0.5341	0.6464
CA>SC	IT>SC	0.7087	0.4265	0.5325
EN>EU	FR>ES	0.5688	0.7549	0.6488
ES>CA	EN>EU	0.9564	0.0787	0.1455
ES>CA	IT>SC	0.8022	0.1934	0.3116

Table 7: Results of the post-hoc analyses on Apertium

6. Bibliographical References

Ahmadi, S., Ojha, A. K., Banerjee, S., and McCrae, J. P. (2021). NUIG at TIAD 2021: Cross-lingual word embeddings for translation inference. In *Proceedings of the Workshops and Tutorials held at LDK 2021*, CEUR Workshop Proceedings. CEUR-WS.org.

Alper, M. (2017). Auto-generating bilingual dictionaries: Results of the TIAD-2017 shared task baseline algorithm. In *Proceedings of the LDK 2017 Workshops*, CEUR Workshop Proceedings, pages 85–93. CEUR-WS.org.

Bestgen, Y. (2021a). LAST at CMCL 2021 shared task: Predicting gaze data during reading with a gradient boosting decision tree approach. In *Proceedings of the Workshop on Cognitive Modeling and Computational Linguistics*, pages 90–96, Online, June. Association for Computational Linguistics.

Bestgen, Y. (2021b). A simple language-agnostic yet strong baseline system for hate speech and offensive content identification. In *Working Notes of FIRE 2021 - Forum for Information Retrieval Evaluation*, CEUR Workshop Proceedings. CEUR-WS.org.

Bestgen, Y. (2022). Please, don't forget the difference and the confidence interval when seeking for the state-of-the-art status. In *Proceedings of the 13th Conference on Language Resources and Evaluation (LREC 2022)*, Marseille, France. European Language Resources Association (ELRA).

Fan, R.-E., Chang, K.-W., Hsieh, C.-J., Wang, X.-R., and Lin, C.-J. (2008). LIBLINEAR: A library for large linear classification. *Journal of Machine Learning Research*, 9:1871–1874.

Goel, S., Gracia, J., and Forcada, M. L. (2022). Bilingual dictionary generation and enrichment via graph exploration. *Semantic Web – Interoperability, Usability, Applicability*.

Gracia, J., Villegas, M., Gomez-Perez, A., and Bel, N. (2018). The APERTIUM bilingual dictionaries on the web of data. *Semantic Web – Interoperability, Usability, Applicability*, 9:231–240.

Gracia, J., Kabashi, B., Kernerman, I., Lanau-Coronas, M., and Lonke, D. (2019). Results of the translation inference across dictionaries 2019 shared task. In *Proceedings of TIAD-2019 Shared Task – Translation Inference Across Dictionaries*, CEUR Workshop Proceedings, pages 1–12. CEUR-WS.org.

Gracia, J., Kabashi, B., and Kernerman, I. (2021). Results of the translation inference across dictionaries 2021 shared task. In *Proceedings of the Workshops and Tutorials held at LDK 2021*, CEUR Workshop Proceedings. CEUR-WS.org.

Mausam, Soderland, S., Etzioni, O., Weld, D., Skinner, M., and Bilmes, J. (2009). Compiling a massive, multilingual dictionary via probabilistic inference. In *Proceedings of the Joint Conference of the 47th Annual Meeting of the ACL and the 4th International Joint Conference on Natural Language Processing of the AFNLP*, pages 262–270, Suntec, Singapore, August. Association for Computational Linguistics.

McCrae, J. P. and Arcan, M. (2020). NUIG at TIAD: Combining unsupervised NLP and graph metrics for translation inference. In *Proceedings of the 2020 Globalex Workshop on Linked Lexicography*, pages 92–97.

Steingrimsson, S., Loftsson, H., and Wa, A. (2021). PivotAlign: Leveraging high-precision word alignments for bilingual dictionary inference. In *Proceedings of the Workshops and Tutorials held at LDK 2021*, CEUR Workshop Proceedings. CEUR-WS.org.

Tanaka-Ishii, K. and Umemura, K. (1994). Construction of a bilingual dictionary intermediated by a third language. In *Proceedings of The 5th International Conference on Computational Linguistics (COLING'94)*, pages 297–303.

Torregrosa, D., Arcan, M., Ahmadi, S., and McCrae, J. P. (2019). TIAD 2019 shared task: Leveraging knowledge graphs with neural machine translation for automatic multilingual dictionary generation. In *Proceedings of TIAD-2019 Shared Task – Translation Inference Across Dictionaries*, CEUR Workshop Proceedings, pages 24–31. CEUR-WS.org.

Proceedings of the Globalex Workshop on Linked Lexicography @LREC2022, pages 32–41
Marseille, 20 June 2022

Compiling a Highly Accurate Bilingual Lexicon by Combining Different Approaches

Steinþór Steingrímsson[1,2], Luke O'Brien[1], Finnur Ingimundarson[2], Hrafn Loftsson[1], and Andy Way[3]
[1]Department of Computer Science, Reykjavik University, Iceland
[2]The Árni Magnússon Institute for Icelandic Studies, Iceland
[3]ADAPT Centre, School of Computing, Dublin City University, Ireland
steinthor18@ru.is, luke20@ru.is, fai@hi.is
hrafn@ru.is, andy.way@adaptcentre.ie

Abstract

Bilingual lexicons can be generated automatically using a wide variety of approaches. We perform a rigorous manual evaluation of four different methods: word alignments on different types of bilingual data, pivoting, machine translation and cross-lingual word embeddings. We investigate how the different setups perform using publicly available data for the English-Icelandic language pair, doing separate evaluations for each method, dataset and confidence class where it can be calculated. The results are validated by human experts, working with a random sample from all our experiments. By combining the most promising approaches and data sets, using confidence scores calculated from the data and the results of manually evaluating samples from our manual evaluation as indicators, we are able to induce lists of translations with a very high acceptance rate. We show how multiple different combinations generate lists with well over 90% acceptance rate, substantially exceeding the results for each individual approach, while still generating reasonably large candidate lists. All manually evaluated equivalence pairs are published in a new lexicon of over 232,000 pairs under an open license.

Keywords: Bilingual Lexicon Induction, Dictionary, Bilingual Corpora, Pivoting, Machine Translation

1. Introduction

Bilingual lexicons are useful for an array of different tasks. First, they can be used for harvesting bitexts from multilingual websites or corpora. For example, *Bicleaner* (Ramírez-Sánchez et al., 2020), a popular tool used for that task, requires a probabilistic lexicon for training. Second, they can be used for cross-language information retrieval (see e.g. Bonab et al. (2020), Steingrímsson et al. (2021b)). Third, they can be exploited in machine translation (MT), e.g. as an additional scoring component (Arthur et al., 2016), for initializing unsupervised MT (Artetxe et al., 2018b; Lample et al., 2018b; Duan et al., 2020), for substituting words in source sentences in pre-training (Lin et al., 2020), for annotating source sentences with possible translations from lexicons (Dinu et al., 2019; Niehues, 2021), or for inputting prior knowledge into the self-attention module of the encoder (Chen et al., 2021).

Among the different approaches to the bilingual lexicon induction (BLI) task are extracting bilingual lexicons from parallel corpora using word alignments (Mihalcea and Pedersen, 2003; Och and Ney, 2003), mining comparable corpora, commonly using cross-lingual word embeddings (Rapp et al., 2020), and pivoting through intermediary languages in available dictionaries (Gracia et al., 2019). The different approaches have contrasting limitations. Pivoting is limited by the availability of dictionaries that connect the source and target languages, and while bitext mining can produce very many candidates it is prone to giving noisy results, both when using word embeddings and candidate pair extraction using word alignments.

We present a methodology to build a moderately large lexicon for the English-Icelandic language pair, a language pair that has basic resources available allowing us to approach the problem from different angles. Previously, only the *Wiktionary*[1] and *Apertium* (Forcada et al., 2011) dictionaries were publicly available for this language pair, containing approximately 18,000 and 23,000 word pairs, respectively. While a wide variety of approaches to automatic bilingual lexicon induction

[1]https://www.wiktionary.org/

Translation Pair		Probabilities	
Icelandic	**English**	**is→en**	**en→is**
ananas	pineapple	1.0	0.82
ananasjurt	pineapple	1.0	0.15
granaldin	pineapple	1.0	0.03
regnhlíf	umbrella	0.70	0.73
regnhlíf	brolly	0.30	1.0
hlífð	umbrella	0.02	0.01
sólhlíf	umbrella	0.31	0.26
sólhlíf	parasol	0.48	1.0
sólhlíf	sunshade	0.21	0.46

Table 1: Example of translation pairs with probability scores from the lexicon resulting from the project. If there is only one translation for a word, the probability is 1.0, if there are many translations the probabilities sum to 1.0, as for the English word *pineapple* or the Icelandic word *regnhlíf*.

(BLI) have been shown to be effective, we experiment extensively with four different methods and perform rigorous manual evaluation with human experts validating a random sample of candidate pair lists from all our experiments. As our goal is to find a quick and efficient way to compile a glossary, we also assess the effectiveness of combining the most promising strategies in order to compile a manually approved lexicon as fast as possible.

Our work results in a manually verified lexicon of over 232,000 pairs, with a probability score attached to each pair for both translation directions. The probability scores are an attempt to order the translations for a given source word from most common to least common. The probability is calculated by tallying the number of times the pair was suggested by our methods and comparing that to how often other translations for the same word were suggested. An example of the lexicon format is shown in Table 1.

Our main contributions are:

- doing rigorous manually verified experiments on four different BLI approaches: 1) using cross-lingual word embeddings trained on comparable corpora, 2) pivoting through available dictionaries, 3) mining bitexts using word alignments, and 4) translating using available MT systems.
- showing that combining outputs of diverse approaches can greatly improve the rate of acceptable candidate pairs, while still retaining a large portion of the acceptable candidate pairs, if the combined approaches are carefully selected.

Furthermore, we publish a new, manually verified English–Icelandic lexicon (Steingrímsson et al., 2021), substantially larger than what was previously available, with probability scores for each translation pair. The lexicon and its availability is described in Section 5.

2. Related Work

A variety of approaches to automatically compile bilingual lexicons have been shown to be successful. Bilingual lexicons have been mined from parallel corpora using word alignments (Mihalcea and Pedersen, 2003; Vulić and Moens, 2012), and from comparable corpora with a variety of approaches, most commonly by learning cross-lingual word embeddings (Lample et al., 2018a; Rapp et al., 2020). Artetxe et al. (2019) use an unsupervised MT system to create a synthetic corpus which they extract the lexicon from.

Comparable corpora can also be exploited by identifying word pairs in the corpus using word alignments. For this purpose, sentence pairs first have to be extracted from the comparable corpora. This has been carried out using various approaches, e.g. using bilingual word embeddings to help calculate a BLEU score (Papineni et al., 2002) to estimate semantic similarity (Bouamor and Sajjad, 2018), using a BERT model (Devlin et al., 2019) to generate a similarity score based on contextualized sentence embeddings (Feng et al., 2020), or using cross-language information retrieval to limit the search space and a classifier, based on a word alignment score and a contextualized embedding score, to select the sentence pairs (Steingrímsson et al., 2021b).

Shi et al. (2021) show that lexicon induction performance correlates with bitext quality, although they are still able to induce a reasonably good bilingual lexicon from their lowest quality bitexts. They also observe that a better word aligner usually leads to a better induced lexicon.

Pivoting through existing dictionaries to infer translations between two languages using an intermediary language, e.g. using L1→L2 and L2→L3 dictionaries to infer translations between L1→L3, can produce a useful lexicon if measures are taken to filter the output of such an approach, as often a monosemous lexical item in one language can be polysemous in its corresponding translation into another language (Ordan et al., 2017). Tanaka and Umemura (1994) consult an inverse dictionary after pivoting and select equivalences based on common elements when source and target language words are translated into the intermediary language.

Mausam et al. (2009) tackle the problem by using multiple Wiktionary dictionaries to build graphs, identify sense cliques and try to identify ambiguity sets to be able to disambiguate between senses. The problem has also been approached by using MT systems to translate the words between languages (Arcan et al., 2019). The highest scoring system in the *2021 shared task for Translation Inference Across Dictionaries* (TIAD 2021) used a combination of pivoting and bitext extraction (Steingrímsson et al., 2021c).

3. Experimental Settings

We designed a number of experiments to explore three research questions:

1. How accurately can we produce equivalence pairs using four different methods: using cross-lingual word embeddings trained on comparable corpora, pivoting through available dictionaries, mining bitexts using word alignments, and translating using available MT systems?
2. To what extent does the frequency of words affect the results in corpus-based approaches?
3. How can we best combine the different approaches to increase accuracy while not reducing the size of the resulting lexicon too much?

Each experiment resulted in a list of translation candidates from which we extracted a random sample for evaluation. The evaluation was carried out by first comparing the list against the following manually curated Icelandic-English/English-Icelandic dictionaries and word lists: English-Icelandic Wiktionary and

Apertium dictionaries, titles of common pages in the Icelandic and English Wikipedia, the Icelandic Term Bank[2], and the Terminology Database of the Ministry of Foreign Affairs[3].

If the candidate pairs were found in these data sets they were accepted, otherwise a human annotator manually evaluated them and categorized into the following categories: *acceptable*, *unacceptable*, *rectifiable/partial*. Four annotators worked on the project, all Icelandic native speakers, educated in linguistics and with excellent knowledge of English. The criteria given to the annotators was that if the word in either language could be translated to the other word, in any environment the annotators could think of, the pair should be categorized as *acceptable*. The *rectifiable/partial* category was used when there was a minor error in one of the words, e.g. a spelling error, lemmatization error or a typo, or when a word in one language had to be translated into a multiword unit, and the translation given only has a part of that unit. Words that fell into neither of these categories were categorized as *unacceptable*.

3.1. Extracting Word Pairs from Bilingual Corpora

We extracted word alignments as accurately as possible using the CombAlign tool (Steingrímsson et al., 2021a), which uses a voting system employing multiple different word aligners, Giza++ (Och and Ney, 2003), fast_align (Dyer et al., 2013), eflomal (Östling and Tiedemann, 2016), two SimAlign (Masoud et al., 2020) models and AWESoME (Dou and Neubig, 2021). If four models agreed on an alignment, it was accepted. In order to increase alignment accuracy and to reduce noise, we lemmatized all the data and collected lemma pairs from the lemmatized sentence pairs. We used SpaCy[4] for lemmatizing English, and after PoS-tagging the Icelandic texts using ABLTagger (Steingrímsson et al., 2019), we lemmatized them using Nefnir (Ingólfsdóttir et al., 2019), which is trained on the Database of Icelandic Morphology (DIM) (Bjarnadóttir et al., 2019). We then calculated a confidence score for each aligned word pair $\langle s,t \rangle$ using Equation (1), as employed by Steingrímsson et al. (2021c):

$$\rho\,(s,t) = \frac{match\,(s,t)}{coc\,(s,t) + \lambda} \quad (1)$$

In Equation (1), $match\,(s,t)$ is the one-to-one matching count, i.e. how often the words are aligned in the corpus, and $coc\,(s,t)$ is the number of one-to-one co-occurrences, i.e. count of $\langle s,t \rangle$ appearing in a sentence pair in the corpus. λ is a non-negative smoothing term. The equation was proposed by Shi et al. (2021). While they set the smoothing variable λ to 20, here it is set to $\log_2 s$ where s is the number of sentence pairs in the corpus under consideration. This way the score is more comparable between corpora of different sizes.

The score is used as a filtering mechanism, by finding cutoff thresholds for six different bilingual corpora of three types: a parallel corpus, comparable corpora, and synthetic corpora. We describe the corpora in the following subsections.

3.1.1. Parallel Corpus

We used the English-Icelandic ParIce corpus (Barkarson and Steingrímsson, 2019), containing 3.6 million sentence pairs, 80% of which are sourced from official EEA documents or movie subtitles.

3.1.2. Comparable Corpora

ParaCrawl (Bañón et al., 2020) is a large project to create parallel corpora by crawling the web. They publish document pairs and sentence pairs extracted from the documents, using various tools in their pipeline, including Bitextor[5] for document alignment, hunalign (Varga et al., 2005), Vecalign (Thompson and Koehn, 2019) and Bleualign (Sennrich and Volk, 2011) for sentence alignment and Bicleaner (Ramírez-Sánchez et al., 2020) for filtering. ParaCrawl has published data for more than 40 languages, low resource and high resource, most of which are paired with English. WikiMatrix (Schwenk et al., 2021) is another publicly available set of sentence pairs, mined from Wikipedia using an approach based on massively multilingual sentence embeddings (Artetxe and Schwenk, 2019b) and a margin criterion (Artetxe and Schwenk, 2019a). WikiMatrix was published for 85 different languages and 1620 language pairs.

The methods applied in these two projects could be applied to most languages that have available monolingual data, comparable to data in another language, although the size of the available monolingual data limits the size of the resulting datasets. As these two publicly available datasets, WikiMatrix and ParaCrawl, have English–Icelandic sentence pairs collected from comparable corpora, we opt to use them instead of creating our own. WikiMatrix has 86K sentence pairs, but ParaCrawl is considerably larger and has 2.4M sentence pairs for version 7.1 and 5.7M sentence pairs for version 8, the two versions we experiment with.

3.1.3. Synthetic Corpora

For synthetic corpora, we used the same methodology as before, i.e. extract word pairs from aligned sentence pairs using word alignment tools. Our synthetic corpora are two back-translated corpora consisting of source sentences and back-translations generated using a transformer network (Símonarson et al., 2020). 44.7M English source sentences were retrieved from Wikipedia, Newscrawl and Europarl, while the 31.3M Icelandic sentences were sourced from the Icelandic Gigaword Corpus (IGC) (Steingrímsson et al., 2018).

[2] https://idordabanki.arnastofnun.is/
[3] https://hugtakasafn.utn.stjr.is/
[4] https://spacy.io
[5] https://github.com/bitextor/bitextor

	Sample from 10,000 most frequent				Sample from 100,000 most frequent			
Corpus	Accept	Unacc.	Partial	Accuracy	Accept	Unacc.	Partial	Accuracy
ParIce	202	**170**	128	0.40	178	**214**	108	0.36
Paracrawl 7.1	**279**	190	31	**0.56**	**212**	228	60	**0.42**
Paracrawl 8	143	339	18	0.29	134	334	32	0.27
WikiMatrix	232	220	48	0.46				
Synthetic is-en	205	258	37	0.41	167	225	108	0.33
Synthetic en-is	272	195	33	0.54	202	227	71	0.40

Table 2: Accuracy of candidate pairs sampled from two different frequency classes in six bilingual corpora. 500 pairs were randomly selected from each frequency class. The table gives numbers for equivalents (accepted), non-equivalents (unaccepted) and partial equivalents in the manually evaluated data. Accuracy is the acceptance ratio, i.e. the number of accepted pairs divided by the total number of pairs.

Synthetic corpora like these can be created for any language pair if an MT model is available, or even by building and using an unsupervised MT model, see e.g. Artetxe et al. (2019).

3.2. Pivoting

We used dictionaries with Icelandic as a source language and pivoted through an intermediate language into English. For collecting translations from Icelandic into intermediary languages we used the ISLEX (Úlfarsdóttir, 2014) and LEXIA dictionaries (Icelandic-Danish / Swedish / Norwegian / Finnish / French) and dict.cc[6] for Icelandic-German. For collecting translations from the intermediary languages into English we used Apertium (Forcada et al., 2011) (Finnish / French / Norwegian / Swedish-English) and dict.cc (German/Finnish/Norwegian/ Swedish/French/English). For each Icelandic source word, we collected all possible translations in the intermediary languages and, for each of the intermediary translations, we collected all English translations.

3.3. Machine Translation

Our most simple approach was translating words into English using four available MT models: Google Translate[7], Microsoft Translator[8], OPUS-MT (Tiedemann and Thottingal, 2020) and M2M100 M2M (Fan et al., 2020). First, we translated the Icelandic source words of the ISLEX/LEXIA dictionaries into English, thereby creating a candidate list. Second, we also translated into English the target language equivalents in these dictionaries, Danish, Swedish, Norwegian, Finnish and French, and then paired the source Icelandic word to the translation of the target words.

While this method is simple and accessible for many languages, using existing commercial MT services can make it difficult to replicate the results of the experiments. As one of our goals is to compile a lexicon as fast as possible we decided to use these services anyway, to see if they could be useful for this purpose.

3.4. Cross-lingual Word Embeddings

Icelandic news texts collected from the IGC and English news texts collected from Newscrawl[9] were used to train two word2vec models (Mikolov et al., 2013), one for English and the other for Icelandic. VecMap (Artetxe et al., 2018a) was then used to build cross-lingual word embeddings by mapping the models to a common vector space.

Three candidate lists were generated. One is based on the most frequent English and Icelandic words in their respective corpus, with the nearest neighbour (NN) to each word in terms of cosine distance. The other two lists contain, on the one hand, words selected based on the lowest cosine distance to a word in the other language and, on the other hand, based on the highest Cross-domain Similarity Local Scaling (CSLS) method, which alleviates the problem of hubs of incorrect translations polluting the vector space (Dinu and Baroni, 2015).

This unsupervised approach is available for all languages if monolingual corpora are available.

4. Evaluation

We performed a thorough evaluation of the different methods, comparing the word pairs against available manually compiled datasets and by performing a manual evaluation as described in Section 3.

For the corpus-based approaches we created classes that could be expected to correlate with the likelihood of the candidate pairs being equivalents. The classes were either based on frequency or similarity as estimated by cross-lingual word embedding models. We tested each of these classes manually. Candidates generated by pivoting and MT were evaluated on a random sample of 500 pairs from each method and class of data evaluated.

[6] `https://www.dict.cc/`

[7] `https://translate.google.com/`, accessed in May 2021

[8] `https://translator.microsoft.com/`, accessed in May 2021

[9] `https://data.statmt.org/news-crawl/en/`

4.1. Bilingual Corpora

We extracted word pairs from six different bilingual corpora, as shown in Table 2, only considering pairs that appear more than five times in each corpus. We created two frequency classes, i.e. for the 10,000 and 100,000 most frequent words in the corpora, respectively. Frequency was calculated as an average of the total count of the Icelandic words in the Icelandic part of the corpus and the English words in the English part. We randomly sampled 500 pairs from both frequency classes in each corpus. For WikiMatrix we did not take a sample from the 100,000 most frequent, as the corpus was too small for us to collect that many samples.

Table 2 shows that the highest accuracy was achieved on the ParaCrawl 7.1 corpus. While it could have been expected to attain the highest scores from ParIce, the parallel corpus, due to it being compiled from known parallel documents, we can see that it has a very high percentage of pairs categorized as partially correct. This may indicate that the texts in ParIce have a higher ratio of multiword units and that if we would extract not only single words from the bilingual corpora, the accuracy might change for this corpus. There is a noticable difference between ParaCrawl 7.1 and 8. As version 8 is more than twice the size of version 7.1, this may indicate that the additional sentence pairs are of lower quality, although this would have to be investigated further.

We used the confidence score (see Equation 1), calculated for each of the word pair candidates, to create ten confidence bands, with the lowest having a score of less than 0.1 and the highest with a score higher than 0.9. We evaluated 250 pairs in each band for each of the corpora. Figure 1 shows that the confidence scores do not represent the same level of accuracy for all corpora. While more than half of the pairs with a confidence score higher than 0.4 were accepted for ParIce, WikiMatrix and ParaCrawl 8, the confidence score for

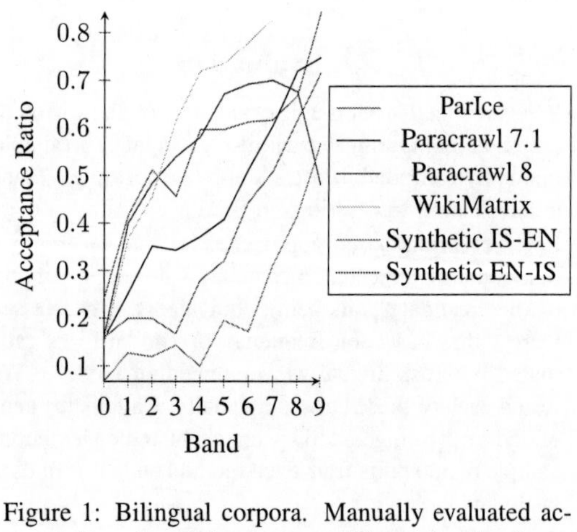

Figure 1: Bilingual corpora. Manually evaluated acceptability of candidate pairs at different bands of confidence, as automatically assessed by our confidence score.

	Apertium		dict.cc	
	acc. ratio	no. pairs	acc. ratio	no. pairs
se	0.64	34,915	0.76	26,622
fi	0.43	214,659	0.75	19,304
no	0.53	15,261	0.74	31,213
fr	0.63	20,865	0.64	39,590
de			0.54	137,970

Table 3: Pivoting. Acceptance ratio and number of pairs yielded by each pivoting path from Icelandic to English connected by an intermediary language in ISLEX and the Apertium and dict.cc dictionaries.

	acc. ratio	no. pairs
se (A+D)	0.85	10,805
fi (A+D)	0.89	12,969
fr (A+D)	0.83	11,012
fi (A) + de (D)	0.91	17,681
fi (A) + se (D)	0.93	13,962
fi (A) + no (D)	0.93	14,750
fi (A) + fr (D)	0.94	13,743

Table 4: Pivoting combinations. Acceptance ratio and number of candidate pairs yielded with different combinations of two pivoting paths. A=Apertium, D=dict.cc.

the synthetic corpora had to be at least 0.7 in order to obtain the same results.

4.2. Pivoting

We compiled candidate lists for each of the intermediary languages, using both Apertium and dict.cc for obtaining English translations from the intermediary language words. The dictionaries vary in size and that is reflected in the candidate lists. For each list, 500 randomly selected candidate pairs were evaluated and the acceptance ratio calculated. Results are shown in Table 3. The smaller lists tend to have higher acceptance ratios. This may be because the smaller lists more often only have the most common translation for any given word, and when multiple senses are given for a word, some of these are likely to have different translations in a third language (see e.g. Tanaka and Umemura (1994)).

As seen in Table 3, up to 76% of the translations are acceptable, depending on the language and dictionary used. In order to increase the accuracy even further, we can require the pairs to be suggested by two or more pivoting paths. We combined two pivoting approaches by selecting an intersection of the result of each. This substantially raised the accuracy, especially when two different language pairs and dictionaries are combined. Table 4 shows the accuracy and number of candidate pairs for all combinations that yield more than 10,000 pairs.

	Opus	M2M	Google	MS	no. pairs
is			0.59	0.60	53,151
da	0.52		0.59	0.63	80,074
sv	0.56	0.32	0.65	0.65	69,884
fi	0.53	0.27	0.66	0.62	62,876
no			0.59	0.61	66,129
fr	0.56	0.35	0.67	0.71	48,533

Table 5: Machine translation. Acceptance ratio in 500 randomly selected candidate pairs for each language and system. For all languages except Icelandic, we pivoted through intermediary languages using dictionaries and translated the intermediary languages to English using MT.

	acc. rate (%)	no. pairs
se+fr	97.7	11,274
se+fi	97.1	14,931
se+de+no	95.8	13,151
fr+fi	97.7	9,914

Table 6: Machine translation combinations. Acceptance rate and number of pairs yielded by an intersection of MT outputs. All combinations listed are an intersection of both Google Translate and Microsoft Translate for each of the languages listed.

4.3. Machine Translation

As described in Section 3.3, we employed MT using two approaches. The more straightforward one was to translate the Icelandic source words from the ISLEX dictionary into English using two different MT engines. The other one was translating the target language words in the ISLEX dictionary into English using up to four different MT engines, and then replacing the ISLEX target word with the Icelandic source word to create an Icelandic–English candidate list. All the systems except M2M resulted in over 50% acceptable translations for all languages. The pivoting process yielded a different number of words to translate, depending on the dictionary, ranging from 48,000-80,000 words. For most languages, Microsoft Translator gave the best results, as shown in Table 5. By combining results from multiple systems and using multiple intermediary languages, accuracy can be raised substantially. We tried taking an intersection of candidate pairs produced for all six languages using both Microsoft Translator and Google Translate. When all these twelve outputs were in agreement, the human annotators agreed with the outputs 99.6% of the time, but the number of candidate pairs yielded went down to only only 2,358. By combining fewer outputs, a higher number of candidates is produced while the acceptance rate is still very high. For the experiments yielding such high accuracy we raised the number of pairs to evaluate to 2,000 for each combination. Table 5 shows the highest resulting

Lang. Direction	Retrieval method	Classification High	Medium	Low
en-is	NN	0.39	0.20	0.03
	CSLS	0.59	0.38	0.14
	freq.	0.71	0.50	0.14
is-en	NN	0.48	0.26	0.15
	CSLS	0.63	0.40	0.19
	freq.	0.67	0.44	0.22

Table 7: Cross-lingual word embeddings. Acceptance ratio for candidate lists in different similarity or frequency classes, for each of the methods employed.

combinations of 2-3 languages yielding close to 10,000 candidate pairs or more.

While Table 6 shows that combining the results of different MT systems can yield a highly acceptable list of candidate pairs, a downside to the MT approach is that each system only outputs one equivalence suggestion for each source word, which when correct is usually a very common translation. Accordingly, this does not seem to be an effective way to obtain translations for low-frequency senses or rare words.

4.4. Cross-Lingual Word Embeddings

Three approaches are used to extract word pairs from our cross-lingual word embeddings, as described in Section 3.4. For each of these approaches we divide the results into three classes: *High*, for the top 2,000 pairs, *Medium*, for the next 8,000 pairs, and *Low* for the next 90,000 pairs. The pairs are ordered by similarity in terms of NN or CSLS, or by frequency in the corpora used to train the embedding models. Table 7 shows that while we obtain decent scores for the most frequent words in the corpora and most similar word pairs according to the model, the scores fall sharply as word frequency and similarity decrease.

4.5. Combining different approaches

Based on the results presented above, we created two lists. One contains all candidate pairs obtained through pivoting or MT, being in classes where acceptance rate of candidate pairs is over 50%. The other list was created from all six bilingual corpora, but only from confidence bands with over 50% acceptance rate (see Figure 1). Taking an intersection of these resulted in a list of 29,609 candidates, of which 93.2% were accepted after manual evaluation. Detailed results are shown in Table 8.

Furthermore, if the confidence bands are ignored and the second list has all pairs from the six bilingual corpora, the intersection of the two lists results in a list of 57,818 candidates, of which 84.1% were accepted.

5. Availability

We publish all word pairs accepted in the evaluation process. The final dataset, resulting from evaluation

		Confidence Scores with over 50% Acceptability			Also in Pivoting/MT Candidate Lists		
Corpus	Total Pairs	Acceptance Ratio (%)	Number of Pairs	Estimated Correct	Acceptance Ratio (%)	Number of Pairs	Estimated Correct
ParIce	346,723	51.6	45,646	23,553	90.4	3,713	3,356
Paracrawl 7.1	107,989	59.6	70,281	41,887	95.8	18,836	18,045
Paracrawl 8	342,444	62.6	93,850	58,750	96.2	16,522	15,894
WikiMatrix	15,781	77.2	6,944	5,360	97.4	3,343	3,256
Synthetic is–en	191,934	67.2	13,215	8,880	97.3	4,986	4,851
Synthetic en–is	229,661	60.2	132,381	79,693	94.4	19,423	18,335
Total	938.354	46.6	249,872	116,440	93.2	29,609	27,595

Table 8: Combining different methods. Evaluation of the combination of different approaches, using bitexts on the one hand and pivoting/MT on the other.

of all the experiments carried out during this research, contains 232,950 pairs, with 105,442 different Icelandic lexical items, of which 84,812 are single words and 20,630 multiword units, and 116,744 different English items, of which 45,147 are unique English words and 71,597 multiword units. The published dataset includes the probability scores described in Section 1 and word class information, in cases where that could be retrieved automatically from Wiktionary or the DIM (Bjarnadóttir et al., 2019). The published dataset also contains information on which methods produced the pairs included in the dataset and how often. The data is available for download at a CLARIN repository[10].

6. Conclusion and Future Work

We have compared four different approaches to automatically compile an English-Icelandic bilingual lexicon. We have shown that by using a combination of bilingual corpora, pivoting and MT approaches, we can build a highly accurate candidate list for lexicon translations between languages. Our combined approach yields a candidate list of almost 30,000 pairs of which 93.2% are acceptable translations. Using individual approaches yields more data, but with less accuracy. Very high accuracy can be achieved using individual approaches by combining the resulting candidate pairs from different data sets, while still yielding a decently sized candidate lists, as shown in Table 4 for pivoting combinations and Table 6 for MT combinations. While using an unsupervised approach such as cross-lingual word embeddings did not result in many useful candidate pairs, extracting candidate pairs from back-translated data using word alignments gives promising results for our language pair.

The results indicate that there are multiple feasible ways to extend the lexicon. Adding more dictionaries for pivoting and by pivoting through more than one intermediary language would produce more candidates. To limit the noise as much as possible we could use a variant of inverse consultation (Tanaka and Umemura, 1994).

While pivoting and MT can yield multiword units, our methods for extracting from bilingual corpora only identifies single word units. The high number of partial equivalents in our parallel corpus is an indication that there is still room for improvement in extracting equivalence pairs from bitexts with the help of word alignments if we have a mechanism for retrieving not only single words but multiword units. We want to explore that further using a similar hybrid approach as Semmar (2018). We are also interested in extracting candidate pairs from other bilingual corpora, e.g. version 9 of ParaCrawl, and creating additional synthetic corpora.

Furthermore, the new compiled lexicon can be a valuable asset to better align and filter parallel corpora or for better extracting parallel sentences from comparable corpora. It could be worthwhile to use the dataset created in this project to explore an iterative approach, where the new English-Icelandic lexicon is used to refine the parallel and comparable corpora used, and then to repeat this experiment and investigate if it then yields more candidates or more accurate candidate lists.

7. Acknowledgements

This project was funded by the Language Technology Programme for Icelandic 2019–2023. The programme, which is managed and coordinated by Almannarómur[11], is funded by the Icelandic Ministry of Education, Science and Culture and by the ADAPT Centre for Digital Content Technology which is funded under the Science Foundation Ireland (SFI) Research Centres Programme (Grant No. 13/RC/2106) and is co-funded under the European Regional Development Fund. We would also like to thank all the annotators that helped evaluate the data: Árni Davíð Magnússon, Þórdís Dröfn Andrésdóttir and Inga Guðrún Eiríksdóttir.

[10] `https://repository.clarin.is/repository/xmlui/handle/20.500.12537/144`

[11] `https://almannaromur.is/`

8. Bibliographical References

Arcan, M., Torregrosa, D., Ahmadi, S., and McCrae, J. P. (2019). Inferring Translation Candidates for Multilingual Dictionary Generation with Multi-Way Neural Machine Translation. In *Proc. of TIAD-2019 Shared Task - Translation Inference Across Dictionaries co-located with the 2nd Language, Data and Knowledge Conference (LDK 2019)*, pages 13–23, Leipzig, Germany.

Artetxe, M. and Schwenk, H. (2019a). Margin-based Parallel Corpus Mining with Multilingual Sentence Embeddings. In *Proceedings of the 57th Annual Meeting of the Association for Computational Linguistics*, pages 3197–3203, Florence, Italy.

Artetxe, M. and Schwenk, H. (2019b). Massively Multilingual Sentence Embeddings for Zero-Shot Cross-Lingual Transfer and Beyond. *Transactions of the Association for Computational Linguistics*, 7:597–610, March.

Artetxe, M., Labaka, G., and Agirre, E. (2018a). A robust self-learning method for fully unsupervised cross-lingual mappings of word embeddings. In *Proceedings of the 56th Annual Meeting of the Association for Computational Linguistics (Volume 1: Long Papers)*, pages 789–798, Melbourne, Australia.

Artetxe, M., Labaka, G., Agirre, E., and Cho, K. (2018b). Unsupervised Neural Machine Translation. In *Proceedings of the Sixth International Conference on Learning Representations*.

Artetxe, M., Labaka, G., and Agirre, E. (2019). Bilingual Lexicon Induction through Unsupervised Machine Translation. In *Proceedings of the 57th Annual Meeting of the Association for Computational Linguistics*, pages 5002–5007, Florence, Italy.

Arthur, P., Neubig, G., and Nakamura, S. (2016). Incorporating Discrete Translation Lexicons into Neural Machine Translation. In *Proceedings of the 2016 Conference on Empirical Methods in Natural Language Processing*, pages 1557–1567, Austin, Texas.

Bañón, M., Chen, P., Haddow, B., Heafield, K., Hoang, H., Esplà-Gomis, M., Forcada, M. L., Kamran, A., Kirefu, F., Koehn, P., Ortiz Rojas, S., Pla Sempere, L., Ramírez-Sánchez, G., Sarrías, E., Strelec, M., Thompson, B., Waites, W., Wiggins, D., and Zaragoza, J. (2020). ParaCrawl: Web-Scale Acquisition of Parallel Corpora. In *Proceedings of the 58th Annual Meeting of the Association for Computational Linguistics*, pages 4555–4567, Online.

Barkarson, S. and Steingrímsson, S. (2019). Compiling and Filtering ParIce: An English-Icelandic Parallel Corpus. In *Proceedings of the 22nd Nordic Conference on Computational Linguistics*, pages 140–145, Turku, Finland.

Bjarnadóttir, K., Hlynsdóttir, K. I., and Steingrímsson, S. (2019). DIM: The Database of Icelandic Morphology. In *Proceedings of the 22nd Nordic Conference on Computational Linguistics*, pages 146–154, Turku, Finland.

Bonab, H., Sarwar, S. M., and Allan, J. (2020). Training Effective Neural CLIR by Bridging the Translation Gap. In *Proceedings of the 43rd International ACM SIGIR Conference on Research and Development in Information Retrieval*, pages 9–18.

Bouamor, H. and Sajjad, H. (2018). H2@BUCC18: Parallel Sentence Extraction from Comparable Corpora Using Multilingual Sentence Embeddings. In *Proceedings of the 11th Workshop on Building and Using Comparable Corpora*, pages 43–47, Miyazaki, Japan.

Chen, K., Wang, R., Utiyama, M., and Sumita, E. (2021). Integrating Prior Translation Knowledge into Neural Machine Translation. *IEEE/ACM Transactions on Audio, Speech, and Language Processing*.

Devlin, J., Chang, M.-W., Lee, K., and Toutanova, K. (2019). BERT: Pre-training of deep bidirectional transformers for language understanding. In *Proceedings of the 2019 Conference of the North American Chapter of the Association for Computational Linguistics: Human Language Technologies, Volume 1 (Long and Short Papers)*, pages 4171–4186, Minneapolis, Minnesota.

Dinu, G. and Baroni, M. (2015). Improving zero-shot learning by mitigating the hubness problem. In Yoshua Bengio et al., editors, *3rd International Conference on Learning Representations, ICLR 2015, San Diego, CA, USA, May 7-9, 2015, Workshop Track Proceedings*.

Dinu, G., Mathur, P., Federico, M., and Al-Onaizan, Y. (2019). Training Neural Machine Translation to Apply Terminology Constraints. In *Proceedings of the 57th Annual Meeting of the Association for Computational Linguistics*, pages 3063–3068, Florence, Italy.

Dou, Z.-Y. and Neubig, G. (2021). Word Alignment by Fine-tuning Embeddings on Parallel Corpora. In *Proceedings of the 16th Conference of the European Chapter of the Association for Computational Linguistics: Main Volume*, pages 2112–2128, Online.

Duan, X., Ji, B., Jia, H., Tan, M., Zhang, M., Chen, B., Luo, W., and Zhang, Y. (2020). Bilingual Dictionary Based Neural Machine Translation without Using Parallel Sentences. In *Proceedings of the 58th Annual Meeting of the Association for Computational Linguistics*, pages 1570–1579, Online.

Dyer, C., Chahuneau, V., and Smith, N. A. (2013). A Simple, Fast, and Effective Reparameterization of IBM Model 2. In *Proceedings of the 2013 Conference of the North American Chapter of the Association for Computational Linguistics: Human Language Technologies*, pages 644–648, Atlanta, Georgia.

Fan, A., Bhosale, S., Schwenk, H., Ma, Z., El-Kishky, A., Goyal, S., Baines, M., Çelebi, O., Wenzek, G., Chaudhary, V., Goyal, N., Birch, T., Liptchinsky,

V., Edunov, S., Grave, E., Auli, M., and Joulin, A. (2020). Beyond English-Centric Multilingual Machine Translation. *ArXiv*, abs/2010.11125.

Feng, F., Yang, Y.-F., Cer, D. M., Arivazhagan, N., and Wang, W. (2020). Language-agnostic BERT Sentence Embedding. *ArXiv*, abs/2007.01852.

Forcada, M. L., Ginestí-Rosell, M., Nordfalk, J., O'Regan, J., Rojas, S. O., Pérez-Ortiz, J. A., Sánchez-Martínez, F., Ramírez-Sánchez, G., and Tyers, F. M. (2011). Apertium: a free/open-source platform for rule-based machine translation. *Machine Translation*, 25:127–144.

Gracia, J., Kabashi, B., Kernerman, I., Lanau-Coronas, M., and Lonke, D. (2019). Results of the Translation Inference Across Dictionaries 2019 Shared Task. In *Proceedings of TIAD-2019 Shared Task – Translation Inference Across Dictionaries*, pages 1–12.

Ingólfsdóttir, S. L., Loftsson, H., Daðason, J. F., and Bjarnadóttir, K. (2019). Nefnir: A high accuracy lemmatizer for Icelandic. In *Proceedings of the 22nd Nordic Conference on Computational Linguistics*, pages 310–315, Turku, Finland.

Lample, G., Conneau, A., Ranzato, M., Denoyer, L., and Jégou, H. (2018a). Word translation without parallel data. In *International Conference on Learning Representations*.

Lample, G., Denoyer, L., and Ranzato, M. (2018b). Unsupervised Machine Translation Using Monolingual Corpora Only. In *International Conference on Learning Representations*.

Lin, Z., Pan, X., Wang, M., Qiu, X., Feng, J., Zhou, H., and Li, L. (2020). Pre-training Multilingual Neural Machine Translation by Leveraging Alignment Information. In *Proceedings of the 2020 Conference on Empirical Methods in Natural Language Processing (EMNLP)*, pages 2649–2663, Online.

Masoud, J. S., Dufter, P., Yvon, F., and Schütze, H. (2020). SimAlign: High Quality Word Alignments Without Parallel Training Data Using Static and Contextualized Embeddings. In *Findings of the Association for Computational Linguistics: EMNLP 2020*, pages 1627–1643, Online.

Mausam, Soderland, S., Etzioni, O., Weld, D., Skinner, M., and Bilmes, J. (2009). Compiling a massive, multilingual dictionary via probabilistic inference. In *Proceedings of the Joint Conference of the 47th Annual Meeting of the ACL and the 4th International Joint Conference on Natural Language Processing of the AFNLP*, pages 262–270, Suntec, Singapore.

Mihalcea, R. and Pedersen, T. (2003). An Evaluation Exercise for Word Alignment. In *Proceedings of the HLT-NAACL 2003 Workshop on Building and Using Parallel Texts: Data Driven Machine Translation and Beyond*, pages 1–10, Edmonton, Canada.

Mikolov, T., Chen, K., Corrado, G., and Dean, J. (2013). Efficient Estimation of Word Representations in Vector Space. In *1st International Conference on Learning Representations, ICLR 2013, Workshop Track Proceedings*, Scottsdale, Arizona.

Niehues, J. (2021). Continuous Learning in Neural Machine Translation using Bilingual Dictionaries. In *Proceedings of the 16th Conference of the European Chapter of the Association for Computational Linguistics: Main Volume*, pages 830–840, Online.

Och, F. J. and Ney, H. (2003). A Systematic Comparison of Various Statistical Alignment Models. *Computational Linguistics*, 29(1):19–51.

Ordan, N., Gracia, J., and Kernerman, I. (2017). Autogenerating Bilingual Dictionaries. In *Proceedings of fifth biennial conference on electronic lexicography (eLex 2017)*, Leiden, Netherlands.

Östling, R. and Tiedemann, J. (2016). Efficient word alignment with Markov Chain Monte Carlo. *Prague Bulletin of Mathematical Linguistics*, 106:125–146.

Papineni, K., Roukos, S., Ward, T., and Zhu, W.-J. (2002). Bleu: a Method for Automatic Evaluation of Machine Translation. In *Proceedings of the 40th Annual Meeting of the Association for Computational Linguistics*, pages 311–318, Philadelphia, Pennsylvania, USA, July.

Ramírez-Sánchez, G., Zaragoza-Bernabeu, J., Bañón, M., and Ortiz-Rojas, S. (2020). Bifixer and Bicleaner: two open-source tools to clean your parallel data. In *Proceedings of the 22nd Annual Conference of the European Association for Machine Translation*, pages 291–298, Lisboa, Portugal.

Rapp, R., Zweigenbaum, P., and Sharoff, S. (2020). Overview of the Fourth BUCC Shared Task: Bilingual Dictionary Induction from Comparable Corpora. In *Proceedings of the 13th Workshop on Building and Using Comparable Corpora*, pages 6–13, Marseille, France.

Schwenk, H., Chaudhary, V., Sun, S., Gong, H., and Guzmán, F. (2021). WikiMatrix: Mining 135M Parallel Sentences in 1620 Language Pairs from Wikipedia. In *Proceedings of the 16th Conference of the European Chapter of the Association for Computational Linguistics: Main Volume*, pages 1351–1361, Online.

Semmar, N. (2018). A Hybrid Approach for Automatic Extraction of Bilingual Multiword Expressions from Parallel Corpora. In *Proceedings of the Eleventh International Conference on Language Resources and Evaluation (LREC 2018)*, pages 311–318, Miyazaki, Japan.

Sennrich, R. and Volk, M. (2011). Iterative, MT-based Sentence Alignment of Parallel Texts. In *Proceedings of the 18th Nordic Conference of Computational Linguistics*, pages 175–182, Riga, Latvia.

Shi, H., Zettlemoyer, L., and Wang, S. I. (2021). Bilingual Lexicon Induction via Unsupervised Bitext Construction and Word Alignment. In *Proceedings of the 59th Annual Meeting of the Association for Computational Linguistics and the 11th Interna-*

tional Joint Conference on Natural Language Processing (Volume 1: Long Papers), pages 813–826, Online.

Steingrímsson, S., Helgadóttir, S., Rögnvaldsson, E., Barkarson, S., and Guðnason, J. (2018). Risamálheild: A Very Large Icelandic Text Corpus. In *Proceedings of the Eleventh International Conference on Language Resources and Evaluation (LREC 2018)*, pages 4361–4366, Miyazaki, Japan.

Steingrímsson, S., Kárason, Ö., and Loftsson, H. (2019). Augmenting a BiLSTM Tagger with a Morphological Lexicon and a Lexical Category Identification Step. In *Proceedings of the International Conference on Recent Advances in Natural Language Processing (RANLP 2019)*, pages 1162–1169, Varna, Bulgaria.

Steingrímsson, S., Loftsson, H., and Way, A. (2021a). CombAlign: a Tool for Obtaining High-Quality Word Alignments. In *Proceedings of the 23rd Nordic Conference on Computational Linguistics (NoDaLiDa)*, pages 64–73, Online.

Steingrímsson, S., Lohar, P., Loftsson, H., and Way, A. (2021b). Effective Bitext Extraction From Comparable Corpora Using a Combination of Three Different Approaches. In *Proceedings of the 14th Workshop on Building and Using Comparable Corpora (BUCC 2021)*, pages 8–17, Online.

Steingrímsson, S., Loftsson, H., and Way, A. (2021c). Pivotalign: Leveraging High-Precision Word Alignments for Bilingual Dictionary Inference. In *Proc. of LDK 2021 workshops and tutorials [IN PRESS]*. CEUR-WS.

Tanaka, K. and Umemura, K. (1994). Construction of a Bilingual Dictionary Intermediated by a Third Language. In *COLING 1994 Volume 1: The 15th International Conference on Computational Linguistics*, pages 297–303, Kyoto, Japan.

Thompson, B. and Koehn, P. (2019). Vecalign: Improved Sentence Alignment in Linear Time and Space. In *Proceedings of the 2019 Conference on Empirical Methods in Natural Language Processing and the 9th International Joint Conference on Natural Language Processing (EMNLP-IJCNLP)*, pages 1342–1348, Hong Kong, China.

Tiedemann, J. and Thottingal, S. (2020). OPUS-MT – Building open translation services for the World. In *Proceedings of the 22nd Annual Conference of the European Association for Machine Translation*, pages 479–480, Lisboa, Portugal.

Úlfarsdóttir, Þ. (2014). ISLEX — a Multilingual Web Dictionary. In *Proceedings of the Ninth International Conference on Language Resources and Evaluation (LREC 2014)*, pages 2820–2825, Reykjavik, Iceland.

Varga, D., Halaácsy, P., Kornai, A., Nagy, V., Németh, L., and Trón, V. (2005). Parallel corpora for medium density languages. In *Proceedings of the RANLP 2005 Conference*, pages 590–596, Borovets, Bulgaria.

Vulić, I. and Moens, M.-F. (2012). Sub-corpora Sampling with an Application to Bilingual Lexicon Extraction. In *Proceedings of COLING 2012*, pages 2721–2738, Mumbai, India.

9. Language Resource References

Símonarson, Haukur Barri and Snæbjarnarson, Vésteinn and Þorsteinsson, Vilhjálmur. (2020). *En-Is Synthetic Parallel Corpus.* CLARIN-IS, http://hdl.handle.net/20.500.12537/70.

Steingrímsson, Steinþór and Obrien, Luke James and Ingimundarson, Finnur Ágúst and Magnússon, Árni Davíð and Andrésdóttir, Þórdís Dröfn and Eiríksdóttir, Inga Guðrún. (2021). *English-Icelandic/Icelandic-English glossary 21.09.* CLARIN-IS, http://hdl.handle.net/20.500.12537/144.

Proceedings of the Globalex Workshop on Linked Lexicography @LREC2022, pages 42–51
Marseille, 20 June 2022

A Category Theory Framework for Sense Systems

David Strohmaier*, Gladys Tyen*
University of Cambridge
{david.strohmaier, gladys.tyen}@cl.cam.ac.uk

Abstract

Sense repositories are a key component of many NLP applications that require the identification of word senses, a task known as word sense disambiguation. WordNet synsets form the most prominent repository, but many others exist and over the years these repositories have been mapped to each other. However, there have been no attempts (until now) to provide any theoretical grounding for such mappings, causing inconsistencies and unintuitive results. The present paper draws on category theory to formalise assumptions about mapped repositories that are often left implicit, providing formal grounding for this type of language resource. We introduce notation to represent the mappings and repositories as a category, which we call a *sense system*; and we propose and motivate four basic and two guiding criteria for such sense systems.

Keywords: Sense Repositories, Word Sense Disambiguation, Category Theory

1. Introduction

Sense repositories are a key language resource for word sense disambiguation (WSD), semantic inference, specifying lexical relations, and other downstream tasks like question answering. For these purposes, researchers have created many sense repositories with varying levels of granularity, along with mappings between them. In particular, the popular WordNet synsets (Miller et al., 1990; Fellbaum, 1998) have been mapped to many coarser-grained repositories.

The value of systematically mapped repositories has been repeatedly shown (Navigli, 2006; Palmer et al., 2007). However, the particular characteristics of the mappings produced are often the byproduct of practical or engineering decisions, instead of being motivated by theoretical considerations. For example, clustered senses are restricted to one cluster per sense, whereas senses that are mapped to domain labels do not have this restriction and are often associated with multiple labels. Additionally, the lack of constraints on mappings often results in problems during implementation. For example, converting sense labels in a corpus from one type to another (e.g. synsets to domain labels) is not always consistent, because sometimes there are several correct labels.

The present paper provides the theoretical grounding to allow for more systematic understanding of mappings and how they might assist researchers in solving tasks such as WSD. As far as we know, no such theory has been proposed before. Our contributions are twofold:

1. Drawing from category theory, we formalise mapped sense repositories as a category which we call a *sense system*; and

2. Using category theoretic notation, we propose and formally describe criteria for such a sense system.

* Both authors contributed equally.

We hope that future researchers building or adapting sense repositories and mappings will find it useful to consider how their new language resource fits into our framework, and adjust their methodology accordingly.

In the following sections, we first discuss the existing literature on sense repositories and mappings between them. We then introduce sense systems and present the surrounding category-theoretic notation. With these foundations in place, we propose and provide motivation for **basic** and **guiding** criteria for such sense systems.

2. Previous work

2.1. Word Sense Disambiguation

As suggested, word sense disambiguation (WSD), i.e. picking the correct sense of a word in a context, is one of the most prominent uses of sense repositories. Typically, a WSD classifier[1] selects from a pre-determined and enumerative repository of candidate senses (Navigli, 2009).

Different NLP techniques for WSD have been developed over the years, including approaches based on lexical similarity, graphs, and supervised learning. Lesk (1986) offers an influential lexical similarity approach, which uses a) the overlap between context of the word to be disambiguated, and b) the dictionary entry of candidate senses, in order to select a sense. Graph-based approaches make use of the graph structure of some sense repositories such as WordNet and BabelNet to select senses (Moro et al., 2014).

In recent years, machine learning has become the dominant approach. WSD is treated as a supervised classification task, where a trained model selects from a pre-determined list of senses. Earlier methods depend on extracting feature vectors (Zhong and Ng, 2010; Mihalcea and Faruque, 2004), while later methods make

[1]We refrain from using the term *word sense disambiguation system* in this paper to avoid any confusion with *sense systems*.

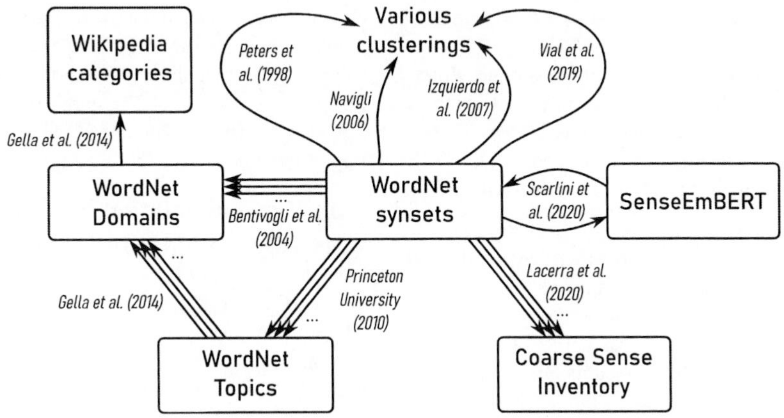

Figure 1: Graph showing mappings between select repositories. ... denotes further possible mappings.

use of word embeddings (Mikolov et al., 2013) and shifted towards neural approaches (Kågebäck and Salomonsson, 2016; Vial et al., 2019; Wiedemann et al., 2019), giving rise to some of the best performing models in WSD. Word embeddings have also been used as features for non-neural machine learning methods (Iacobacci et al., 2016), as well as more traditional lexical similarity approaches (Oele and Noord, 2017).

2.2. Sense representations

Sense repositories are sets of word senses, i.e. representations of lexical meaning. Existing sense repositories range widely in terms of how senses are represented and how fine-grained they are. Sense representations can be roughly divided into 4 types: dictionary definitions, clusters, domain labels, and embedding vectors.

1. **Dictionary definitions** typically consist of a piece of text describing the sense in question. A dictionary is an enumerative listing of such senses, though in practice such a list is unlikely to be exhaustive. WordNet (Miller et al., 1990; Fellbaum, 1998), one of the most widely used sense repository in WSD, is a prime example of a dictionary-like repository: it consists of gloss definitions, each of which is linked to a set of corresponding synonymous words, called a synset.

   Outside of WordNet, there are many repositories where senses are represented as definitions. For example, BabelNet (Navigli and Ponzetto, 2012), MultiWordNet (Pianta et al., 2002), and EuroWordNet (Vossen, 1998) are three multilingual repositories similar to WordNet; and many conventional dictionaries like the *Longman Dictionary of Contemporary English* (LDOCE) and the *Oxford Dictionary of English* (ODE) have also been used for WSD. Due to the popularity of WordNet, much of the WSD work cited in this paper pertains to mappings from WordNet, but many of the techniques can be applied to other repositories as well.

2. **Clusters of senses** are obtained by grouping fine-grained senses by various metrics, which typically approximate semantic similarity. For example, the semantic relations encoded in WordNet have been used to cluster WordNet synsets (Peters et al., 1998; Vial et al., 2019; Izquierdo et al., 2007); similarly, Dolan (1994) clustered definitions from the LDOCE according to semantic information extracted from the dictionary; Agirre and Lacalle (2003), working on clustering WordNet synsets, investigated 4 different sources of information to measure similarity: topic signatures, confusion matrices, translation equivalences, and the context of occurrence.

   Senses within a cluster can be represented as dictionary definitions, embedding vectors, or otherwise — crucially, there is no unified way of determining its semantic content, as it often depends on the clustering technique. For example, clusters that are formed from hypernym/hyponym relations have explicit, shared semantic content, because each cluster member is a hyponym of the highest level hypernym. In other cases, such as WordNet synsets clustered according to confusion matrices, there may not be any semantic content explicitly associated with each cluster.

3. **Domain labels** are very coarse-grained senses represented by a word or short phrase that denotes a topic domain, such as *biology*, *economics*, etc. Domain label repositories aim to cover the largest semantic space with the fewest possible domain labels (Lacerra et al., 2020; Izquierdo et al., 2007).

   Mappings to domain labels can be determined manually, automatically, or both. For example, Magnini and Cavaglia (2000) began with a small set of manual annotations, then extended them automatically based on a semantic hierarchy; Camacho-Collados and Navigli (2017) produced their mappings according to similarity metrics and other heuristics, then evaluated a subset according to manual annotations. Many dictionary repositories like WordNet and the LDOCE also comes with manually annotated domain labels.

Unlike clusters, there is no way to ensure that all fine-grained senses can be mapped to a substantive domain, so a miscellaneous or "catch-all" label is sometimes used for uncategorised senses. For example, the WordNet Domains Hierarchy (Bentivogli et al., 2004) contains the label "factotum" for when no better label is available. Additionally, it is possible for fine-grained senses to be mapped to multiple domain labels.

4. **Embedding vectors** represent senses as a dense vector. Early word embedding techniques like Word2Vec (Mikolov et al., 2013) produce one embedding per word type, but later techniques such as ELMo (Peters et al., 2018) and BERT (Devlin et al., 2019) can be used to produce contextualised embeddings, which are effectively very fine-grained senses. Scarlini et al. (2020a; Scarlini et al. (2020b) have also created embeddings for WordNet synsets.

2.3. Mapping sense repositories

Most work on mapping sense repositories is motivated by a common concern: that WordNet synsets are too fine-grained to achieve reasonable results on the WSD task (Ide and Wilks, 2007; Lacerra et al., 2020). Some researchers advocate for multiple levels of grain, so that downstream applications are free to select the level as appropriate. For example, Palmer et al. (2004) employ WordNet synsets, synset groupings, and framesets as three repositories at different levels of grain. It has been argued that there is no single correct repository of senses that is independent of the use case (Kilgarriff, 2003).

It has been established that using multiple mapped repositories can improve the performance on the WSD task, demonstrating the practical value of mappings. Navigli (2006) clustered WordNet synsets based on partial mappings to the *Oxford Dictionary of English*, and showed that this mapping-based clustering improved the performance on the WSD task. Similarly, Palmer et al. (2007) showed that the possibility of backing off to coarse-grained sense groups improves WSD, further supporting the usefulness of mapping sense repositories of different grain.

None of this work, however, provides general theoretical grounding and restrictions for the mappings between multiple sense repositories. Formal features such as the transitivity of mappings are more often the result of practical exigencies and methodological choices rather than theoretical motivations. For example, some WordNet synsets were mapped to the Coarse Sense Inventory (CSI) indirectly via BabelDomains (Lacerra et al., 2020), suggesting that sense mappings are transitive. The present paper will make such implicit assumptions explicit using category theory.

3. Formal notation for a sense system

We introduce the term *sense system* to denote an interconnected system of sense repositories and mappings. We represent a sense system as a small category S, where the object set of S, denoted by $\mathbf{Ob}(S)$, is a set of sense repositories; and the homomorphism set or hom-set of S, denoted by $\mathbf{Hom}(S)$, is a set of mappings between these repositories. The set of mappings from repository R to repository R' in S is denoted by the hom-set $\mathbf{Hom}_S(R, R')$. The general hom-set $\mathbf{Hom}(S)$ is the union of all these repository-specific hom-sets.

Note that each R in $\mathbf{Ob}(S)$ only contains senses – other information such as word type exists separately (see Section 4.1.2) and we make no assumptions about the form or content of the senses themselves. Our sense system representation will be applicable regardless of whether the senses are dictionary definitions, embeddings, domain labels, or otherwise.

As a category, S has the following two properties:

1. **$\mathbf{Hom}(S)$ is closed under function composition.** If, in $\mathbf{Hom}(S)$, R is mapped to R' and R' is mapped to R'', then there must be some composite mapping that maps R to R'' in $\mathbf{Hom}(S)$.

2. **Each repository in $\mathbf{Ob}(S)$ has an identity function id in $\mathbf{Hom}(R, R)$ mapping R to itself.**

Both of these properties are trivially fulfilled by the common understanding of sense mappings.

We conceptualise each mapping as a way of converting a label from one repository to another label from another repository. For example, if WordNet synsets are mapped to WordNet Domains, one could take a corpus like SemCor (Landes et al., 1998), which is labelled with WordNet synsets, and convert the synset labels to Domain labels.

Since there can be multiple ways of converting, in principle multiple mappings from one repository to another can coexist. For example, the WordNet 2.0 synset for *amethyst* is linked to three WordNet Domain labels, as seen in Figure 2. When encountering the word *amethyst* in SemCor, one could select a label randomly, or according to some arbitrary order, or by frequency, etc. Each of these methods would correspond to a different mapping between the two repositories.

Mappings in $\mathbf{Hom}(S)$ have the following properties:

1. **Mappings are unidirectional.** A mapping from R to R' does not entail a mapping from R' to R.

   While this property is often assumed, it is not always made explicit. For example, WordNet

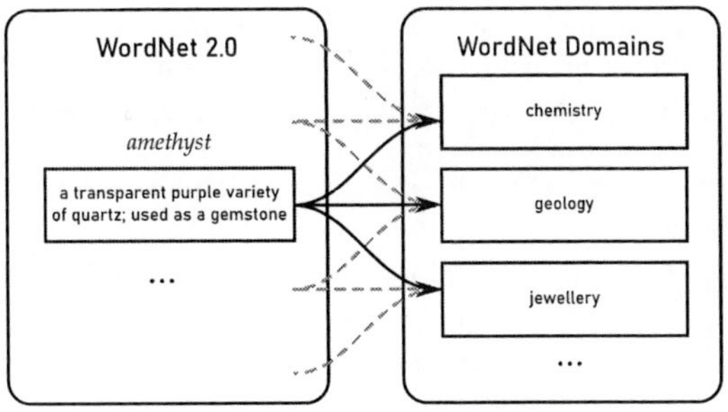

Figure 2: Example mapping from the WordNet 2.0 synset for *amethyst* to WordNet Domains.

synsets are often mapped to domain labels or clusters that are coarser-grained, making it impossible to reverse the mapping.[2] Therefore, repositories are typically mapped from finer-grained ones to coarser-grained ones, not vice versa. Bidirectional mappings would only be possible between repositories that are of equal grain and mapped one-to-one to each other, e.g. when embeddings are created specifically for WordNet synsets (Scarlini et al., 2020a).

2. **Mappings are not multivalued.** That is, each mapping in $\mathbf{Hom}_S(R, R')$ maps each sense in R to at most one sense in R', though multiple senses in R can be mapped to the same sense in R'.

   This is consistent with the idea that mappings represent a way of converting labels (as suggested above), because each conversion method takes one input and gives only one output.

3. **Mappings are total functions.** A mapping from R to R' ensures that all senses in R are mapped to at least one sense in R'.

   In practice, there are some cases where mappings are not total. For example, Navigli (2006) partially mapped WordNet synsets to definitions in the Oxford Dictionary of English, leaving synsets that are not mapped to any ODE senses. There may also be repositories that were built for a reduced vocabulary, such as dictionaries for learners, or repositories that only contain certain types of words, such as English verbs (Green et al., 2001).

   For the purposes of this theory, we follow Navigli (2006), Navigli and Ponzetto (2012), etc. and use ϵ as a null value, so senses that are not mapped to anything are instead mapped to ϵ.

The category theoretic properties described in this section will be assumed throughout this paper. Formalising a sense system as a category posits very minimal assumptions about sense repositories and their mappings, and should therefore be applicable to most existing sense systems.

However, such a flexible representation of sense systems is not very informative. Previous work on mapping repositories often impose further assumptions, resulting in sense systems that are more useful and informative. In the following sections, we formally describe these assumptions and formulate them as **basic** and **guiding** criteria for sense systems.

4. Basic criteria for sense systems

In this section, we formalise and motivate 4 **basic** criteria for sense systems. These criteria capture linguistic intuitions that are often implicitly assumed, while simultaneously accounting for downstream application concerns.

1. **Correctness preservation: Mappings should preserve the correctness of sense labels in all contexts.**

   Intuitively, if the correct sense for a word token is mapped to another sense, this sense should also be correct. To formalise this criterion, we postulate the existence of a WSD oracle Ω, which evaluates to 0 or 1 depending on whether a given word token in a usage context has a given sense. Note that Ω makes no assumption about the number of correct senses.

   We formalise the preservation of correctness as follows:

$$\begin{aligned} &\forall R, R' \in \mathbf{Ob}(S) \\ &\quad \forall m \in \mathbf{Hom}_S(R, R') \\ &\quad \forall s \in R \\ &\quad \forall t \in T \\ &\Omega(t, s) = 1 \Rightarrow \Omega(t, m(s)) = 1 \end{aligned} \tag{1}$$

   where t denotes any given word **t**oken from the set of tokens T covered by both R and R'.

2. **Candidacy preservation: Mappings should preserve the lexical candidacy of sense labels.**

[2] One notable exception to this is the sense compression technique developed by Vial et al. (2019), which allows for mappings from coarse to fine senses in virtue of the way they were produced.

To introduce the concept of candidacy, we distinguish word types from word tokens: word tokens are words in a usage context; word types, also known as a lemma, refer to the abstract notion of a word, and is independent of morphological variants.

We postulate that word types exist separately for each repository R as the set W_R, which are mapped to senses in R like in a dictionary, i.e. each word type is associated with a set of candidate senses. We formalise this dictionary function as $d_R : W_R \rightarrow \mathcal{P}(R)$, where $\mathcal{P}(R)$ denotes the power set of R.

For a sense s in R to be a candidate for a word type w, the dictionary function d_R must map w to a set that contains s. For example, in WordNet 3.1, the word *manuscript* is mapped to the set of two synsets: "the form of a literary work submitted for publication", and "handwritten book or document". Both of these senses are candidates of *manuscript*.

Having introduced the dictionary function, candidacy preservation can then be formulated as follows: if a sense s that is a candidate for a word type w is mapped to another sense, that sense must also be a candidate for w. Formally,

$$\begin{gathered} \forall R, R' \in \mathbf{Ob}(S) \\ \forall w \in (W_R \cap W_{R'}) \\ \forall m \in \mathbf{Hom}_S(R, R') \\ s \in d_R(w) \Rightarrow m(s) \in d_{R'}(w) \end{gathered} \tag{2}$$

3. **Uniqueness criterion: There should be at most one mapping from one repository to another.**

The uniqueness criterion states that for each pair of repositories R and R', there is at most one mapping from R to R', and at most one mapping from R' to R, making S a *posetal* or *thin* category. Note that this criterion is direction-sensitive, so for each pair of repositories, there can be at most two mappings, one in each direction. For example, SensEmBert embeddings are mapped one-to-one to WordNet synsets, and vice versa. This criterion prevents WordNet embeddings from being mapped to a different WordNet synset, or vice versa.

Formally:

$$\forall R, R' \in \mathbf{Ob}(S) \quad |\mathbf{Hom}_S(R, R')| = 1 \tag{3}$$

4. **Connectivity: A sense system should be a connected category.**

The connectivity criterion states that S is a connected category, i.e. all repositories in $\mathbf{Ob}(S)$ and their mappings in $\mathbf{Hom}(S)$ must form a single connected graph. For example, WordNet synsets are mapped to CSI labels, but neither are mapped to or from, say, the *Macmillan English Dictionary*. This means that the sense system formed by these three repositories does not fulfil the connectivity criterion.

Formally, for any two repositories R and R' in $\mathbf{Ob}(S)$, there is a sequence $R = R_0, R_1, R_2, \ldots R_n = R'$ where $(R_0, \ldots, R_n) \in \mathbf{Ob}(S)$, and for each i up to (but not including) n, there is at least one mapping in either $\mathbf{Hom}_S(R_i, R_i + 1)$ or $\mathbf{Hom}_S(R_i + 1, R_i)$.

4.1. Motivation

4.1.1. Correctness preservation

This criterion is endorsed by virtually all existing mappings. Without this assumption, existing mappings would be unusable. Nonetheless, repositories occasionally contain errors, particularly ones which are automatically mapped. Because of this, manual annotations are more highly valued (Pradhan and Xue, 2009), while automatically mapped repositories are often evaluated afterwards to reveal errors. For example, Seppälä et al. (2016) checked their automatically generated mappings against their manually identified mappings for medicine-related words, and discovered that only 85% were correctly identified automatically. They also found two "obvious mistakes" made during manual annotation, which were promptly corrected.

Since mappings are not multivalued (section 3), preserving correctness allows us to cross-check labelled data for any inconsistencies. Using the word *mouse* as an example, one annotator or classifier might select the WordNet synset referring to the rodent, and another might select the WordNet Domain label of "computer science". Since the rodent synset is not mapped to "computer science", we know (by *modus tollens*) that there was a disagreement between the two annotators/classifiers, even though they make use of different sense repositories.

Note that the correctness preservation is only defined with respect to the selection of the correct sense, but does not place any restrictions on candidacy and word type.

4.1.2. Candidacy preservation

Candidacy preservation is intuitive from a semantic perspective. If a word sense s is mapped to a semantically more encompassing word sense s', it must be the case that this broader sense is also a candidate. This criterion is trivially fulfilled by clustering-based approaches, but is not typically explicitly stated for repositories.

A violation would only occur if an instance of a word type could carry the sense s without also being able to carry s' in any context. Such a violation would suggest that s' has some semantic specificity that s lacks. For example, the WordNet synset `mind.n.01` (with the gloss definition "that which is responsible for one's

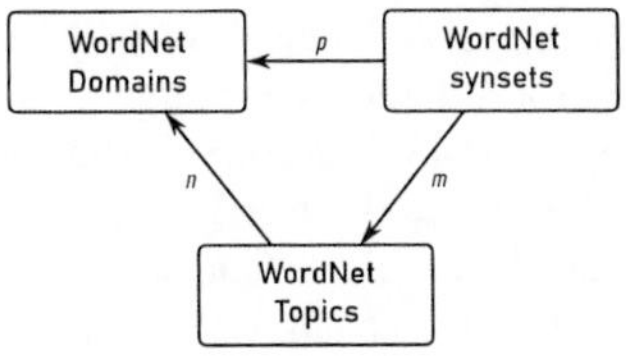

Figure 3: Mappings for WordNet synsets, WordNet Domains, and WordNet Topics have been created. By the compositionality of morphisms and the uniqueness criterion, $n \circ m = p$.

thoughts and feelings; the seat of the faculty of reason") is a candidate sense for the word types *brain*, *head*, *psyche*, and *nous*. If this synset is mapped to a domain label called "anatomy", it would be a violation of candidacy preservation, because "anatomy" is not a candidate sense for "psyche" or "nous".

Relatedly, candidacy preservation is required for a straightforward way of comparing granularity levels for each word type: by counting the number of senses. For example, WordNet 3.1 contains 42 senses for *head*, while the online *Oxford Learner's Dictionary* contains 20. If we map all of WordNet's synsets to OLD entries and preserve candidacy, we can postulate that the 20 senses are coarser-grained than the 42 in WordNet. On the other hand, if we do not preserve candidacy, it may be the case that semantic content was lost in applying the mapping, and hence the fewer senses of the *Oxford Learner's Dictionary* might not be more coarse-grained, but just leave semantic gaps.

4.1.3. Uniqueness

For many existing mappings that were produced through clustering (Dolan, 1994; Vial et al., 2019), the uniqueness criterion is assumed implicitly, because each sense can belong to at most one cluster. The same is true for embedding-based senses that are mapped one-to-one to a dictionary-based repository.

However, there are other types of mappings that do not fulfil this criterion. As mentioned in Section 3, WordNet Domains maps the synset for *amethyst* to the domains of "chemistry", "geology", and "jewellery". Similarly, the Coarse Sense Inventory (CSI) (Lacerra et al., 2020) maps the synset for *abbatoir* to "craft, engineering, and technology", "art, architecture, and archaeology", and "food, drink, and taste".

We argue that enforcing the uniqueness criterion provides several benefits:

1. Repositories in S would form a partial preorder, which would roughly correspond to the notion of granularity. Since mappings are total and cannot be multivalued, the range (or image) of the mapping must have cardinality less than or equal to that of the domain. The cardinality thus reflects a notion of granularity that is measured numerically.[3]

2. There would be more consistency when converting between labels. For example, Izquierdo et al. (2007) mapped each WordNet synset to one Base Level Concept (BLC), so one could consistently convert from the former to the latter. A WSD tool or downstream application that uses BLC-annotated corpora can automatically make use of a WordNet-annotated corpus such as SemCor (Landes et al., 1998), because the labels can be directly converted into BLCs.

3. In a similar vein, evaluation metrics that depend on converted labels would be more reliable. A WSD classifier using BLCs can easily be evaluated according to SemCor, because there is only one correct BLC that each word is mapped to. On the other hand, if WordNet synsets are mapped to multiple BLCs, it is not clear how the classifier should be evaluated. The BLCs might all be considered correct, resulting in inflated scores; or if a random one is chosen, the scores may not accurately reflect the classifier's performance.

4. In conjunction with function composition (see Section 3), the uniqueness criterion would also enforce transitivity. Consider WordNet synsets, WordNet topics, and WordNet Domains in Figure 1: if the mappings between these repositories fulfil the uniqueness criterion, there would only be at most one mapping between each repository, as in Figure 3. Under function composition, $n \circ m = p$ (where n, m, and p correspond to mappings in Figure 3).

One might argue that the domain labels for *amethyst* and *abbatoir* should not be interpreted as separate labels, but instead as a set containing all relevant domains; so one would map WordNet synsets to the *power set* of CSI or Domain labels. However, adapting classifier models (for WSD or otherwise) to handle multiple labels instead of one is not always straightforward, so ideally a sense system should only contain sets of senses, not sets of sets of senses.

Another practical solution is to designate one main CSI or Domain label for each WordNet synset, so that all conversions and comparisons will be made according to one label. This main label could be chosen based on inter-annotator agreement or frequency or another metric, as long as it is consistent across all synsets. Other non-designated labels can still be made available for classifiers that can handle multiple labels.

[3]This correspondence of course only applies to the range, but not the whole co-domain. In practice, mappings are usually surjective (so the co-domain *is* the range) — exceptions are limited to newer or more specialised vocabulary. For example, English WordNet (`https://en-word.net/`) contains the definition of *dab* that refers to the dance move, which is not in Princeton WordNet 3.1.

In either case, formalising the uniqueness criterion explicitly provides a better understanding of the potential problems and associated tradeoffs when the criterion is not met. It also allows researchers to evaluate current and future repositories according to specific needs and resources.

4.1.4. Connectivity

Previous work on WSD have focused on building mappings between repositories rather than a complete sense system, so connectivity is rarely assumed. However, in the few cases where more than two repositories were mapped (Gella et al., 2014; Palmer et al., 2004), the resulting sense systems do fulfil the connectivity criterion.

The connectivity criterion on its own is not very informative, but it enables other criteria by extending their benefits to the rest of the sense system. After all, an unconnected sense system technically fulfils all the other criteria in this paper, but is not very useful. As mentioned above, the previous three criteria each had their own practical and theoretical benefits: 1) correctness preservation allowing cross-checking; 2) candidacy preservation allowing comparison of grain level; and 3) uniqueness allowing consistent label conversion. If the connectivity criterion is fulfilled, these benefits can be extended to any two repositories in $\mathbf{Ob}(S)$.

With a sufficient number of repositories in $\mathbf{Ob}(S)$, one can leverage these benefits on a larger scale, opening up new opportunities for WSD research. For example, ensemble classifiers based on different sense repositories can be built: if there are three WSD classifiers that use senses from R, R', and R'' respectively, their outputs can be aggregated and cross-checked, as long as R, R', and R'' are connected to each other in a single graph.

5. Guiding criteria for sense systems

While all criteria listed in this paper are desirable for various reasons, the **basic** criteria are ones which can be fulfilled both in theory and in practice, while the **guiding** criteria may be impossible to fulfil in certain situations, and should be considered more as approximate guidelines than strict criteria.

In addition to the 4 basic criteria, we propose two additional guiding criteria:

1. **Non-contradiction: Mappings cannot exist between senses that semantically contradict each other.**

   The non-contradiction criterion forbids mappings between senses whose (strict) implications contradict each other. Examples of such contradictions can easily be found in the literature: the word *monograph* has (at least) two fine-grained senses, one referring to the physical printed volume by an author, another referring to the abstract piece of work instantiated by such a volume. These two senses might be mapped to one coarse-grained sense in a different repository, where it is categorised as a physical object. Thus arises a contradiction where the fine-grained sense referring to the abstract work is mapped to a coarse-grained sense referring to a physical object.

   We formalise the non-contradiction criterion as follows:

$$\begin{aligned} &\forall R, R' \in \mathbf{Ob}(S) \\ &\quad \forall m \in \mathbf{Hom}_S(R, R') \\ &\quad \forall s \in R \\ &\quad s \models P \Rightarrow \neg(m(s) \models \neg P) \end{aligned} \tag{4}$$

   where $\models$ indicates strict entailment and P is any proposition.

   Note that the correctness criterion does not entail the non-contradiction criterion. In the *monograph* example, the mapping fulfils the correctness preservation because a WSD oracle would consider the coarse-grained sense to be correct, despite the contradiction.

2. **Inter-annotator agreement: Mappings should correspond to a partial preorder of inter-annotator agreement levels.**

   It has been observed that, when annotating corpora with senses from a given sense repository, inter-annotator agreement tends to drop when the repository is more fine-grained (Ng et al., 1999; Navigli, 2009). Therefore, if R is coarser-grained than R', one can expect agreement levels to be higher when annotating corpora with senses in R, compared to R'.

   We formalise this criterion as follows:

$$\begin{aligned} &\forall R, R' \in \mathbf{Ob}(S) \\ &(\exists m \in \mathbf{Hom}_S(R, R')) \Rightarrow (a(R) \leq a(R')) \end{aligned} \tag{5}$$

   where a refers to the inter-annotator agreement, defined by $a : \mathbf{Ob}(S) \to \mathbb{R}$. $\exists m \in \mathbf{Hom}_S(R, R')$ means that there is at least one mapping from R to R'.

5.1. Motivation

5.1.1. Non-contradiction

Non-contradiction is considered a guiding criterion because, while it is desirable, it is also a difficult criterion to meet. Firstly, some sense representations (such as embeddings) do not come with explicit semantics, so it would be impossible to determine if their implications contradict one another. Secondly, semantic implications are often subtle and difficult to identify: even WordNet, a repository known for its fine-grained senses, does not distinguish the two senses in the *monograph* example above.

However, mappings that do meet the non-contradiction criterion can be useful in downstream tasks that require natural language inference, such as question answering or information extraction. For example, with the correct sense labels, an information extraction tool could eliminate the possibility of an abstract *book* having the same referent as a physical *monograph*. Alternatively, mappings that do not meet the criterion might cause errors in these downstream applications. For the question "When was this monograph created?", a question-answering system might incorrectly assume the physicality of the object in question, and describe the time when the monograph was printed instead of when the text was written.

Some sense repositories that are formed through clustering techniques do not contain any semantic content. For example, clustering WordNet synsets based on confusion matrices (Agirre and Lacalle, 2003) would create clusters that are not explicitly associated with a label or definition. These mappings trivially fulfil the non-contradiction criterion. However, there are also clustering techniques where this criterion does apply: for example, Navigli (2006) makes use of the hierarchical semantic structures in the *Oxford Dictionary of English* to cluster WordNet synsets. As a result, the clusters produced are associated with a textual definition and other semantic information.

5.1.2. Inter-annotator agreement

We previously demonstrated that mapped repositories in a posetal sense system (fulfilling the uniqueness criterion) form a partial preorder of granularity. If the inter-annotator agreement criterion is fulfilled, mapped repositories would also form a partial preorder of inter-annotator agreement levels.

This criterion is considered a guiding criterion because, unlike basic criteria, it cannot be directly enforced — researchers have no reason to artificially inflate or lower inter-annotator agreement. Additionally, this criterion cannot be applied to sense representations that are not used for human annotation, such as word embeddings. Nevertheless, this criterion not only reflects existing expectations for a sense system, but strong violations suggest that the sense distinctions of the coarse-grained sense repository are unnatural, i.e. not in accordance with human linguistic intuitions, since the annotators appear to struggle more despite a reduction in labels.

6. Conclusion

This paper develops a representation of sense systems as categories, and proposes a list of criteria that serve as guidelines for future sense repositories and mappings. The list is by no means exhaustive, as there are other properties that may be desirable depending on the downstream application.

A sense system that fulfils our list of criteria brings multiple benefits and opportunities to the WSD task: not only does it provide theoretical grounding for sense mappings, it also opens up other opportunities to improve existing WSD tools, such as extending them to ensemble classifiers that can crosscheck annotation from multiple sense repositories.

Agirre, E. and Lacalle, O. L. D. (2003). Clustering Wordnet Word Senses. In *Proceedings of the Conference on Recent Advances on Natural Language (RANLP'03)*. http://ixa3.si.ehu.es/cgi-bin/ signatureak/signaturecgi.cgi http://ixa2.si.ehu.es/pub/webcorpus.

Bentivogli, L., Forner, P., Magnini, B., and Pianta, E. (2004). Revising the Wordnet Domains Hierarchy: Semantics, Coverage and Balancing. In *Proceedings of the Workshop on Multilingual Linguistic Resources*, pages 94–101, Geneva, Switzerland, August. COLING.

Camacho-Collados, J. and Navigli, R. (2017). Babeldomains: Large-scale domain labeling of lexical resources. In *Proceedings of the 15th Conference of the European Chapter of the Association for Computational Linguistics: Volume 2, Short Papers*, page 223–228. Association for Computational Linguistics.

Devlin, J., Chang, M.-W., Lee, K., and Toutanova, K. (2019). BERT: Pre-training of Deep Bidirectional Transformers for Language Understanding. *arXiv:1810.04805 [cs]*, May. arXiv: 1810.04805.

Dolan, W. B. (1994). Word sense ambiguation: Clustering related senses. In *Proceedings of the 15th conference on Computational linguistics-Volume 2*, page 712–716. Association for Computational Linguistics.

Christiane Fellbaum, editor. (1998). *WordNet: An Electronic Lexical Database*. Language, speech, and communication. MIT Press, Cambridge, Mass.

Gella, S., Strapparava, C., and Nastase, V. (2014). Mapping WordNet Domains, WordNet Topics and Wikipedia Categories to Generate Multilingual Domain Specific Resources. In *LREC*, pages 1117–1121.

Green, R., Pearl, L., Dorr, B. J., and Resnik, P. (2001). Mapping lexical entries in a verbs database to WordNet senses. In *Proceedings of the 39th Annual Meeting of the Association for Computational Linguistics*, pages 244–251, Toulouse, France, July. Association for Computational Linguistics.

Iacobacci, I., Pilehvar, M. T., and Navigli, R. (2016). Embeddings for word sense disambiguation: An evaluation study. In *Proceedings of the 54th Annual Meeting of the Association for Computational Linguistics (Volume 1: Long Papers)*, page 897–907. Association for Computational Linguistics.

Ide, N. and Wilks, Y. (2007). Making Sense About Sense. In Eneko Agirre et al., editors, *Word Sense Disambiguation: Algorithms and Applications*, Text, Speech and Language Technology, pages 47–73. Springer Netherlands, Dordrecht.

Izquierdo, R., Suarez, A., and Rigau, G. (2007). Exploring the Automatic Selection of Basic Level Concepts. In *Recent Advances in Natural Language Processing*, pages 298–302, Borovets, Bulgaria.

Kågebäck, M. and Salomonsson, H. (2016). Word sense disambiguation using a bidirectional lstm. In *Proceedings of the 5th Workshop on Cognitive Aspects of the Lexicon (CogALex - V)*, page 51–56. The COLING 2016 Organizing Committee, Dec.

Kilgarriff, A. (2003). "I Don't Believe in Word Senses". In Brigitte Nerlich, et al., editors, *Polysemy*. DE GRUYTER MOUTON, Berlin, New York, January.

Lacerra, C., Bevilacqua, M., Pasini, T., and Navigli, R. (2020). CSI: A Coarse Sense Inventory for 85% Word Sense Disambiguation. In *Proc. of AAAI*.

Landes, S., Leacock, C., and Tengi, R. I. (1998). Building semantic concordances. In *WordNet: an electronic lexical database*, chapter 8, pages 199–216. MIT Press, Cambridge, MA.

Lesk, M. (1986). Automatic sense disambiguation using machine readable dictionaries: How to tell a pine cone from an ice cream cone. In *Proceedings of the 5th Annual International Conference on Systems Documentation*, SIGDOC '86, page 24–26. ACM.

Magnini, B. and Cavaglia, G. (2000). Integrating Subject Field Codes into WordNet. In *LREC*, pages 1413–1418.

Mihalcea, R. and Faruque, E. (2004). Senselearner: Minimally supervised word sense disambiguation for all words in open text. In *Proceedings of SENSEVAL-3, the Third International Workshop on the Evaluation of Systems for the Semantic Analysis of Text*, page 155–158. Association for Computational Linguistics, Jul.

Mikolov, T., Sutskever, I., Chen, K., Corrado, G., and Dean, J. (2013). Distributed Representations of Words and Phrases and Their Compositionality. In *Proceedings of the 26th International Conference on Neural Information Processing Systems - Volume 2*, NIPS'13, pages 3111–3119, USA. Curran Associates Inc. event-place: Lake Tahoe, Nevada.

Miller, G. A., Beckwith, R., Fellbaum, C., Gross, D., and Miller, K. J. (1990). Introduction to WordNet: An On-line Lexical Database*. *International Journal of Lexicography*, 3(4):235–244, December. Publisher: Oxford Academic.

Moro, A., Raganato, A., and Navigli, R. (2014). Entity linking meets word sense disambiguation: a unified approach. *Transactions of the Association for Computational Linguistics*, 2:231–244.

Navigli, R. and Ponzetto, S. P. (2012). BabelNet: The automatic construction, evaluation and application of a wide-coverage multilingual semantic network. *Artificial Intelligence*, 193:217 – 250.

Navigli, R. (2006). Meaningful Clustering of Senses Helps Boost Word Sense Disambiguation Performance. In *Proceedings of the 21st International Conference on Computational Linguistics and the 44th annual meeting of the ACL - ACL '06*, pages 105–112, Sydney, Australia. Association for Computational Linguistics.

Navigli, R. (2009). Word Sense Disambiguation: A Survey. *ACM Computing Surveys*, 41(2):1–69, February.

Ng, H. T., Lim, C. Y., and Foo, S. K. (1999). A Case Study on Inter-Annotator Agreement for Word Sense Disambiguation. In *SIGLEX99: Standardizing Lexical Resources*.

Oele, D. and Noord, G. v. (2017). Distributional lesk: Effective knowledge-based word sense disambiguation. In *IWCS 2017 — 12th International Conference on Computational Semantics: Short papers*, pages W17–6931.

Palmer, M., Babko-Malaya, O., and Dang, H. T. (2004). Different Sense Granularities for Different Applications. In *Proceedings of the 2nd International Workshop on Scalable Natural Language Understanding (ScaNaLU 2004) at HLT-NAACL 2004*, pages 49–56.

Palmer, M., Dang, H. T., and Fellbaum, C. (2007). Making Fine-Grained and Coarse-Grained Sense Distinctions, Both Manually and Automatically. *Natural Language Engineering*, 13(2):137–163, June.

Peters, W., Peters, I., and Vossen, P. (1998). Automatic Sense Clustering in Eurowordnet. In *Proceedings of LREC'1998*.

Peters, M., Neumann, M., Iyyer, M., Gardner, M., Clark, C., Lee, K., and Zettlemoyer, L. (2018). Deep Contextualized Word Representations. In *Proceedings of the 2018 Conference of the North American Chapter of the Association for Computational Linguistics: Human Language Technologies, Volume 1 (Long Papers)*, pages 2227–2237, New Orleans, Louisiana, June. Association for Computational Linguistics.

Pianta, E., Bentivogli, L., and Girardi, C. (2002). Multiwordnet: developing an aligned multilingual database. In *First international conference on global WordNet*, pages 293–302.

Pradhan, S. S. and Xue, N. (2009). OntoNotes: The 90% solution. In *Proceedings of Human Language Technologies: The 2009 Annual Conference of the North American Chapter of the Association for Computational Linguistics, Companion Volume: Tutorial Abstracts*, pages 11–12, Boulder, Colorado, May. Association for Computational Linguistics.

Scarlini, B., Pasini, T., and Navigli, R. (2020a). SensEmBERT: Context-Enhanced Sense Embeddings for Multilingual Word Sense Disambiguation. In *Proc. of AAAI*.

Scarlini, B., Pasini, T., and Navigli, R. (2020b). With More Contexts Comes Better Performance: Contextualized Sense Embeddings for All-Round Word Sense Disambiguation. In *Proceedings of the 2020*

Conference on Empirical Methods in Natural Language Processing. Association for Computational Linguistics.

Seppälä, S., Hicks, A., and Ruttenberg, A. (2016). Semi-automatic mapping of WordNet to Basic Formal Ontology. In Verginica Barbu Mititelu, et al., editors, *Proceedings of the Eighth Global WordNet Conference*, pages 369–376, Bucharest, Romania, January 27-30.

Vial, L., Lecouteux, B., and Schwab, D. (2019). Sense Vocabulary Compression through the Semantic Knowledge of WordNet for Neural Word Sense Disambiguation. *ArXiv*.

Piek Vossen, editor. (1998). *EuroWordNet: A multilingual database with lexical semantic networks*. Springer Netherlands.

Wiedemann, G., Remus, S., Chawla, A., and Biemann, C. (2019). Does bert make any sense? interpretable word sense disambiguation with contextualized embeddings. In *Proceedings of the 15th Conference on Natural Language Processing (KONVENS 2019): Long Papers*, page 161–170. German Society for Computational Linguistics & Language Technology.

Zhong, Z. and Ng, H. T. (2010). It makes sense: A wide-coverage word sense disambiguation system for free text. In *Proceedings of the 48th Annual Meeting of the Association for Computational Linguistics (ACL*, page 78–83.

Proceedings of the Globalex Workshop on Linked Lexicography @LREC2022, pages 52–59
Marseille, 20 June 2022

Converting a Database of Complex German Word Formation for Linked Data

Petra Steiner
Universität Bayreuth
petra.steiner@uni-bayreuth.de

Abstract

This work combines two lexical resources with morphological information on German word formation, CELEX for German and the latest release of GermaNet, for extracting and building complex word structures. This yields a database of over 100,000 German wordtrees. A definition for sequential morphological analyses leads to a Ontolex-Lemon type model. By using GermaNet sense information, the data can be linked to other semantic resources. An alignment to the CIDOC Conceptual Reference Model (CIDOC-CRM) is also provided. The scripts for the data generation are publicly available on GitHub.
Keywords: CELEX, GermaNet, morphology, German

1. Introduction

Languages with a high lexical productivity in word formation bounce into bottleneck problems if it comes to analysing texts, building terminologies, or finding links between ontologies and other networks. Concerning the German language, there are three main problems:

A. The wealth of ambiguous forms on the level of word formation

B. The lack of deeper structural analyses in current approaches

C. The lack of linkages between morphological analyses and ontologies

The linkage of lemmas, lexical items, ontological entities etc. with morphological complex word forms presupposes their structural disambiguation on the morphological level, either manually or automatically. Only if this is provided, a classification at a high quality level is possible. However, especially for long and complex lexical items, the morphological analyses and with it the semantic interpretations are no trivial task for human and automatic disambiguation.

For example, *Landesentwicklungsgesellschaft* 'state development corporation' and *Stadtentwicklungsgesellschaft* 'urban development company' have two different hyperonyms although their first constituents *Land*'state' and *Stadt* 'urban' are cohyponymns denoting levels of administrative units. However, the first term denotes a corporation, and the second a company, as the German lexeme *Gesellschaft* can be used for both senses. Figure 1 and Figure 2 present the first three levels of the different structures, including the linking elements.[1] The last top level constituents of the morphological structure (here *Entwicklungsgesellschaft* vs. *Gesellschaft*) are usually the heads of the constructions, especially for compounds. By this, they determine not only the grammatical features of the complete lexeme but in most cases also the hyperonymic class of the terms.

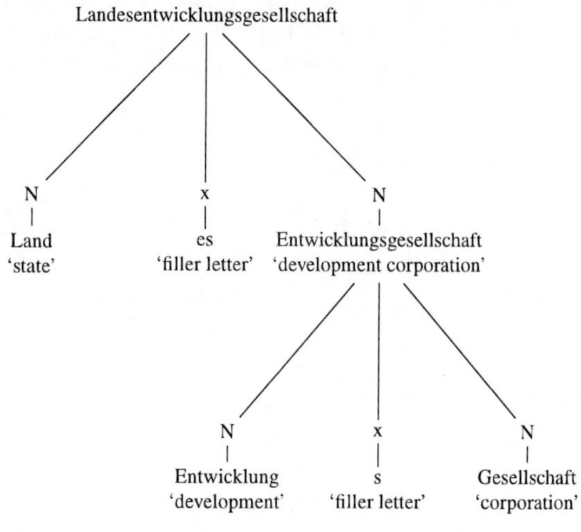

Figure 1: Analysis of *Landesentwicklungsgesellschaft* 'state development corporation'

German compounds can consist of derivatives such as *Entwicklung* and *Gesellschaft*, both ending with suffixes (*ung* and *schaft*). These analyses can further link lexical units to others, e.g. by the verbs they were derived from. On each level of morphological segmentation, the number of possible analyses is 2^n. This number can be reduced by excluding implausible constructions such as suffixes at the beginning of a construct. However, it has to be multiplied by the number of morphological homonyms for the segmented forms. The wealth of such long and structurally ambiguous wordforms necessitates the search for solutions.

This paper provides the development of a lexical resource for complex morphological analyses. Section 2 gives a concise overview of related work in word seg-

[1]By some approaches, linking elements are considered as a special kind of morphemes and called *Fugenmorpheme*. However, the status of morpheme is questionable, therefore the labels *filler letter(s)* or *interfix* are being used here.

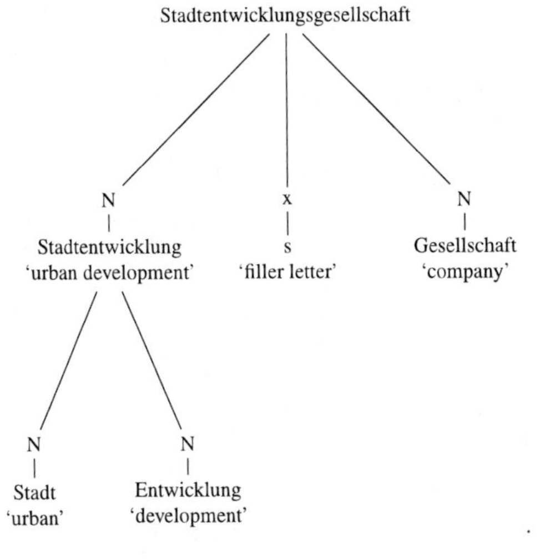

Figure 2: Analysis of *Stadtentwicklungsgesellschaft* 'urban development corporation'

mentation and word parsing for German with a focus on structural analysis. Section 3 describes the lexical resources CELEX and GermaNet on which our morphological database is built and the prerequisites for extracting the required information. Section 4 describes the procedures for the combination of the morphological analyses. Section 5 deals with the representation of morphological information in accordance with the Ontolex-Lemon modules, and links to the CIDOC Conceptual Reference Model (CIDOC-CRM) and WordNet information. The final discussion gives an outlook for future developments.

2. Related Work

Morphological segmentation tools for German such as SMOR (Schmid et al., 2004), Gertwol (Haapalainen and Majorin, 1995), MORPH (Hanrieder, 1996), TAGH (Geyken and Hanneforth, 2006) generate dozens of analyses for relatively simple words. With the exception of Würzner and Hanneforth (2013), the results yield only flat structures though their project was restricted to adjectives.
In most cases, also German morphological data resources are restricted to lists of flat analyses, for instance, the test set of the 2009 workshop on statistical machine translation, which was used by Cap (2014). Henrich and Hinrichs (2011) augmented the GermaNet database with information on noun compound splits of the top-level. DErivBase (Zeller et al., 2013) comprises derivational families (word nests) and could be used to infer derivational trees from its sets and rules, however, it is based on heuristics and therefore contains some errors. Shafaei et al. (2017) use the CELEX German data for inferring derivational families (DErivCELEX) which are more precise than DErivBase. This data is obviously drawn from the original CELEX version with its old orthographical standard (Baayen et al., 1995).

3. Lexical Resources for the Synopsis of Morphological Analyses

3.1. The Refurbished CELEX-German Database

CELEX is a publicly available database of Dutch, English, and German lexical information (Baayen et al., 1995). The German part of the CELEX database (CELEX-German) comprises 51,728 lemmas of all parts of speech. 38,650 entries are derivates or compounds and 2,402 entries are conversions. The compilation of the lemmas is widely overlapping with the one of the dictionary *Der kleine Wahrig* (Wahrig-Burfeind and Bertelsmann, 2007) which represents the core vocabulary for German. CELEX-German comprises not just flat analyses but also German word tree information. The linguistic information is combined with frequency information based on corpora (Burnage, 1995) which makes it useful for automated morphological and phonological analysis of unknown words. Therefore, CELEX-German (Baayen et al., 1995) is a solid standard for building morphological resources.
The drawbacks of the German part of the CELEX database are its outdated format and the use of former orthographical conventions. Therefore, both lemmas and word forms are transferred to a modern standard of encoding by merging the orthographic and the morphophonological information, both for the lemma and the word form data (Steiner, 2016). After these changes, the database with its solid list of base vocabulary yields a foundation for further exploitation. It serves as the foundation for the morphological structure database and can then be augmented by other resources (Steiner and Ruppenhofer, 2018; Steiner, 2017; Steiner, 2019a; Steiner, 2019b), the first of which is the GermaNet database which contains markup for compounds.
Some of the morphological analyses of the CELEX-German database on a deep level are oriented towards diachronic descriptions. For instance, *Gift* 'poison' is analyzed as a derivation from *geben* 'give'. This is certainly of less interest for linking semantic information. On the other hand, the relation between *Ausfuhr* 'export.n' and *ausführen* 'to export' is morphologically manifested in an implicit derivation with *u/ü* ablaut and might lead to interesting connections.
The refurbished database possesses no modification concerning this feature. The decision whether to appreciate, accept, or change this diachronic information is left to the next steps of usage, depending on the respective application.
Examples 1 and 2 show parts of the entries for the derivatives *Entwicklung* 'development' and *Gesellschaft* 'society, corporation, company' with the affixes *ent*, *ung*, and *schaft*.

(1) Entwicklung entwickel+ung\Vx\[...]
(((ent)[V|.V],((Wickel)[N])[V])[V],
(ung)[N|V.])[N]

(2) Gesellschaft gesell+schaft\Vx\[...]
((gesell)[V],(schaft)[N|V.])[N]

3.2. Compound Analyses from GermaNet

Henrich and Hinrichs (2011) augmented the GermaNet (Hamp and Feldweg, 1997) database with information on compound splits. This feature is restricted to nouns. We are using version 17 which was most recently updated in April 2022.[2] This version includes 205.000 lexical units. GermaNet comes with an alignment to Wiktionary entries (Henrich et al., 2011) and connects its senses to EuroWordNet by an interlingual index. Example 3 and 4 present the entries for *Landesentwicklungsgesellschaft* 'state development corporation' and *Stadtentwicklungsgesellschaft* 'urban development company'. The first entry has the hyperonym {Amt, Behörde} 'office, authority'. The parts of interest are marked by bold letters.

(3)
```
<synset id="s151622" category=
    "nomen" class="Gruppe">
<lexUnit id="l196706" sense="1
    " source="core" namedEntity
    ="no" artificial="no"
    styleMarking="no">
<orthForm>
    Landesentwicklungsgesellschaft
    </orthForm>
<compound>
    <modifier
    category="Nomen">Land</modifier>
    <head>Entwicklungsgesellschaft</head>
</compound>
</lexUnit>
</synset>
```

(4)
```
<synset id="s145239" category=
    "nomen" class="Gruppe">
<lexUnit id="l188830" sense="1
    " source="core" namedEntity
    ="no" artificial="no"
    styleMarking="no">
<orthForm>
    Stadtentwicklungsgesellschaft
    </orthForm>
<compound>
    <modifier category="Nomen">
    Stadtentwicklung</modifier>
    <head>Gesellschaft</head>
</compound>
</lexUnit>
</synset>
```

As can be seen, these entries do neither provide filler letters, such as *es* or *s*, nor deep-level structures. Again, it is left the next steps of usage to appreciate, accept, or change this information.

[2]see http://www.sfs.uni-tuebingen.de/GermaNet/compounds.shtml#Download for a description.

4. Procedures

In general, the underlying script permits to restrict the analysis to GermaNet data. Here, both databases are to be combined.

4.1. Fitting the CELEX Data

For the peculiarity of the CELEX database with its diachronically motivated derivations, we added a heuristics based on the Levenshtein distance. For accepting or rejecting two parts of words as derivational relatives, the procedure will calculate the Levensthein distance (LD) for the (sub)strings of the smaller length of the two compared constituents ($min(c_1, c_2)$), and then compare their quotient *dis* to a threshold *t* as in (5):

$$dis = \frac{LD}{min(c_1, c_2)} \leq t \quad (5)$$

For example, for the derivational pair *Gift* - *geb*, the smaller length is 3. The string *Gift* is cut to this length: *Gif*. After this, the quotient of *LD* for *Gif* and *geb* and the length is compared to the threshold. (6) shows that the analysis will stop for a threshold at 0.66 or below.

$$\frac{LD}{min(c_1, c_2)} = \frac{2}{3} \quad (6)$$

4.2. Fitting the GermaNet Data

Different to the CELEX data, the filler letters in the GermaNet data are missing within the analyses. A heuristic method recovers them. A few entries were automatically excluded, as those with missing part-of-speech classes which could not be retrieved from the CELEX database, and compounds with affixoids or fossilized morphemes. Complex components whose analyses are not inside the database are considered as technically simplex lexemes.

4.3. Synopsis of the Databases

The structures are recursively collected, first from the GermaNet data and if no entries can further be found there, then CELEX-German with its rich information on derivations is retrieved. By this, compositional constituents not found within the GermaNet inventory but inside CELEX-German can be analyzed too. Algorithm 1 presents the top-down procedure. Among others, the underlying program has the options presented in Table 1.

We permit compounds with proper names as constituents and foreign expressions, automatically add filler letters and choose a threshold of 0.5 for dissimilarity. Parts of speech tags of GermaNet and CELEX-German are mapped according to Table 2. In GermaNet, there are some orthographic variants of these categories, e.g. *nomen* and *Nomen* for *noun*. The chosen depth for constructions of conversions is 2 and the general depth for the trees is 7, as a depth of 8 did not yield any deeper analyses.

The GermaNet Release 17.0 yields 97,362 compounds, including some with proper names and foreign words as

```
Input: CELEX-German revised, GN flat
    compounds
Output: A Morphological Treebank
initialization of parameters: depth of analysis,
  linguistic information, levenshtein threshold,
  parts of speech, filler letters, conversions
  (Zusammenrückungen), style of output;
add CELEX data to the knowledge base
  according to the requirements
forall entries of GN flat compounds do
    if entry is a compound according to the
      conditions (complete parts of speech, foreign
      words, proper names yes/no) then
        foreach constituent of entry do
            if depth of analysis reached then
                retrieve linguistic information/PoS
                  as required;
                return linguistic information and
                  constituent
            end
            else if constituent not found in GN data
              then
                depth of analysis++;
                analysedeepercelex part with
                  parameters and depth;
                return result of analysedeepercelex
            end
            else
                foreach part of constituent do
                    depth of analysis++;
                    analysedeeper part with
                      parameters and depth;
                    return result of analysedeeper
                end
            end
        end
    end
end

sub analysedeeper part (parameters and level)
  if part is simplex
  or depth of analysis reached
  then
    retrieve linguistic information/PoS as required;
    return linguistic information and part
  end
  else if constituent not found in GN data then
    depth of analysis++;
    analysedeepercelex part with parameters and
      depth;
    return result of analysedeepercelex
  end
  else
    depth of analysis++;
    foreach subpart of part do
        analysedeeper subpart
          return result of analysedeeper subpart
    end
  end
```

Algorithm 1: Building a merged morphological treebank from GermaNet and CELEX

-rmfw	ignore lexemes with foreign expressions
-rmpn	ignore lexemes with proper names
-addfl	add filler letters
-n	iterations for the depth of tree for compounds and derivations
-zn	iterations for the depth of conversions in CELEX
-levperc	Levenshtein based threshold, range 0:1
-celex	use CELEX compounds and derivations
-zcelex	use CELEX conversions
-ctags	map GermaNet tags to CELEX tags
-pos	provide parts of speech
-par	choose parenthesis style for the output

Table 1: Options for Linking the Databases

components but excluding all lexemes with affixoids or fossilized morphemes. The number of deep-level analyses amounts to 119,476.

As examples, the complete analyses of our examples are presented in 7 and 8. Table 3 shows the number of entries for the merged databases, some of them are alternatives for ambiguous parts.

(7)
```
Landesentwicklungsgesellschaft
(Land_N)
(es_x)
(*Entwicklungsgesellschaft_N*
(*Entwicklung_N*
(*entwickeln_V*
(ent_x)
(*wickeln_V*
(Wickel_N)(n_x)))
(ung_x))
(s_x)
(*Gesellschaft_N*
(gesellen_V)
(schaft_x)))
```

(8)
```
Stadtentwicklungsgesellschaft
(*Stadtentwicklung_N*
(Stadt_N)
(*Entwicklung_N*
(*entwickeln_V*
(ent_x)
(*wickeln_V*
(Wickel_N)
(n_x)))
(ung_x)))
(s_x)
(*Gesellschaft_N*
(gesellen_V)
(schaft_x))
```

Part of Speech/morph type	GN	CELEX	Linked Database
noun	nomen, Nomen	N	N
adjective	Adjektiv	A	A
adverb	Adverb	B	B
preposition	Präposition	P	P
verb	Verb, verben	V	V
article	Artikel	D	D
interjection	Interjektion	I	I
pronoun	Pronomen	O	O
abbreviation	Abkürzung	X	X
word group	Wortgruppe	n	n
root/confix	Konfix	R	R
filler letters, affixes	-	x	x

Table 2: Mapping of two morphological tagsets

Structures	GN entries	CELEX entries	Union
flat	97,362	40,097	135,533
GN deep-level merged with CELEX	119,476	40,097	153,992

Table 3: Number of entries for the merged databases

5. Linkages

5.1. Linking Morphological Data to Ontolex-Lemon

Ontolex-Lemon (McCrae et al., 2017) can be considered as the main standard for lexical data on the web. Its core component was tailored for linking ontologies with resources of lexical entries[3], consisting of information of sense and form. Declerck and Racioppa (2019) and Racioppa and Declerck (2019) provide information concerning inflection of word forms. However, standards for the description of (complex) morphological analyses are still under development (Klimek et al., 2019). Morph classes such as *affix* or *prefix* are insufficient for describing structures which are not just defined by hierarchy but also by sequence. Therefore, representing constituency by decomp:Component and decomp:Constituent (Klimek et al., 2019, 585ff.) resources could be accompanied by next markers for making the level and the position of the relation transparent. A next element is easily definable by rdf:first and rdf:rest (the next element is the first element of the rest)[4]. Another option is using expressions of one-level sets with fixed sequence. rdf:seq (`https://www.w3.org/TR/rdf-schema/#ch_seq`) provides this feature, as it is an ordered container. Listing 9 displays the lemma *Landesentwicklungsgesellschaft* with such an analysis.

(9)

```
lexinfo:orderedAnalysis a rdf:seq;
rdfs:comment "A list of ordered
components as defined by decomp:Component";
rdfs:range :decomp:Component;
rdfs:subPropertyOf
lexinfo:morphosyntacticProperty.

:lex_Landesentwicklungsgesellschaft
  a ontolex:LexicalEntry;
lexinfo:partOfSpeech lexinfo:noun;
lexinfo:orderedAnalysis
  [rdf:li lex_Land_N;
   rdf:li interfix_es;
   rdf:li lex_Entwicklungsgesellschaft_N].
```

5.2. Linking Morphological Data to CIDOC

The derived morphological information is intended to be used to link information of cultural heritage. Therefore, it can aligned to the CIDOC Conceptual Reference Model (CIDOC-CRM)[5]. Mambrini and Passarotti (2020) establish the linkage to CIDOC-CRM via the propositional status of etymological assumptions. In case of morphological analyses, the class *E33 Linguistic_Object*[6] is more suitable in analogy to Wettlaufer et al. (2015, 191f.).

[3]The specification can be consulted here: `https://www.w3.org/2019/09/lexicog/`

[4]In LISP notation, this corresponds to the cadr function.

[5]`https://cidoc-crm.org/Version/version-7.2.1`

[6]For the definition, consult `https://cidoc-crm.org/Entity/e33-linguistic-object/version-6.0`.

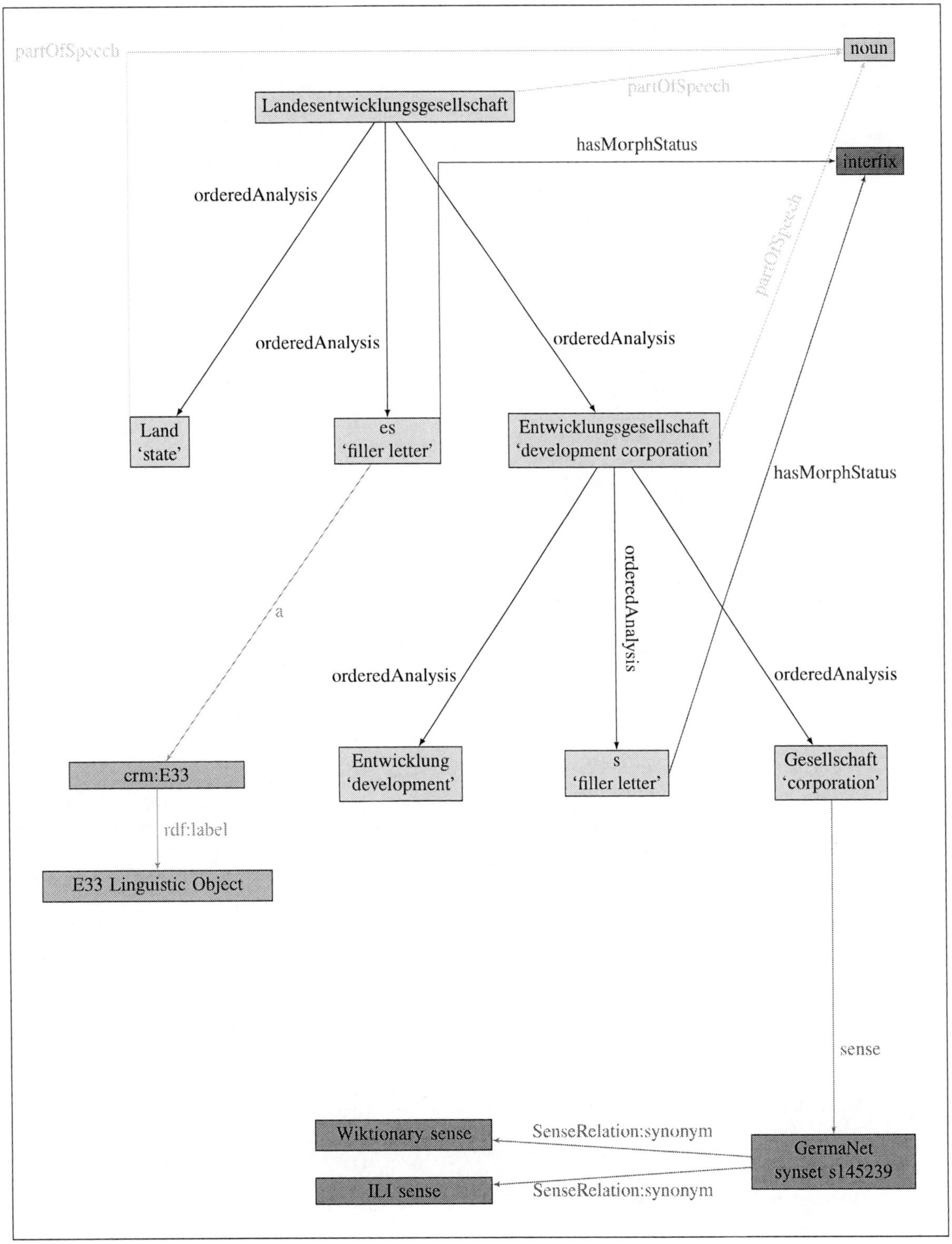

Figure 3: An model for the reprentation of morphological and semantic information of *Landesentwicklungsgesellschaft* 'state development corporation'

5.3. Senses and Synopsis

As minimal linguistic signs, morphemes have meanings and/or functions. As GermaNet provides the synsets for the components of the morphological analyses, the connection to their content side is straightforward. The inventories of the Interlingual Index to EuroWordNet and of the aligned Wiktionary resources open the way to Linked Open Data (Chiarcos et al., 2020).
Figure 3 illustrates a synopsis of these connections. For the sake of clarity, some relations were omitted.

6. Conclusions and Future Work

This paper links the most recent version of GermaNet with the established resource of CELEX-German by recursively connecting their compositions, conversions and derivations, and mapping the annotation sets. Furthermore, it takes a step towards the representation of sequential and hierarchical morphological information for Ontolex-Lemon and similar models by using the `rdfs:Container` class Seq which is defined as an ordered list.
Finally, a transparent connection to CIDOC-CRM is provided to make this linguistic data findable, accessible, interoperable, and reusable for other applications, in the sense of the FAIR data principles (Wilkinson et al., 2016).
The information of the linguistic databases can be considered as on a high-quality level. However, as the inventories of both lexical resources are restricted, hybrid approaches with (more time-consuming) morphological parses and enrichments of the knowledge base are one of the next choice (Steiner, 2019a) for the linguistic work. This would also help to find candidates within the database which could get a more fine-grained analysis. Especially, for new entries whose components are not yet parts of the data, this can be useful. Another very important step will connect the morphological analyses to ontological knowledge via the WordNet synsets by direct mappings of the interlingual index and Wiktionary entries.
The scripts for the data generation are publicly available on `https://github.com/petrasteiner/morphology`.

7. Acknowledgements

Work for this paper was partially supported within the Africa Multiple Cluster of Excellence at the University of Bayreuth, funded by the Deutsche Forschungsgemeinschaft (DFG, German Research Foundation) under Germany's Excellence Strategy – EXC2052/1 – 390713894.

8. Bibliographical References

Baayen, Harald and Piepenbrock, Richard and Gulikers, Léon. (1995). *The CELEX lexical database (CD-ROM)*. Linguistic Data Consortium, University of Pennsylvania, 1.0, ISLRN 204-698-863-053-1.

Burnage, G. (1995). CELEX: A Guide for Users. In Harald Baayen, et al., editors, *The CELEX Lexical Database (CD-ROM)*. Linguistic Data Consortium, Philadelphia, PA.

Cap, F. (2014). *Morphological processing of compounds for statistical machine translation*. Ph.D. thesis, Universität Stuttgart.

Chiarcos, C., Klimek, B., Fäth, C., Declerck, T., and McCrae, J. P. (2020). On the linguistic linked open data infrastructure. In *Proceedings of the 1st International Workshop on Language Technology Platforms*, pages 8–15, Marseille, France. European Language Resources Association.

Declerck, T. and Racioppa, S. (2019). Porting multilingual morphological resources to ontolex-lemon. In *Proceedings of the International Conference on Recent Advances in Natural Language Processing (RANLP 2019)*, pages 233–238, Varna, Bulgaria. INCOMA Ltd.

Geyken, A. and Hanneforth, T. (2006). TAGH: A Complete Morphology for German based on Weighted Finite State Automata. In *Finite State Methods and Natural Language Processing. 5th International Workshop, FSMNLP 2005, Helsinki, Finland, September 1-2, 2005. Revised Papers*, volume 4002, pages 55–66. Springer.

Haapalainen, M. and Majorin, A. (1995). GERTWOL und morphologische Disambiguierung für das Deutsche. In *Proceedings of the 10th Nordic Conference on Computational Linguistics, Helsinki, Finland*.

Hamp, B. and Feldweg, H. (1997). GermaNet - a Lexical-Semantic Net for German. In *In Proceedings of ACL workshop Automatic Information Extraction and Building of Lexical Semantic Resources for NLP Applications*, pages 9–15.

Hanrieder, G. (1996). MORPH - Ein modulares und robustes Morphologieprogramm für das Deutsche in Common Lisp. In Roland Hauser, editor, *Linguistische Verifikation Dokumentation zur Ersten Morpholymics 1994*, pages 53–66. Niemeyer, Tübingen.

Henrich, V. and Hinrichs, E. (2011). Determining Immediate Constituents of Compounds in GermaNet. In *Proceedings of the International Conference Recent Advances in Natural Language Processing 2011*, pages 420–426. Association for Computational Linguistics.

Henrich, V., Hinrichs, E. W., and Vodolazova, T. (2011). Aligning GermaNet senses with Wiktionary sense definitions. In Zygmunt Vetulani et al., editors, *Human Language Technology Challenges for Computer Science and Linguistics - 5th Language and Technology Conference, LTC 2011, Poznań, Poland, November 25-27, 2011, Revised Selected Papers*, volume 8387 of *Lecture Notes in Computer Science*, pages 329–342. Springer.

Klimek, B., McCrae, J. P., Bosque-Gil, J., Ionov, M., Tauber, J. K., and Chiarcos, C. (2019). Challenges for the representation of morphology in ontology lexicons. *Proceedings of eLex*, pages 570–591.

Mambrini, F. and Passarotti, M. (2020). Representing etymology in the LiLa knowledge base of linguistic resources for latin. In Ilan Kernerman, et al., editors, *Proceedings of the 2020 Globalex Workshop on Linked Lexicography*, pages 20–28, Marseille, France. European Language Resources Association.

McCrae, J. P., Bosque-Gil, J., Gracia, J., Buitelaar, P., and Cimiano, P. (2017). The OntoLex-Lemon model: Development and applications. In *Electronic lexicography in the 21st century. Proceedings of eLex 2017 conference.Leiden, the Netherlands, 19–21 September 2017*, pages 587–597.

Racioppa, S. and Declerck, T. (2019). Porting the latin wordnet onto ontolex-lemon. In *Electronic lexicography in the 21st century (eLex 2021) Post-editing lexicography*, pages 429–439.

Schmid, H., Fitschen, A., and Heid, U. (2004). SMOR: A German computational morphology covering derivation, composition and inflection. In *Proceedings of the International Conference on Language Resources and Evaluation (LREC)*.

Shafaei, E., Frassinelli, D., Lapesa, G., and Padó, S. (2017). DErivCELEX: Development and evaluation of a German derivational morphology lexicon based on CELEX. In *Proceedings of the DeriMo workshop*, Milan, Italy.

Steiner, P. and Ruppenhofer, J. (2018). Building a morphological treebank for German from a linguistic database. In *Proceedings of the Eleventh International Conference on Language Resources and Evaluation (LREC 2018)*, Miyazaki, Japan, May. European Language Resources Association (ELRA).

Steiner, P. (2016). Refurbishing a morphological database for German. In *Proceedings of the Tenth International Conference on Language Resources and Evaluation (LREC'16)*, pages 1103–1108, Portorož, Slovenia, May. European Language Resources Association (ELRA).

Steiner, P. (2017). Merging the trees - building a morphological treebank for German from two resources. In *Proceedings of the 16th International Workshop on Treebanks and Linguistic Theories*, pages 146–160, Prague, Czech Republic.

Steiner, P. (2019a). Augmenting a German morphological database by data-intense methods. In *Proceedings of the 16th Workshop on Computational Research in Phonetics, Phonology, and Morphology*, pages 178–188, Florence, Italy, August. Association for Computational Linguistics.

Steiner, P. (2019b). Combining data-intense and compute-intense methods for fine-grained morphological analyses. In *Proceedings of the Second International Workshop on Resources and Tools for Derivational Morphology*, pages 45–54, Prague, Czechia, 19–20 September. Charles University, Faculty of Mathematics and Physics, Institute of Formal and Applied Linguistics.

Wahrig-Burfeind, R. and Bertelsmann, G. L. (2007). *Der kleine Wahrig: Wörterbuch der deutschen Sprache ; [der deutsche Grundwortschatz in mehr als 25000 Stichwörtern und 120000 Anwendungsbeispielen ; mit umfassenden Informationen zur Wortbedeutung und detaillierten Angaben zu grammatischen und orthografischen Aspekten der deutschen Gegenwartssprache]*. Wissen Media Verlag.

Wettlaufer, J., Johnson, C., Scholz, M., Fichtner, M., and Thotempudi, S. G. (2015). Semantic Blumenbach: Exploration of text–object relationships with semantic web technology in the history of science. *Digital Scholarship in the Humanities*, 30(Supplement 1):fqv047.

Wilkinson, M. D., Dumontier, M., Aalbersberg, I. J. J., and Appleton, G. (2016). The FAIR guiding principles for scientific data management and stewardship. *Scientific data*, 3:160018.

Würzner, K. and Hanneforth, T. (2013). Parsing morphologically complex words. In Mark-Jan Nederhof, editor, *Proceedings of the 11th International Conference on Finite State Methods and Natural Language Processing, FSMNLP 2013, St. Andrews, Scotland, UK, July 15-17, 2013*, pages 39–43. The Association for Computer Linguistics.

Zeller, B., Šnajder, J., and Padó, S. (2013). DErivBase: Inducing and evaluating a derivational morphology resource for German. In *Proceedings of the 51st Annual Meeting of the Association for Computational Linguistics (Volume 1: Long Papers)*, volume 1, pages 1201–1211. Association for Computational Linguistics.

Proceedings of the Globalex Workshop on Linked Lexicography @LREC2022, pages 60–67
Marseille, 20 June 2022

Resolving Inflectional Ambiguity of Macedonian Adjectives

Katerina Zdravkova
University Ss, Cyril and Methodius, Faculty of Computer Science and Engineering
Rudjer Boshkovikj, 16, 1000 Skopje, N. Macedonia
katerina,zdravkova@finki.ukim.mk

Abstract

Macedonian adjectives are inflected for gender, number, definiteness and degree, with in average 47.98 inflections per headword. The inflection paradigm of qualificative adjectives is even richer, embracing 56.27 morphophonemic alterations. Depending on the word they were derived from, more than 600 Macedonian adjectives have an identical headword and two different word forms for each grammatical category. While non-verbal adjectives alter the root before adding the inflectional suffixes, suffixes of verbal adjectives are added directly to the root. In parallel with the morphological differences, both types of adjectives have a different translation, depending on the category of the words they have been derived from. Nouns that collocate with these adjectives are mutually disjunctive, enabling the resolution of inflectional ambiguity. They are organised as a lexical taxonomy, created using hierarchical divisive clustering. If embedded in the future spell-checking applications, this taxonomy will significantly reduce the risk of forming incorrect inflections, which frequently occur in the daily news and more often in the advertisements and social media.

Keywords: inflectional ambiguity, lexical taxonomy, linguistic linked open data (LLOD), non-verbal and verbal adjectives

1. Introduction

Macedonian language as a South Slavic language is highly inflective (Bonchanoski and Zdravkova, 2018). Verbs have the richest inflectional paradigm that embraces seven tenses: present, past or aorist (depending on the verb aspect), past undetermined, pluperfect, future, past future, and future told); a conditional form; positive and negative imperative; and a construction with the particle neka (Cyrillic: нека / English: let it), each producing different forms for the three persons and the two numbers (http://vigna.mk/). Verbs have three aspects: progressive, perfective and bi-aspectual (Ljubešić et al, 2021a).

Verbal adjectives can be derived from all the verbs, independently of their aspect (Zdravkova and Petrovski, 2007). Whenever their root is identical with the root of a non-verbal adjective, they trigger the inflectional ambiguity, which is the main subject of this paper.

Inflectional paradigm of Macedonian adjectives is also rich, although unlike most Slavic languages, it does not use cases. Their function in the sentence is determined by the prepositions (Körtvélyessy, 2016). Adjectives are inflected for gender, number, definiteness and degree. In the lexicon MKLex that was annotated according to MULTEXT-East version 4 (Erjavec, 2017), Macedonian adjectives have in average 47.98 inflections per adjectival stem (Table 1.). The lexicon is available from CLASSLA CLARIN knowledge centre for South Slavic languages (https://www.clarin.si/info/k-centre/faq4macedonian/).

The inflection paradigm of qualificative adjectives is even richer, with 56.27 morphophonemic alterations. MKLex is not extended with the verbal adjectives, which introduce more than 30000 headwords (Zdravkova and Petrovski, 2007). Although frequently used, these adjectives are not entered in the official Macedonian dictionaries, which are the core sources of the Digital dictionary of Macedonian language (throughout the paper: DRMJ, http://drmj.eu).

MULTEXT-East version 6 introduced two categories: verbal adjectives, which are participles; and the category general that unites the adjectives such as: takov (таков / such), and gotov (готов / ready), which cannot be classified into any of the previously four mentioned groups. In the project described in this paper, all the adjectives are divided into two threads: verbal, i.e., participle adjectives and non-verbal, i.e., the adjectives belonging to remaining types.

Type	Headwords	All infections
Qualificative	7048	396591
Possessive	2172	65953
Ordinal	307	5200
Total	9749	467744

Table 1: Macedonian adjectives in MKLex

The inflectional base (Laudanna et al., 1992) of non-verbal adjectives is created by dropping the most right vowel before it gains the inflection suffixes (Table 2). When the headword ends with the consonant ~n (~н), which is preceded by two vowels, they are altered to ~jn (~јн). Dropping of the rightmost vowel of the adjectives ending with: ~dok (~док), ~zok (~зок) and ~zhok (~жок) causes morphonemic alterations: ~tk (~тк), ~sk (~ск) and shk (~шк). Exclusion are the endings: ~sten (~стен), which are transformed into ~sn (~сн), and ~on (~он), while the suffix remains unchanged, equally to all verbal adjectives.

Headword endings	Base endings	Headwords - base
~aen	~jn	traen – trajn
~ar	~r	dobar – dobr
~dok	~tk	redok – retk
~een	~jn	ideen - idejn
~ien	~jn	stihien – stihijn
~en	~n	temen - temn
~oen	~jn	bezboen - bezbojn
~ol	~l	topol – topl
~on	~on	avtohton - avtonton
~ov	~v	ednakov - ednakv
~uen	~jn	buen - bujn
~sten	~sn	mesten – mesn
~zhok	~shk	zhezhok – zheshk
~zok	~sk	blizok – blisk

Table 2: Alterations of non-verbal adjectives

	Masculine	Feminine	Neuter	Plural
No	/	~a	~o	~i
Yes	~iot	~ata	~oto	~ite
Distal	~iov	~ava	~ovo	~ive
Proximal	~ion	~ana	~ono	~ine

Table 3: Inflectional suffixes of Macedonian adjectives

The inflections are formed by adding the suffixes to the inflectional base (Table 3). The columns present the suffixes for the three genders in singular and the plural, which are identical for all genders. Rows correspond to definiteness. Similarly to nouns and pronouns, definiteness is expressed by the three suffixed articles: undetermined (yes), distal, and proximal. Distal and proximal definiteness are language specific and they do not exist in other Slavic languages (Stojanovska, 2019).
Many non-verbal adjectives are derived from nouns, such as: boen (боен), which is derived from the noun boj (бој / battle) and the verb boi (бои / to colour); vozen (возен), derived from the noun voz (воз / train) and the verb vozi (вози / to drive); soboren (соборен), derived from the noun sobor (собор / gathering, feast), and the verb sobori (собори / to knock down, shoot down, demolish). Their stems are identical: boen (боен), vozen (возен), soboren (соборен), but the inflections for the same morpho-syntactic description and the translations are different.
In the daily news and yet more often in the advertisements, the inflections of non-verbal and verbal adjectives are usually mixed. Of these two options, the former occurs because the spell-checking applications do not recognise them as incorrect, while the latter is usually due to illiteracy of people. For example, masculine, singular, definite and positive form of the adjective boen (боен) is either bojniot (бојниот / military, battle) or boeniot (боениот / painted, coloured, stained, dyed), which, if wrongly used, produce the collocations: bojniot dzid (бојниот ѕид / the military wall), instead of boeniot dzid (боениот ѕид / the painted wall), and boeniot otrov (боениот отров / the dyed poison), instead of bojniot otrov (бојниот отров / the military poison). The phrase boeniot otrov (боениот отров / the dyed poison) exists 6 times on the Web, compared to 282 correct collocations. Even more frequent is the collocation soboreniot hram (соборениот храм / the overthrown temple), that apears 125 times instead of the correct soborniot hram (соборниот храм / the cathedral temple), which occurs more than 100000 times. Google Translate translates both: the incorrect soborniot avion (соборниот авион) and the correct soboreniot avion (соборениот авион) as the downed plane. The translations for soboreniot hram and soborniot hram are: the overthrown temple and the cathedral, confirming that Google Translate recognises both forms of the adjective soboren (соборен).
Depending on the word they were derived from, more than 600 adjectives have an identical stem and two word forms for each grammatical category. In parallel with the morphological differences, both types of adjectives have different translations, depending on the category of the word they have been derived from. They are the subject matter of the research presented in this paper.
The paper proposes a solution intended to resolve inflectional ambiguity of non-verbal and verbal adjectives with the same headword and different meanings. Section 2 presents several examples of inflectional ambiguities and the proposed solutions for their disambiguation. Particular attention is paid to lexical taxonomies, which are the proposed approach for the resolution of inflectional ambiguity. Section 3 introduces the process of extracting the adjectives with inflectional ambiguity, as well as the hierarchical classifiers that enable the disambiguation. Section 4 is dedicated to created taxonomy. Section 5 summarises the introduced approach and announces further extensions and practical use of the project.

2. Inflectional ambiguity and lexical taxonomies

Inflectional ambiguity is not uniquely defined. Branco and Nunes (2012) introduce it at two independent layers, according to different substrings that qualify a given word form, as well as according to admissible affixes, the latter conveying more than one admissible value. The main goal of their project was disambiguation of Portuguese verbs, which can have identical third person with the infinitive verb form; identical forms for first and third person; as well as inconsistency between the inflected infinitive and the subjunctive future. All the three experiments implemented the machine learning based MFF algorithm supported by a verbal lemmatization tool (Branco and Nunes, 2012).
The inflection ambiguity of the Finish language encompasses two aspects: ambiguity of words with two decomposable readings and ambiguity due to homographic stem allomorphs (Järvikivi et al., 2009). The disambiguation is based on early segmentation of inflected words. Both aspects achieved similar results for unambiguous, partly or completely ambiguous inflected forms (Järvikivi et al., 2009).
Third explanation of inflectional ambiguity relates to the possibility of implementing several conjugation rules for the verbs in Arabic (Ismail et al, 2017). More detailed explanation and the disambiguation process are not presented in the paper.
The first two examples of inflectional ambiguity are not similar to ambiguity of Macedonian adjectives. They include lemmatisation (removing inflectional endings to return the lemma (Schütze, 2008)), or word recognition (selection of the correct lexical representation from a set of candidates (Segui and Grainger, 1990)). Our approach is related to morphological synthesis, i.e. determination of inflected word forms (Bickel and Nichols, 2005).
No matter the target result: headword or word form, the disambiguation is heavily dependent on the available contextual information. For the resolution of inflection ambiguity of Macedonian adjectives, such contextual information can be extracted from the adjective-noun collocations. The nouns collocating with the non-verbal and verbal adjectives are mutually disjunctive, defining the two branches of the hierarchical taxonomy that entirely resolve the ambiguity.
The first association of successful lexical taxonomies is WordNet (Miller, 1998). Nouns within WordNet are hierarchically organised by connecting the hyponyms are hypernyms via is-a relationship. Knowledge structure is convenient for resolving the inflectional ambiguity. Although ambitiously announced (Saveski and Trajkovski. 2010), the Macedonian language is still not included in WordNet, and even if it was, this semantically organised lexical database is far too massive for the problem. Nevertheless, it remains the greatest inspiration for the creation of our hierarchical taxonomy.
Another valuable lexical taxonomy was proposed by Burtăverde and De Raad (2019). This hierarchical structure was obtained by splitting the personality-descriptive Romanian adjectives using different levels of abstraction.
Taxonomy enrichment of Russian language has recently been efficiently done (Nikishina et al, 2020). Based on the defined set of potential hypernyms, this project had an intention to correctly classify new words that do not have any definition.

The capacity to efficiently cluster the words of the above mentioned projects was the major inspiration for the disambiguation of Macedonian adjectives. It was broken down into seven phases:

- Extraction of candidate non-verbal and verbal adjectives with different inflections
- Elimination of all the candidate adjectives that are not frequently used
- Elimination of the candidate adjectives that do not have full collocations for both types
- Determination of all the nouns belonging to mutually disjunctive sets of collocations
- Hierarchical classification of the extracted nouns
- Creation of the lexical taxonomy
- Labelling of the adjectives

They will be explained in more detail in the next section.

3. Disambiguation process

Candidate adjectives were extracted from non-commercial version of Macedonian lexicon MKLex, which can be downloaded from the CLASSLA CLARIN.SI repository (http://www.clarin.si/info/k-centre/). It consists of roughly 76000 headwords and more than 1300000 word forms presented as tab-separated triples: word form, headword, and annotation according to MULTEXT-East version 4. Since the development of MKLex, MSDs were upgraded and new dictionaries were published, unfortunately, none is available in a machine readable form. Therefore, the extraction was done by following these steps:

- Extraction of the pairs with two forms for definite masculine singular (358 pairs or 179 headwords);
- Extraction of the adjectives that have an identical or a similar root with the verbs from the lexicon (182 headwords);
- Extraction of the adjectives that have an identical or a similar root with the nouns from the lexicon (6 headwords);
- Extraction of nouns and verbs with an identical or similar root (420 headwords);
- Addition of the eligible adjectives that do not exist in the lexicon (17 headwords)
- Union of the five sets: in total, 634 headwords.

The most valuable resource for the next two steps was the digital dictionary DRMJ (http://drmj.edu). It presents all the words existing in the printed dictionaries, including many new words that were found in the dictionary embedded corpus of Macedonian literature. Each headword is accompanied with a ranking. The higher the value of the rank is, the lower is the frequency of word's occurrence in the embedded corpus. The most important feature of the digital dictionary is its linked structure. Namely, each headword is connected with a list of sentences from the corpus where it occurs in all the feasible word forms.

The creation of lexical taxonomy started with the pre-processing of candidate adjectives. It included two eliminations, followed by the creation of the taxonomy skeleton. The procedure included the following steps:

- Exclusion of the least frequent adjectives
- Exclusion of the adjectives without adjective–noun collocations for both threads
- Extraction of the adjective-noun collocations from DRMJ embedded corpus
- Creation of mini taxonomies for each adjective
- Joining mini taxonomies into a final taxonomy

First elimination was done by examining the ranking of the candidates. The adjectives with a rank above 35000 were removed. For the adjectives that were not found in DRMJ, the ranking of the noun or the verb they are derived from was also checked. High rankings did not necessarily mean that the adjective would not be included in the taxonomy. For example, the adjective broen (броен / non-verbal: number, numerical, numerous; verbal: counted, numbered) has a rank 1781 and almost no collocations for the verbal adjective: broeniot denar (броениот денар / counted pennies), broeno kolichestvo (броено количество / counted quantity), broeni denovi (броени денови / numbered days, and broeni pari (броени пари / counted money). Conversely, the adjective vklopen (вклопен / non-verbal: timed, time switch; verbal: blended, embedded, assembled) with a rank 32007 is completely populated for both threads.

For each of the remaining adjectives, DRMJ embedded corpus was manually checked to extract the adjective-noun collocations for each gender and number. The adjectives without at least three out of the four possible combinations (masculine, feminine, neuter, plural) for both threads were excluded. The absence of corresponding collocations does not necessarily mean that they do not exist. Missing examples of common adjectives were searched on the Web. For example, the adjective loven (ловен / non-verbal: hunting; verbal: hunted) has only two non-verbal collocations in DRMJ corpus: lovniot trofej (ловниот трофеј / the hunting trophy) and lovna oprema (ловна опрема / hunting equipment), and no collocations for the verbal adjective. On the other hand, they are very frequent on the Web: lovno drushtvo (ловно друштво / hunting union), loveniot zajak (ловениот зајак / the hunted rabbit), lovena mechka (ловена мечка / hunted bear), lovenoto zhivotno (ловеното животно / the hunted animals), and loveni srni (ловени срни / hunted dears).

Since DRMJ is not available for crawling, interlinking of the adjectives and the corpus was manually done for each of the 634 candidate adjectives. They were stored in a large spreadsheet consisting of five columns. First column presents the headword of the adjective, the second and third correspond to all possible occurrences of nominal and verbal adjectives respectively, whereas the fourth column presents the headword of verbal adjective derived from the perfective pair of the headword with the same meaning, and the last column presents its occurrence. All the values were extracted from DRMJ. Although these five nominal adjectives are not frequent, they were kept for further processing, because the nouns in adjective-noun collocations of both verbal adjectives are identical. After these two stages, 96 headwords remained in the corpus (Table 4). Most of them are simultaneously nominal and verbal, and make their inflections implementing the rules presented in the Tables 2 and 3.

Derived from	Nouns and verbs	Verbs	Nouns
In total	60	34	2

Table 4: Distribution of ambiguous adjectives

Several ambiguous verbal adjectives are derived from a negated verb, which is formed by adding the particle ne (не / not) to the main verb. In the verbal adjectives, this particle becomes is transformed into a prefix: nezasiten (не засити → незаситен / greedy); and neodgovoren (не одговори → неодговорен / irresponsible).

The extraction process was done in parallel with the second elimination. All the possible adjective-noun collocations existing on the interpretation part of DRMJ and the existing collocations from the embedded corpus were stored in a spreadsheet together with their English translations and the superordinate and subordinate categories the corresponding nouns belong to. These categories are a combination of suggested categories within DRMJ, WordNet Domains Hierarchy suggested by Bentivogli et al. (2004) and English WordNet (Fellbaum, 2005), which is accessible from http://wordnetweb.princeton.edu/perl/webwn.

After the extraction, only 96 eligible adjectives remained in the corpus (see Appendix 1). They are presented with Macedonian Cyrillic script, their Latin transliteration, the ranking according to DRMJ, and the corresponding English translations of nonverbal and verbal adjective.

4. Creation of lexical taxonomy

The creation of mini taxonomies for each adjective is divisive (or top-down), starting from the root node toward the leaf nodes (Roux, 2018). The organisation of noun categories is hierarchical, with a root node divided into superordinate nodes, each a parent of at least one node at subordinate layer. Subordinate categories become superordinates if they can further be divided into subtler categories. Initially, the idea was to create the lexical taxonomy by combining the extracted clusters, but the creation of mini taxonomies and their merging was more convenient. It started with the adjective vlezen (влезен / non-verbal: entry, input; verbal: entered), which is alphabetically the first adjective that determines at least 10 distinct categories. It is the seed lexical taxonomy. Collocation nouns of verbal adjective vlezen (влезен / entered), in which the inflectional base is identical with the headword are Living beings, which are direct descendants of the root, so they belong to layer B (Figure 1).

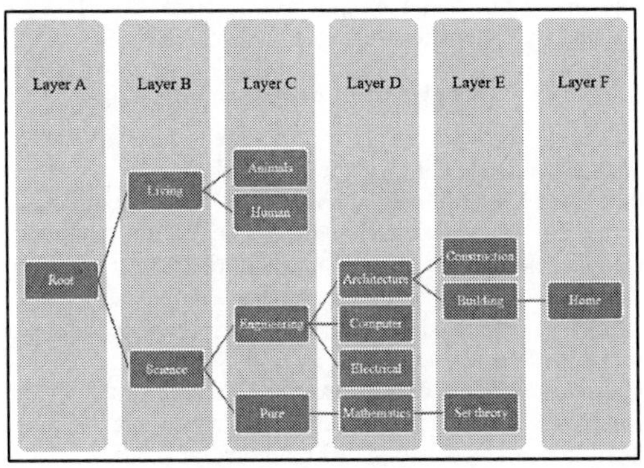

Figure 1: Seed lexical tree

Each layer is marked with a letter, staring with the root node. The nodes within one layer are marked with integers, starting from the topmost node, which is 1. Each noun belonging to one cluster is labelled with the pair: letter of the layer, and number of the node within the layer. Living beings are divided into two clusters: Animal, which unites animal species (cats, dogs, horses, etc.) and Human (boys, girls, men, women, etc.). These clusters are terminal, so they are nodes belonging to leaf categories: C1 for animals, C2 for human. If some adjectives collocate with a specific part of the terminal cluster, it can further be divided.

The nouns collocating with the nominal adjective vlezen (влезен / entry, input), in which the inflectional base is formed by dropping the rightmost vowel are disjunctive with the clusters Animal and Human. They are part of the superordinate category Science. Science is divided into two subordinate layers: Engineering and Pure science. Engineering is a superordinate category for Architecture, Computer and Electrical Engineering. Architecture is further divided into Constructions, where the nouns from the first collocation of vlezna porta (влезна порта / entry gate) belong. The second embraces the nouns related to Home, where vlezna porta (влезна порта / entry doorway) belongs. Collocations: vlezna porta (влезна порта / input port) and vlezni uredi (влезни уреди / input devices) are terms belonging to Computer engineering, while vlezniot prikluchok (влезниот приклучок / the input switch) is related to Electrical engineering. Pure sciences have one subordinate category: Mathematics, where the nouns such as vlezno mnozhestvo (влезно множество / input set) belong. To distinguish Set theory from other mathematical branches, Mathematics can further be extended.

In the lexical tree of adjective vlezen, all the labels belong to the leaf nodes. The leaves from the layer C (C1 for animals, C2 for human) collocate with the verbal adjective. The nouns of the leaves from layer D: D2 for Computer engineering, D3 for Electrical engineering and D4 for Mathematics collocate with the nominal adjective, together with the nouns from layer E: E1 for Constructions and E2 for Home. This is the initial stage of the lexical taxonomy. The same strategy was implemented for all the adjectives in the corpus. The taxonomy creation continues according to the algorithm presented on Figure 2.

```
Lexical taxonomy creation:
While list of adjectives is not empty
    Get the lexical taxonomy of the new adjective
    Merge the taxonomy of new adjective with the existing
    Remove the adjective from the list
endwhile

Merge:
If superordinate category exists
    While list of subordinates is not empty
        Get the name of the top subordinate category
        If new name is alphabetically prior to existing one
            While list of subordinates is not empty
                Increment the numerical value of the labels
                Go to next layer
            endwhile
            Go to next subordinate
        endif
        Go to next subordinate
    endwhile
endif
```

Figure 2. Pseudocode of taxonomy creation

Merging of the seed lexical taxonomy with the mini taxonomy of the adjective boen (боен / non-verbal: military; verbal: coloured, dyed, painted, stained) starts with the nodes from layer B. The new superordinate category Objects, which is a parent of Physical objects is alphabetically between Living organisms (node B1), and Sciences (before the addition, node B2). After adding the superordinate category Objects, the numerical value of the label for Science is incremented: Science (node B3).

The new category B2 has its own children node in the layer C: Physical objects. This node becomes the new C3 node. This addition causes an increase of the numerical values of all the nodes after the first child of the former category B2: Engineering (node C4) and Pure (node C5). Since the node C3 (Physical objects) has no children, the procedure continues with the new Science, which is a node at layer C.

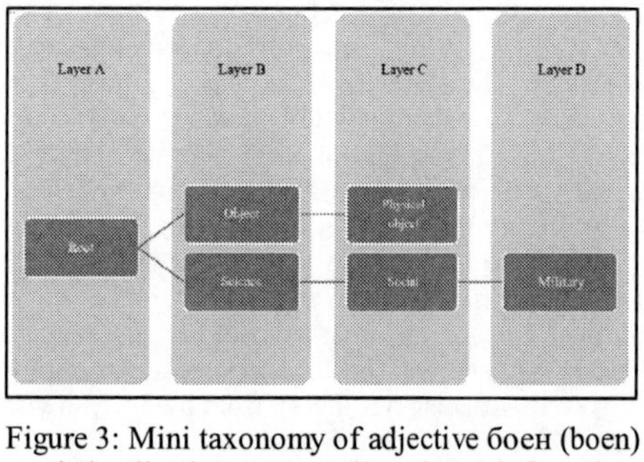

Figure 3: Mini taxonomy of adjective боен (boen)

Non-verbal adjective-noun collocations define the new scientific subordinate category Social as a child category of Science (Bentivogli et al., 2004). Its subordinate category is Military (Figure 4.). Both new nodes do not affect the previous alphabetic ordering of sciences, thus the node will be labelled as C6: Social and its subordinate nodes continue the previous numbering at all the descendant layers, in this case only the new subordinate at layer D, which becomes D5: Military.

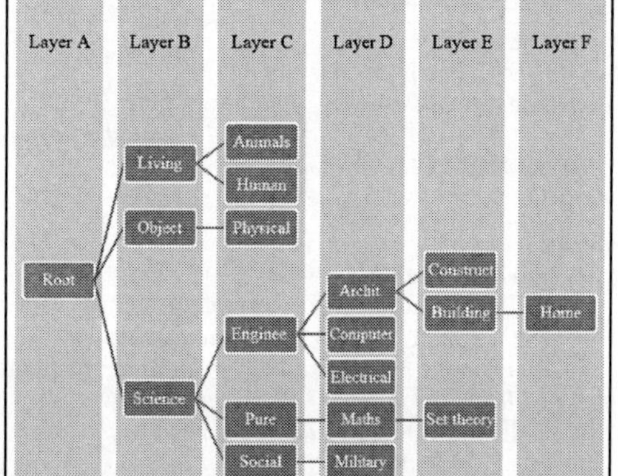

Figure 4: Lexical taxonomy after adding the first adjective

By continuing the procedure, the final lexical taxonomy was created. It embraces 138 meanings (and consequently, English translations) of the adjectives belonging to non-verbal thread, and 118 meanings from verbal thread. All the meanings from both threads are mutually disjunctive, proving that the division was worthwhile.

4.1 Nouns that collocate with non-verbal adjectives

Non-verbal thread introduced these 105 clusters: abstract, actions, activity, administration, analysis, anatomy, animal, approach, architecture, authorization, beauty, birds, body, bomb, character, chemistry, church, civil engineering, computing, consequences, construction, data, dermatology, disease, document, documentation, economy, effort, electrical engineering, emotion, emotion, event, exam, examples, finance, finance, food, furniture, gastronomy, genetics, geometry, goods, grammar, house, human, image, institution, instrument, justice, law, letter, line, material, mathematics, measures, medicine, military, music, nature, paper made, part, path, payment, person, pet, philosophy, physical object, place, plan, post, price, profession, religion, reply, results, river, road, scene, science, season, senses, sentence, signs, smooth material, soil, solution, speech, states, technology, temperature, text, theory, thing, time, topology, traffic, transport, transport means, travel, view, water, weapon, weather, words, and work.

4.2 Nouns that collocate with verbal adjectives

The verbal thread that unites participle adjectives introduce 58 clusters, almost half of clusters for the non-verbal thread, mainly because the agents are either human beings or animals. They are: abstract, animal, article, chemistry, clothes, company, construction, drink, duty, economy, effort, facts, finance, flammable, food, garden, gastronomy, goods, group of people, human, image, industry, inflammable, inheritance, justice, law, life, living organism, lock, medicine, money, movement, object, obligation, part of animal, part of body, people, philosophy, physical object, price, profession, property, quantity, question, religion, senses, shoes, sound, space, task, technology, territory, thing, vegetables, vehicle, wire, words, and yarn.

While the adjectives belonging to both threads are disjunctive, the clusters of nouns they collocate with them intersect. In total, both threads define 137 clusters, 27 belonging to both: abstract, animal, chemistry, construction, economy, effort, emotion, finance, finance, food, gastronomy, goods, human, image, justice, law, medicine, part of body, philosophy, physical object, price, profession, religion, senses, technology, thing, and words. The maximum depth of the taxonomy is 7, and it was reached by the clusters related to both threads.

5. Conclusions and further work

Macedonian adjectives are specific due to their inflectional ambiguity. Depending on their etymology and derivation, they have two inflectional bases. The inflectional base of verbal adjectives coincides with the headword, while non-verbal adjectives are morphonologically altered. Unfortunately, these simple rules are not obeyed by online published news, and particularly not in advertisements and social media.

Main resource for extraction of inflectionally ambiguous adjectives was MKLex, a lexicon that was created more than 15 years ago with NooJ (Silberztein, 2005). MKLex was annotated with MULTEXT-East version 4 classifying the ambiguous adjectives as qualificative, although most of them are also participles.

Within the pilot project presented in this paper, a new approach for their disambiguation has been proposed. It suggests a division of all the adjectives into two different threads depending on the inflectional base. The first thread embraces the non-verbal adjectives, and the second are those that are derived from verbs. Although obvious, such distinction is not made in the new dictionary of Macedonian language, but it can be found in the digital dictionary, which explicitly points to the verb the adjective was derived from.

So far, lexical taxonomy has not been practically evaluated. It was manually checked with several incorrect inflections on the Web, and the intersection of adjective-noun collocations with wrong adjective inflection and adjective-noun collocation from the taxonomy was always empty, proving the correctness of the approach. This optimistic finding is the main motivation for further work.

Recently, two valuable text collections of Macedonian language have been released: comparable corpus collection consisting of Wikipedia dumps that were crawled in 2020 (Ljubešić et al, 2021b) and Macedonian web corpus MaCoCu-mk 1.0, which was built by dynamic crawling of ".mk" and ".мкд" internet top-level domains in 2021 (Bañón et al., 2022). These large corpora will be exhaustively researched in the following several months, in order to examine the availability of the selected inflectionally ambiguous adjectives and their collocations, to examine whether the adjectives that lacked adjective-noun collocations for some genders can be added to the existing collection and to discover new adjectives that were not discovered so far.

Unlike DRMJ corpus, these two large corpora are publicly available, so they will enable semiautomatic and automatic processing of available collocations, and well as successful evaluation of the created lexical taxonomy.

If powered with the forthcoming Macedonian WordNet, it will permanently resolve the inflectional ambiguity due to different etymology, different derivational morphological rules and different semantic properties of those adjectives that should be presented with two headwords, one belonging to qualificative, the second to participle adjectives.

Once created and accepted, this lexical taxonomy will facilitate the correct inflection of ambiguous adjectives in the online published news that are not proofread. It can also become a valuable resource for foreign language learners, because collocations are crucial for acquiring native-like fluency (Basal, 2019).

6. Acknowledgements

This paper is based upon work from action CA18209: European network for Web-centred linguistic data science supported by COST (European Cooperation in Science and Technology). It was partially financed by the Faculty of Computer Science and Engineering.

7. Bibliographical References

Bañón, M. et al. (2022). Macedonian web corpus MaCoCu-mk 1.0, Slovenian language resource repository CLARIN.SI, http://hdl.handle.net/11356/1512

Basal, A. (2019). Learning collocations: Effects of online tools on teaching English adjective-noun collocations. *British Journal of Educational Technology*, 50(1), pp. 342-356.

Bentivogli, L., et al. (2004). Revising the wordnet domains hierarchy: semantics, coverage and balancing. *Proceedings of the workshop on multilingual linguistic resources*, pp. 94-101.

Bickel, B., and Nichols, J. (2005). Inflectional synthesis of the verb. *The world atlas of language structures*, pp. 94-97.

Bonchanoski, M., and Zdravkova, K. (2018). Learning syntactic tagging of Macedonian language. *Computer Science and Information Systems*, 15(3), pp. 799-820.

Branco, A., and Nunes, F. (2012). Verb analysis in a highly inflective language with an MFF algorithm. In *International Conference on Computational Processing of the Portuguese Language*, pp. 1-11.

Burtăverde, V., and De Raad, B. (2019). Taxonomy and structure of the Romanian personality lexicon. *International Journal of Psychology*, 54(3), 377-387.

Erjavec, T. (2017). MULTEXT-East. In *Handbook of Linguistic Annotation*, pp. 441-462

Fellbaum, C. (2005). WordNet and wordnets. In: *Brown, Keith et al. (eds.), Encyclopedia of Language and Linguistics*, Oxford: Elsevier, pp. 665-670.

Ismail, S., Maraoui, H., Haddar, K., and Romary, L. (2017). ALIF editor for generating Arabic normalized lexicons. In *2017 8th International Conference on Information and Communication Systems (ICICS)*, pp. 70-75.

Järvikivi, J., Pyykkönen, P., and Niemi, J. (2009). Exploiting degrees of inflectional ambiguity: Stem form and the time course of morphological processing. *Journal of Experimental Psychology: Learning, Memory, and Cognition*, 35(1), 221

Körtvélyessy, L. (2016). Word-formation in Slavic languages. Poznan Studies in Contemporary Linguistics, 52(3), pp. 455-501.

Laudanna, A., Badecker, W., and Caramazza, A. (1992). Processing inflectional and derivational morphology. *Journal of Memory and Language*, 31(3), pp 333-348.

Ljubešić, N., et al. (2021a). The CLASSLA-StanfordNLP model for morphosyntactic annotation of standard Macedonian 1.1.

Ljubešić, N., et al., (2021b), Comparable corpora of South-Slavic Wikipedias CLASSLA-Wikipedia 1.0, *Slovenian language resource repository CLARIN.SI*, http://hdl.handle.net/11356/1427.

Miller, G. (1995). WordNet: A Lexical Database for English, *Communications of the ACM* 38(11): pp. 39-41.

Nikishina, I., Logacheva, V., Panchenko, A. and Loukachevitch, N. (2020). *RUSSE'2020: Findings of the First Taxonomy Enrichment Task for the Russian language.* arXiv preprint arXiv:2005.11176.

Roux, M. (2018). A comparative study of divisive and agglomerative hierarchical clustering algorithms. *Journal of Classification*, *35*(2), pp. 345-366.

Saveski, M., and Trajkovski, I. (2010). Automatic construction of wordnets by using machine translation and language modeling. In 13th *Multiconference Information Society*, Ljubljana, Slovenia.

Schütze, H., Manning, C. D., and Raghavan, P. (2008). Introduction to information retrieval (Vol. 39), pp. 234-265. Cambridge: Cambridge University Press.

Segui, J., and Grainger, J. (1990). Priming word recognition with orthographic neighbors: Effects of relative prime-target frequency. *Journal of Experimental Psychology: Human Perception and Performance*, 16(1), 65.

Silberztein, M. (2005). NooJ: a linguistic annotation system for corpus processing. In *Proceedings of HLT/EMNLP 2005 Interactive Demonstrations*, pp. 10-11.

Stojanovska, B. (2019). The Definite Article in the Macedonian Language. DEIXIS IN LANGUAGE, 22.

Zdravkova, K., and Petrovski, A. (2007). Derivation of Macedonian verbal adjectives. In *Proceedings of international conference recent advances in natural language processing" (RANLP'07)*, pp. 661-665.

Appendix: Inflectionally ambiguous adjectives (part 1)

Cyrilic	Latin	Ranking	Translation of nonverbal adjective	Translation of verbal adjective
боен	boen	4932	military, battle	painted, coloured, stained, dyed
броен	broen	1781	number, numerical, numerous	counted, numbered
буден	buden	2000	awake, watchful, vigilant	awaken
варен	varen	6124	limestone, lime	boiled
вграден	vgraden	7091	built-in	implanted, embedded, installed
верен	veren	1512	faithful, devoted	engaged
виден	viden	28385	prominent, noticeable, visible	seen
вклопен	vklopen	32007	timed, time switch	blended, embedded, assembled
вкусен	vkusen	7570	tasty, tasteful, delicious	tasted
влезен	vlezen	188	entry, input	entered
возен	vozen	9779	driving	driven
вратен	vraten	6399	neck	returned, repaid
гасен	gasen	35739	gas	extinguished
гледан	gledan	6653	view	groomed, viewed
горен	goren	1624	upper, higher	burned
граден	graden	5720	chest	built
грешен	greshen	5622	sinful	erroneous
димен	dimen	27006	smoke, smoking	smoked
договорен	dogovoren	6274	contractual	agreed
дрвен	drven	990	wood	wooden
дробен	droben	9429	tiny, small, little	minced, chopped
забавен	zabaven	4640	entertaining	slow
заборавен	zavoraven	2689	forgetful	forgotten
завршен	zavrshen	1678	final	completed
заглавен	zaglaven	13856	initial	stuck
задоволен	zadovolen	1247	content	fulfilled
задушен	zadushen	11557	part of memorial service	stuffy, silenced
заклучен	zakluchen	8166	final	locked
заложен	zalozhen	32151	security	pawned, pledged
залуден	zaluden	9075	fruitless, futile, vain, wasted	insane, mad, spoony
занесен	zanesen	3790	exhilarating, enchanting	absent-minded
заобиколен	zaobikolen	12033	detour	indirect, surrounded
запален	zapalen	2327	combustible	inflamed
заразен	zarazen	18869	infectious, catching	infected
заслужен	zasluzhen	6199	deserving	justified
заштитен	zashtiten	3602	protective	protected
земен	zemen	8716	earthy	taken
извршен	izvrshen	2889	executive, effective	executed, finished
излезен	izlezen	169	exiting	output
искусен	iskusen	5242	experienced, skilful	tried
исправен	ispraven	4747	correct	upright, straight
исцрпен	iscrpen	7610	exhaustive, comprehensive	exhausted
јаден	jaden	20211	pitiable, angry	eaten
книжен	knizhen	10571	paper	registered
кожен	kozhen	4073	skin	leather
ладен	laden	2586	cool, cold	cooled, chilled
ловен	loven	34882	hunting	hunted
матен	maten	2578	obscure, unclear, dull	stirred
мачен	machen	2481	difficult, suffering	forced, tormented
набавен	nabaven	35836	purchase	purchased
нагазен	nagazen	23924	stepping	stepped
нагорен	nagoren	13771	rising, steep, upward	burned

Appendix: Inflectionally ambiguous adjectives (continued)

Cyrilic	Latin	Ranking	Translation of nonverbal adjective	Translation of verbal adjective
нареден	nareden	1659	next	arranged, ordered, lined up
наследен	nasleden	8182	heritance, hereditary	inherited
научен	nauchen	1365	scientific	learned
нацртан	nacrtan	2995	descriptive	drawn, made up
незаситен	nezasiten	27589	greedy	unsaturated
неизмерен	neizmeren	14721	immeasurable	unmeasured
неодговорен	neodgovoren	17393	irresponsible	unanswered
неуреден	neureden	22040	untidy	disorderly, messy
носен	nosen	22247	nasal	worn
обиколен	obikolen	23361	bypass	bypassed, surrounded
одговорен	odgovoren	2189	responsible	answered
одделен	oddelen	1963	separate, different, individual	separated
отсечен	otsechen	11882	decisive	cut off
пазарен	pazaren	4969	market	negotiated, purchased
платен	platen	4942	salary, buying	paid
погоден	pogoden	2807	suitable	hit, affected, agreed
погубен	poguben	11778	deadly	killed, executed
поздравен	pozdraven	29809	welcoming	welcomed
поправен	popraven	11868	correctional	corrected
попречен	poprechen	14116	crosswise	disabled
поразен	porazen	8529	disastrous, devastating	defeated
потврден	potvrden	11257	confirmed	proven
потресен	potresen	6958	shocking	shocked, worried
потрошен	potroshen	10454	expendable	spent
пофален	pofalen	18247	lauding, commendable	praised
правен	praven	1229	legal	made, prepared, completed
преден	preden	2208	frontal	spun, spinning
преселен	preselen	17541	migratory	moved, relocated
пресечен	presechen	9173	intersection	cut off
пријавен	prijaven	35015	reported	registered
присвоен	prosvoen	26513	possessive	seized
речен	prechen	10142	river	said
роден	roden	769	fruitful, native	born, talented
следен	sleden	431	next, following	pursued, stalked
сложен	slozhen	1407	united	complex
соборен	soboren	15432	cathedral	overthrown
составен	sostaven	2158	composite, compound	joined, composed
среден	sreden	1437	middle, medium, average	ordered
товарен	tovaren	7030	transport	loaded
точен	tochen	3288	accurate, correct	draft, pour
украсен	ukrasen	6653	decorative	decorated
употребен	upotreben	7617	practiced	used
уреден	ureden	5775	tidy, orderly	arranged

Proceedings of the Globalex Workshop on Linked Lexicography @LREC2022, pages 68–74
Marseille, 20 June 2022

Morpholex Turkish: A Morphological Lexicon for Turkish

**Bilge Nas Arıcan[♡], Aslı Kuzgun[♡], Büşra Marşan[♡], Deniz Baran Aslan[♡], Ezgi Sanıyar[♡]
Neslihan Cesur[♡], Neslihan Kara[♡], Oğuzhan Kuyrukçu[♡], Merve Özçelik[♡]
Arife Betül Yenice[♡], Merve Doğan[♡], Ceren Oksal[♡], Gökhan Ercan[♠], Olcay Taner Yıldız[◇]**
Starlang Yazılım Danışmanlık[♡], Işık University[♠], Ozyegin University[◇]
Istanbul, Turkey
{bilge, asli, busra, deniz, ezgi, neslihanc, neslihank, oguzhan, merve}@starlangyazilim.com
gokhan.ercan@isik.edu.tr, olcay.yildiz@ozyegin.edu.tr

Abstract

MorphoLex is a study in which root, prefix and suffixes of words are analyzed. With MorphoLex, many words can be analyzed according to certain rules and a useful database can be created. Due to the fact that Turkish is an agglutinative language and the richness of its language structure, it offers different analyzes and results from previous studies in MorphoLex. In this study, we revealed the process of creating a database with 48,472 words and the results of the differences in language structure.

Keywords: MorphoLex, Turkish MorphoLex

1. Introduction

Turkish, which has many meaningful words, has a very rich content for Natural Language Processing. With DDI, texts, sounds and data in a language can be analyzed by a computer. For DDI, the structures of words are important as well as their meanings. Morphemes are formed from the meaningful root of a word. The word is divided into its suffixes and descended to the correct root that forms it. In polysemous languages such as Turkish, it is very difficult to find the root of the word. Examples of morpholex studies, which have not been studied much internationally, can be found in English and French. Although the structures of these languages are different from Turkish, the basic work is done in a similar way. After the root of a word is obtained, similar words derived from that word can be determined and even new words can be created.

Since Turkish is an agglutinative language, it always uses suffixes in word processing, unlike the languages studied in MorphoLex before. Words of Turkish origin do not have a prefix, but words of foreign origin can have a prefix. The structure of Turkish has made the analysis part of the MorphoLex study quite different from other languages. For this reason, it is important to understand Turkish structurally in order for the study to be understandable. In this way, the difference in the content of the study will be shown and it will be a pioneer in the studies to be carried out in agglutinative languages such as Turkish.Turkish MorphoLex

This paper is organized as follows: We first give a very brief review of Turkish in Section and discuss the relevant literature on MorphoLexes in Section. We explain how we generated the Turkish MorphoLex. The statistics and experimental results regarding this MorphoLex are given in Section. Lastly, we conclude in Section.

2. Literature Review

Currently, there are two morpholex studies in English and French. These are MorphoLex (Mailhot et al., 2018) and MorphoLex-FR (Mailhot et al., 2020). The English work, Morpholex, has a volume of 68,624 words formed by root words from the English Lexicon Project. It contains six new variants for affixes and three for roots. In the study, it was seen that root density and length, root family size, suffix family size and suffix frequency had a facilitating effect. Suffix length is important and the group in which an affix is included is also important in terms of separating other words. On the other hand, MorphoLex-FR (Mailhot et al., 2020) focused on approximately 70,000 words taken from English. Although the study in English is an important example for Morpholex-FR, the differences between languages also affected the content of the root distinction. In English, two different words can be combined to form a new word, adjectives can be used as verbs in sentences. In French, there are few cases of zero derivation, which relies on derivational processes. To reveal these typological differences, MorpholexFR based on 38,840 words of the French Dictionary Project is presented, using procedures similar to those used in English for segmentation and calculation of morphological variables.

The same inconsistencies were reached in both studies. Although the role of root frequency and the interaction of family size with word frequency are controversial for French, there is extensive evidence for the influence of root frequency on morphological processing in French. Meunier and Segui show that root-sum frequency modulates the effect of whole word frequency on the LD delays of suffixed words (Meunier and Segui, 1999). It is also claimed to modulate the effects of whole word frequency, root frequency and morphological root family size on LD delays, but this effect is only found for suffixed words (Cole et al., 1989). There are many different methodological studies in Morpholex-FR, what is tried to be shown here is to make reliable comparisons between studies.

Studies have been carried out in the field of vocabulary for many years. It can be said that the studies and methods used in fields such as word recognition form an important basis in terms of linguistics and affect current studies. (Morton, 1969) logogen model is an important example for word recognition. Similar studies on the use of words have also been studied on a smaller scale for Turkish (Cetinkaya et al., 2016). (Bagriacik et al., 2019) and (İbrahim Delice, 2009) also did a Turkish study on affixes and prefixes.

Turkish, which belongs to a different language family, is structurally different from English and French. (Akbaba, 2007) work on verbs is important to see its difference from European languages. Although this difference has limited the similarity between the studies, basically the aim and the result are the same. English and French morpholex studies have been an important source for Turkish MorphoLex. The method applied with these sources has been transferred to Turkish, and a comprehensive morpholex study has been put forward.

3. Turkish MorphoLex

Turkish is an end-to-end language group regarding structure among world languages. It is quite easy to derive new words and terms in additive languages. The most common sentence structure is in the form of subject-object-verb. Transitional sentences are frequently used in daily life. Short narration in Turkish is in the foreground. It is one of the agglutinative languages. In Turkish, all inflectional changes are built on the roots, which remain unchanged. Suffixes follow this structure in specific rules. Derivational changes allow one to make dozens of new words from a single root. There are no prefixes (articles) and no grammatical gender in Turkish grammar. Therefore, there is no change in sentences due to gender differences. When word derivation and conjugation performed with the suffixes, no change occurs on roots. For example, there is a difference between the third-person possessive suffix -(s)I, which is added to nouns to indicate possessiveness, and the compound marker, CM, -(s)I, which is used to form lexicalized noun compounds by specifying their basic semantic and structural differences. (Aslan and Altan, 2006) The richness and diversity of the appendices are remarkable. Regarding the relevance of the elements that make up the sentence, sentences are set up as a natural hierarchy of completed thought, not in the order of developing thoughts.

KeNet (Bakay et al., 2021) is a Turkish Lexicon Project containing 77,330 synsets, 109,049 synset members and 80,956 distinct synset members KeNet has both in-tralingual semantic relations and is linked to PWN through interlingual relations. The fact that KeNet, which was used in the creation of Turkish morpholex, is rich in the number of nouns and verbs, has been a very important resource for the study. Before finding root, the words and their meanings were taken from KeNet.

The words are divided into meaningful units with the data received over KeNet and ordered based on the suffix of the word. According to (Goksel and Kerslake, 2005), almost all suffixes in Turkish have more than one form. The first consonant in some suffixes and the vowels in almost all suffixes depend on the consonant or vowel that precedes them. For example, the suffixes of the words optician and bookstore were considered. The root of the word gözlükçü (optician) is göz (eye), the second word derived from it is gözlük (glasses), and the third word is gözlükçü (optician). A similar derivation applies to the word kitapçı (bookstore). The word kitapçı (bookseller) derives from the word kitap (book).

After all the words were sorted and checked according to their meanings according to their suffixes, a second control stage was carried out. In this second stage, the words were sorted according to their roots, so that the group that a root belongs to and the words derived from this root is seen. In the second control phase, the meaning of the word was a major factor in determining the roots.

In Turkish, when determining the root of a word, taking the smallest semantically meaningful unit of that word as a basis does not produce an accurate result. For example, while the word ab (water) is a meaningful word on its own, it cannot be thought that the root of the word aba (a type of fabric) is ab (water). In Turkish, which is a very rich language, words can have more than one meaning. Therefore, reaching the root of the word by evaluating it semantically has revealed a healthier result.

When examining words in Turkish MorphoLex, it is seen that the ratio of suffixes is much higher than prefixes due to the structure of the language. In languages where prefixes are used frequently, when a prefix at the beginning of a word is considered, the ratio between prefixed and pseudo-prefixed words starting with the same spelling sequence is in favor of prefixed words. (Laudanna et al., 1994) Since Turkish is an agglutinative language, new words are generally not derived with prefixes. These few examples are mostly encountered in reinforced adjectives and examples of foreign origin. For example, the word çare (help) is prefixed and turns into the word biçare (wretched).

Turkish is an agglutinative language. The roots of the words do not change in Turkish, there are stems derived from these roots and construction and inflectional suffixes added to the root stems. Since Turkish is an agglutinative language, it always uses suffixes in word derivation. Originally, there is no prefix in Turkish. But, Turkish has been under the influence of foreign languages throughout its history. Firstly, Arabic and Persian and then French and English. There are also prefixed words among these words. This situa-

Word	Definition	Prefix	Root
anormal (abnormal)	Those who are against the general, customary and rule, abnormal - Those who have lost their minds	a	normal
anormalleşmek (become abnormal)	Become abnormal	a	normal
anormalleştirmek (abnormalize)	Make abnormal	a	normal
anormallik (abnormality)	State of being abnormal	a	normal

Table 1: Derivations of the word "normal" and its "prefixes".

Word	Definition	Prefix	Root
antialerjik (antiallergic)	Characteristics of drugs used in the prevention or treatment of allergies - Non allergic	anti	alerji
antiasit (antacid)	Contains alkali	anti	asit
antibakteriyel (antibacterial)	antibacterial	anti	bakteri

Table 2: Examples of "anti" prefix.

Word	Definition	Prefix	Root	Suffix
apacı (veri hot)	Very hot	ap	acı	
apaçık (obvious)	Very clear, very obvious	ap	Aç	yHk

Table 3: Examples of prefixes in Turkish intensive adjectives.

tion has led to the use of prefixed words in Turkish. Also, in the studies of finding correspondences to foreign words, while transforming the prefixed words into Turkish, compound words were formed. There compound words in Turkish were sometimes perceived as prefixed words.

Table 1 shows the word "normal" and its derivatives, along with their definitions, prefixes and roots. It comes from the French word abnormal. The French word is derived from the French word "normal" with the prefix an+. It is a suitable example of words taken

Word	Definition	Root1	Root2	Suffix
biyoekonomi (bioeconomics)	All economic activities related to research, development, production, trade and consumption of plants, animals and all other living things.	biyo	ekonomi	
biyoelektrik (bioelectricity)	Electricity produced by living things	biyo	elektrik	
biyoelektronik (bioelectronics)	The part of molecular biology that studies the electrostatic forces between the molecules that enter the structure of cells.	biyo	elektron	ik

Table 4: Examples of double-root words.

Word	Definition	Root1	Comb. Letter	Root2
adedimürettep	Fractional number - The number that is agreed upon for singles that make up a whole	adet	i	mürettep
esericedit	Large writing paper used in official correspondence	eser	i	cedit

Table 5: Examples of words of Arabic and Persian origin.

from the languages that Turkish is influenced by. It can take a prefix because it is a word of foreign origin.

Anti is also a prefix used in Turkish with words from other languages. It means "against" in Turkish too. Table 2 contains examples of words with the prefix "anti".

One of the prefix structure used in Turkish is prefixes that are used to derive intensive adjectives. Most of them are formed by ending the first syllable of the word with one of the P, R, M or S consonants. Table 3 shows

Word	Definition	Root1	Comb. Letter	Root2	Suffix
açıkgözlük (astuteness)	Taking advantage by being vigilant, taking advantage of opportunities shrewdly or behavior befitting this situation	aç	yHK	göz	lük
gerilimölçer (tensiometer)	Instrument for measuring stresses related to steam decomposition, surface, etc.	geril	Hm	ölç	Ar

Table 6: Examples of combinative letter.

Word	Definition	Root	Suffix1	Suffix2	Suffix3	Suffix4	Suffix5	Suffix6
akışkanlaştırıcılık	Having the property of making so me-thing fluid	Ak	Hş	GAn	lAş	DHr	HCH	lHk
ölümsüzleştirilme	to be immortalized	öl	yHm	sHz	lAş	DHr	Hl	mA
şekillendirilebilir	that can be put into a certain format	şekil	lAn	dHr	Hl	yAbil	Hr	

Table 7: Examples of suffixes.

examples of intensive adjectives.

Some foreign-origin words can be considered as double-rooted. As the example shows, "bio" is not considered as a prefix. Instead, they are considered words consisting of a combination of two roots. In addition, although "biyo" (bio) is not a root in Turkish, it has been accepted as a root in the study. This is due to the large number of words starting with "biyo" (bio). Table 4 shows examples of double-rooted words.

This is also seen in words from Arabic and Persian (Table 5). However, there is a difference in these words. These words have combinative letters that combine two roots.

These combinative letters are also found in words of Turkish origin (Table 6). While the roots of words formed by the combination of two words are separated, the suffix of the first root is accepted as a combinative letter. It should be added that the combinative letters in these examples are actually suffixes. Certain roots in words of foreign origin are standard in Turkish. For example, the suffix -loji (logy) is frequently encountered in words of foreign origin. This is also important in terms of distinguishing word origins. Although there was no original logy root in Turkish, -loji (logy) was accepted as a suffix due to the excess of words of foreign origin.

Suffixes are mostly used in Turkish. These suffixes can derive a new noun from the noun, a verb from the noun, a verb from the verb, or a noun from the verb. The number of these suffixes is more than sixty.

The three words with the most suffixes in Turkish MorphoLex are shown in the Table 7. In the work, suffixes are separated according to the specific format shown in the example. For example, the first suffix in the "ölümsüzleştirilme" example is taken as yHm, not -üm. These rules ensure a certain order between suffixes. This order is very important for the consistency of the study. An annotator can easily understand what the main word is just by looking at the root and suffixes. Also, while deciding on the root, it is very important to check the meaning of the main word. In this way, the same root words with different meanings are easily separated from each other. And the annotater can easily understand what the root is. This significantly increases the accuracy of root words and the prefixes and suffixes they take.

# of suffixes	# of # of suffixes
6	2
5	28
4	327
3	2,169
2	9,373
1	16,618
0	19,954

Table 8: Number of number of suffixes.

4. Statistics

It is important to give some statistics to reveal the details of the study. For this, we extracted the statistics of different values such as the number of prefixes, the number of suffixes, the number of roots.

As can be seen in Table 8, almost 40% of the words in the study do not have suffixes. However, words without this suffix often form the root of other suffixed words. As was given before, the word "göz" (eye) has no suffixes. However, the root of the word "gözlük" (glasses) is "göz" (eye) and has one suffix (which is -lük), the root of the word "gözlükçü" (optician) is also "göz" (eye) and has two suffixes (which is -lük, -çü).

In the study, there are a total of 458 prefixed words. The most common prefixes, how many words these prefixes are in and examples of these words are shown in Table

Prefix	Number	Example
mü	55	mütedavül, mütehevvür
anti	42	antiserum, antitoksik
gayri	28	gayriresmi, gayrisafi
a	20	anormal, amoralist
na	19	namert, namüsait
bi	19	biseksüel, bizat, bibaht
re	19	reprodüksiyon, rekreasyon
poli	13	polietilen, poligami
oto	13	otomobil, otokontrol

Table 9: Most common prefixes.

# of Roots	# of # Roots
4	1
3	72
2	5,345
1	43,053

Table 10: Number of roots.

Total # of roots	# of Distinct Roots
53,963	19,115

Table 11: Number of total roots and distinct roots.

Root Form	# of Root Form
Baş	296
Et	246
Hane	183
Bil	157
Kara	127
Ol	117
Ot	114
Metre	101
Taş	99
Göz	98

Table 12: Most common root words.

9. Comparing the number of suffixes and prefixes, it can be seen that the number of prefixes is very minimal. Table 10 shows how many roots a word has. The vast majority of them are words with one root. And these one root words are divided into two among themselves. Some get at least one suffix, while others get no suffix. Tables 11 and 12 show the total root numbers, distinct root numbers and the most common root words. There are a total of 53802 roots, of which 19369 are different from each other. The fact that the most common root word is the root of 295 words reveals how rich a language Turkish is and that its meaning should be taken into account when finding a root word.

Tables 13, 14 and 15 show the total number of suffixes, the number of distinct suffixes, the number of most used suffixes and their description. It should be stated again that the number of suffixes used in Turkish

# of suffixes	# of distinct suffixes
43263	286

Table 13: Number of suffixes.

Suffix	# of suffix
mAk	5,051
lHk	4,847
CH	3,384
lH	3,158
mA	2,266
sHz	2,200
lA	1,944
sH	1,836
lAş	1,535
CA	958
DHr	903
lAn	884
yHm	872
yHk	714
Hl	526
lAr	500
Hn	499
Ht	499
HcH	455
Hş	452

Table 14: Most common suffixes.

is more than sixty.

5. Conclusion

This study is about MorphoLex, which has not been studied in Turkish before. The study was based on the Turkish Dictionary Project KeNet (Bakay et al.) and the words used in the study were taken from KeNet. The fact that each word has its own meaning in KeNet has been very useful when creating the database. In Turkish, the meaning of the word is also very important when deciding what the root of a word is. Without the meaning of the word, annotater can never be sure of the correctness of a root. Therefore, the meaning of the word should be related to the main word and root and the analysis should be made accordingly.

When the literature is examined, it is seen that both the English MorphoLex and the French MorphoLex were created for basically the same purposes but using different methods. In Turkish MorphoLex, words are obtained from dictionary projects, just like in English and French versions. But unlike the other two studies, all analysis is done manually. Manual annotating has been an appropriate choice for a comprehensive language such as Turkish. The annotater evaluated word meanings with words and analyzed accordingly. In addition to the word meanings, the second annotating was also important in terms of ensuring accuracy. In the first annotating, the annotater started from the end of the prefix-root-suffix sequence and in the second annotat-

Suffix	Description
mAk	Form nouns: Ekmek 'bread', çakmak 'lighter'.
lHk	Nouns from nouns, adjectives or adverbs to indicate: Krallık 'kingship', sağırlık 'deafness'.
CH	A productive suffix: Güreşçi 'wrestler', palavracı 'liar'.
lH	A productive suffix: Atlı 'horseman', hızlı 'rapid'.
mA	Form nouns: Kıyma 'minted meat', inme 'paralysis'. Adjectives: Dökme 'of metal cast'.
sHz	Productive suffix added to nouns to form adjectives: Parasız 'peniless'. Nouns and pronouns to form adverbs denoting the non-involment in an event of whatever is: Arabasız 'without the car'.
lA	Attaches to nouns to designate a place associated with the concept in the root: Yayla 'plateau', tuzla 'salt mine'.
sH	Expresses approximation to particular quality. Added only to nouns to form adjectives: Kadınsı 'feminine'.
lAş	Added to adjectives of quality to form intransitive verbs that indicate the process of attaining that particular quality: Güzelleş- 'become beautiful'.
CA	A productive suffix which creates adjectives from nouns: Çocukça 'childish'. From the pluralized form of a round numeral: Binlerce 'thousands of'. / Creates nouns, adjectives or adverbs denoting a language from nouns of nationality: Japonca 'in Japanese'.
DHr	Indicates intensive or repetitive action: Araştır- 'investigate'.
lAn	Passive/reflexive, added to adjectives: Avlan- 'hunt'.
yHm	Forms nouns from underived verb roots: Bölüm 'department'.
yHk	Forms nouns: Konuk 'guest', kayık 'boat'.
Hl	Forms nouns: Okul 'school', kural 'rule'.
lAr	The plural suffix. Çocuklar 'children', kediler 'cats'.
Hn	Forms nouns: Basın 'press', yayın 'publication'.
Ht	Forms nouns: Geçit 'crossing', umut 'hope'.
HcH	A person practising a certain profession or having a certain occupation: Koruyucu 'guardian'. A tool, machine or substance performing a particular function: Yazıcı 'printer'.
Hş	Form nouns: Direniş 'resistance', giriş 'entrance'.

Table 15: Description of most common suffixes.

ing, the annotater followed the opposite path. The double control system has increased the accuracy of roots and prefix-suffixes.

At the end of the study, a database consisting of 48,472 roots emerged. It is seen that a very small part of these 48,472 roots have prefixes, most of them have suffixes and most of them are root only. As the statistics show, the fact that Turkish is a language rich in suffix has been one of the reasons that made the analysis work difficult. The study shows a result both showing that Turkish has a different structure when considering English and French studies, and the values that emerge when creating a database based on this different structure. Turkish, which is an agglutinative language, has quite a lot of suffixes compared to other languages. Statistics show the differences between languages and the effect of the differences on the prefix-root-suffix.

We believe that this database contains most of the Turkish roots and has been properly analysed. In this way, we think that automatic analysis can be done with MorphoLex and this database will be useful in modern technology.

6. Bibliographical References

Akbaba, D. E. (2007). Compound verbs with a noun-verb in structure in Turkish. *Journal of Language Studies*, 12.

Aslan, E. and Altan, A. (2006). The role of -(s)i in Turkish indefinite nominal compounds. *Journal of Language*, pages 57–75, 03.

Bagriacik, M., Goksel, A., and Ralli, A. (2019). Two Turkish suffixes in pharasiot. pages 116–147, 04.

Bakay, O., Ergelen, O., Sarmis, E., Yildirim, S., Kobalcioglu, A., Arican, B. N., Ozcelik, M., Saniyar, E., Kuyrukcu, O., Avar, B., and Yildiz, O. T. (2021). Turkish wordnet kenet. In *Proceedings of GWC 2021*, 01.

Cetinkaya, G., Ulper, H., and Bayat, N. (2016). Analysing errors reference to use of connectives. *Journal of Theoretical Educational Sciense*, pages 198–213, 04.

Cole, P., Beauvillain, C., and Segui, J. (1989). On the representation and processing of prefixed and suffixed derived words: A differential frequency effect. *Journal of Memory and Language*, pages 1–13, 01.

Goksel, A. and Kerslake, C. (2005). *Turkish: A Comprehensive Grammar*. Routledge, 1st edition.

Laudanna, A., Burani, C., and Cermele, A. (1994). Prefixes as processing units. *Language and Cognitive Processes*, pages 295–316, 01.

Mailhot, H., Sanchez-Gutiérrez, C. H., Deacon, S. H., Wilson, M. A., and Macoir, J. (2018). Morpholex: A derivational morphological database for 70,000 English words. 08.

Mailhot, H., Sanchez-Gutiérrez, C. H., Deacon, S. H., Wilson, M. A., and Macoir, J. (2020). Morpholex-fr: A derivational morphological database for 38,840 French words. 06.

Meunier, F. and Segui, J. (1999). Frequency effects in auditory word recognition: The case of suffixed words. *Journal of Memory and Language*, 01.

Morton, J. (1969). Interaction of information in word recognition. *Psychological Review*, page 165, 03.

İbrahim Delice, H. (2009). Prefixes in Turkish and structure which have prefixes. *International Periodical For the Languages, Literature and History of Turkish or Turkic*, 01.

Proceedings of the Globalex Workshop on Linked Lexicography @LREC2022, pages 75–84
Marseille, 20 June 2022

Time Travel in Turkish: WordNets for Modern Turkish

Ceren Oksal[♡], Hikmet Nur Oğuz[♡], Mert Çatal[♡], Nurkay Erbay[♡], Aslı Duvarcı[♡], Özgecan Yüzer[♡] İpek Binnaz Ünsal[♡], Oğuzhan Kuyrukçu[♡], Arife Betül Yenice[♡], Aslı Kuzgun[♡], Büşra Marşan[♡] Ezgi Sanıyar[♡], Bilge Nas Arıcan[♡], Merve Doğan[♡], Özge Bakay[♠], Olcay Taner Yıldız[◇]
Starlang Yazılım Danışmanlık[♡], University of Massachussetts Amherst[♠] Ozyegin University[◇]
Istanbul, Turkey
{ceren, hikmet, mert, nurkay, asli, ozgecan, ipek}@starlangyazilim.com
{oguzhan, arife, asli, busra, ezgi, bilge, merve}@starlangyazilim.com, obakay@umass.edu, olcay.yildiz@ozyegin.edu.tr

Abstract

Wordnets have been popular tools for providing and representing semantic and lexical relations of languages. They are useful tools for various purposes in NLP studies. Many researches created WordNets for different languages. For Turkish, there are two WordNets, namely the Turkish WordNet of BalkaNet and KeNet. In this paper, we present new WordNets for Turkish each of which is based on one of the first 9 editions of the Turkish dictionary starting from the 1944 edition. These WordNets are historical in nature and make implications for Modern Turkish. They are developed by extending KeNet, which was created based on the 2005 and 2011 editions of the Turkish dictionary. In this paper, we explain the steps in creating these 9 new WordNets for Turkish, discuss the challenges in the process and report comparative results about the WordNets.

Keywords: WordNet, Turkish, Modern Turkish

1. Introduction

Wordnets are large online lexical databases that are created for various machine related uses. WordNets include the lexical units and the relations that these units have between each other in a relational semantic network. Usually, they are created for general purposes by including as many words as possible, but they can be domain specific as well, such as WordNets specific for tourism, architecture etc. WordNets mostly contain open-class words like nouns, verbs, adjectives and adverbs. There can also be closed-class words such as prepositions, pronouns and conjunction. In WordNets, synsets are created by grouping the word senses with their synonyms. These synsets are representations of unique senses and they enable us to combine the relevant senses.

Linking synsets by making use of nodes provides the relational semantic networks in WordNets. Relations between the nodes in WordNets can be of two kinds; semantic or lexical. This means that WordNets are able to make both semantic and lexical information available. Because of this, WordNets have been a common tool in Natural Language Processing (NLP) studies. These tools can be used for machine translation, word sense disambiguation, information retrieval and sentiment analysis. Wordnets are incredibly useful for these fields since they provide data in an organized way and they are accessible. This also explains their popularity in recent years. The first development of the WordNet which is the Princeton WordNet (PWN) established at Princeton University was in English (Miller, 1995). Over the years, various WordNets have been created for different languages and new and improved versions have been released for existing ones. Moreover, thanks to multilingual WordNets, multiple languages have been linked to each other in multilingual WordNets.

Building a WordNet, or even extending an existing one, is a time-consuming process with multiple steps that requires both human and machine labor. In this paper, we offer a time travel journey on Modern Turkish by presenting a comparative analysis on 9 WordNets on Modern Turkish. For this study, we have taken the first 9 editions of the Turkish dictionary and created the WordNets for these editions (Türk Dil Kurumu Yayınları, 1944; Türk Dil Kurumu Yayınları, 1955; Türk Dil Kurumu Yayınları, 1959; Türk Dil Kurumu Yayınları, 1966; Türk Dil Kurumu Yayınları, 1969; Türk Dil Kurumu Yayınları, 1974; Türk Dil Kurumu Yayınları, 1983; Türk Dil Kurumu Yayınları, 1988; Türk Dil Kurumu Yayınları, 1998). We compared these new WordNets to the comprehensive WordNet KeNet (Bakay et al., 2021; Ehsani et al., 2018), which was created based on the last two editions of the Turkish dictionary. All of these WordNets are online, free and available for 7 different programming languages[1]. The outline of this paper is as follows. In Section 2, we present a literature review on WordNets for various languages, including those on Turkish. We give information about the structure of Turkish in Section 3. In Section 4, we describe and explain the steps that we have taken for the creation of our WordNets of Modern Turkish. In Section 5, we summarize the challenges and interest-

[1] https://github.com/StarlangSoftware/TurkishWordNet
https://github.com/StarlangSoftware/TurkishWordNet-Py
https://github.com/StarlangSoftware/TurkishWordNet-Cy
https://github.com/StarlangSoftware/TurkishWordNet-C#
https://github.com/StarlangSoftware/TurkishWordNet-CPP
https://github.com/StarlangSoftware/TurkishWordNet-Js
https://github.com/StarlangSoftware/TurkishWordNet-Swift

ing cases that we faced during this process. In Section 6, we present the statistical results from the WordNets and finally, in Section 7, we conclude with a discussion on the possible uses of our WordNets.

2. Literature Review

Research on WordNets was pioneered by G.A. Miller when he created the first WordNet, the Princeton WordNet (PWN) on English (Miller, 1995). After this, many other researchers started working on different WordNets for different languages. French WordNet WOLF (Sagot and Fiser, 2008), Arabic WordNet (AWN) (ElKateb et al., 2006), Polish Word-Net (Derwojedowa et al., 2008), Japanese WordNet (Isahara et al., 2008), Finnish WordNet FinnWord-Net (Linden and Carlson, 2010), NorwegianWord-Net (Fjeld and Nygaard, 2009) and Danish WordNet (Pedersen et al., 2009) are a few examples of these works. There are also projects that link WordNets of different languages to create a multilingual WordNet such as EuroWordNet (EWN) (Vossen, 2007), MultiWordNet (Pianta et al., 2002) and BalkaNet (Tufis et al., 2004). MultiWordNet includes Italian, Spanish, Portuguese, Hebrew, Romanian and Latin. BalkaNet consists of Bulgarian, Czech, Greek, Romanian, Serbian and Turkish.

Regarding Turkish WordNets, TR-WordNet of BalkaNet (Bilgin et al., 2004) is the first Turkish WordNet. It includes 14,626 synsets and 19,834 intralingual semantic relations. BalkaNet was constructed by automatically extracting synonyms, antonyms and hyponyms from a core set of lemmas that are common across different languages. The other WordNet for Turkish is KeNet which is the more recent and more comprehensive one (Bakay et al., 2021; Ehsani et al., 2018). Rather than starting from a core set like the BalkaNet, KeNet was created with a bottom-up approach. KeNet was prepared by starting with the whole set of lemmas in the two latest editions of the Turkish Dictionary, the 2005 and 2011 editions (Türk Dil Kurumu Yayınları, 2005; Türk Dil Kurumu Yayınları, 2011). It includes 77,110 synsets and has 107,839 intralingual semantic relationships such as hypernymy, meronymy and antonymy. It is also integrated to the Princeton WordNet through interlingual relationships (Bakay et al., 2019). In our study, we create 9 new WordNets for different historical versions of Modern Turkish by expanding KeNet. This study, to our knowledge, is the first to link WordNets that are based on earlier editions of the Turkish dictionary with KeNet, which is created based on later editions.

3. Turkish

In this chapter, we present a brief overview of Turkish in relation to our current work. Turkish has subject-object-verb (SOV) order and it is an agglutinative language (Göksel and Kerslake, 2005). Morphologically complex words have the "ROOT-SUFFIX1-SUFFIX2-. . ." structure.

Inflectional suffixes in Turkish mark grammatical features. They include those that mark the voice features of verbs such as active, passive, reciprocal and causative. For example, passive voice is formed by attaching the -Il or –(I)n suffixes to verbs. While *açmak* is the active form of the verb meaning "to open", its passive form is *aç***ıl***mak*, where "-mAk" is the infinitive suffix. Causative voice has four different morphemes: -DIr, -(I)t, -(I)r, -Ar. An example is *gül***dür***mek* "to make somebody laugh". Derivational suffixes, on the other hand, can change the meaning as well as the grammatical category of words. For instance, the suffix -CI forms nouns from nouns. An example is *av*-**cı** "hunter" in which *av* means "prey". Another exemplary suffix that changes the category of the word is -sIz, which forms adjectives out of nouns. An example is *anlam*-**sız** "meaningless" in which *anlam* means "meaning".

Spelling rules in Turkish have changed over the years. Some of these changes are a result of the attempts to adapt the phonological structure of borrowed words to that of Turkish. Turkish does not allow consonant clusters at the beginning of words (Göksel and Kerslake, 2005). For example, for borrowed words such as *plan* or *tren*, [i] is inserted in between the first two consonants during articulation, and this inserted vowel was sometimes included in the spelling of these words in Turkish. Another example is circumflex ˆ. It is used in borrowed words from Arabic and Persian with [a] and [u] that occurred after [k] and [g], e.g., *hâl*. It is also used to indicate longer vowels as in *âdet*. However, the use of the circumflex was abandoned from time to time; although it is now used in Turkish orthography, it is not commonly used by Turkish speakers anymore. Turkish Dictionaries reflects these spelling changes.

4. Steps in Creating Turkish Wordnets

There are currently 11 editions of the Turkish dictionary that were written in the Latin alphabet; the 1944, 1955, 1959, 1966, 1969, 1974, 1983, 1988, 1998, 2005 and 2011 editions[2]. All of these dictionaries are prepared by the Turkish Language Association. 1944 edition is composed of around 15.000 entries and this number increases with each subsequent dictionary. In this study, we present 9 new WordNets that we have created for the first 9 editions. None of these editions are available digitally. These new WordNets were created based on KeNet, which was created with the 2005 and 2011 editions. Thus, we provide a complete picture for the comparative analysis on different editions of the Turkish dictionary.

For the annotation of the first dictionary, i.e., the 1944 edition, an Excel sheet with the entries in KeNet was prepared. This excel sheet had 7 columns. The first column was named "R" and this column was used to indicate whether or not an entry in KeNet occurred in the 1944 edition of the dictionary. We wrote "1" for the words that were in the dictionary, "0" for the ones

[2]www.tdk.gov.tr

R	WORD	ID	POS	DEFINITION	SYNSET	EXAMPLE SENTENCE
1	abaküs	TUR10-0670670	NOUN	Basit sayma ve hesap işleri yapmakta kullanılan, her teline onar boncuk geçirilmiş hesap aracı	abaküs sayı boncuğu çörkü	
1	abanmak	TUR10-0000380	VERB	Birine yük olarak onun sırtından geçinmeye bakmak	abanmak	Ekonomik ihtiyaçları için tamamen annesine abandı.
1	abramak	TUR01-0100170	VERB	Yönetmek; idare etmek	abramak	
1	cerrar	TUR07-0300100	ADJECTIVE	Zorla para alan	cerrar	
1	cahilane	TUR07-0300020	ADJECTIVE	Cahilce, cahile yakışır	cahilane	
1	cahilane	TUR10-0130440	ADVERB	Öğrenim görmemiş veya bir konuda bilgisi olmayan kimseye yakışır biçimde	cahilane	
1	firari	TUR01-0701240	NOUN	NO DEFINITION	firari	

Table 1: Example seven entries in the annotation sheet

that were not. Other columns included words, IDs of the senses, definitions, synset members and exemplary sentences. Each letter had its own sheet where entries were alphabetically ordered. The letters were distributed among 13 linguistically-informed annotators. Annotators went through the dictionary and the Excel sheet. Additionally, we created a list of the words that were included in KeNet but not in the dictionary in the same format. This list was created to check the differences between the different editions. These steps were followed for each edition of the dictionary. For later editions, the final version of the Excel sheet, i.e., the one for the previous version of the dictionary, was used. This was because we expected less changes to occur between consequent editions. Table 1 presents an example of seven entries from an Excel sheet for one of the dictionaries.

Checking each word in the dictionaries took the longest time. We also checked whether the definitions and the POS tags in the dictionaries were the same as those in the Excel sheets. If the POS tags were different, we put a new ID for that word. We marked the words that were present in the Excel sheet as well as the dictionary as "1", and the rest as "0". If a word in the dictionary was absent in the Excel sheet, we checked the list of words from KeNet that were left out in the earlier edition(s). If the entry occurred in that list, we added it to our original excel sheet; if not, we highlighted it to add later. This was because our priority was to use definitions from KeNet. We did not change the definitons based on those in the dictionaries as it would unnecessarily complicate the process.

KeNet had meaning IDs that started with "TUR10-". We kept the IDs the same unless there was a new meaning in the dictionary that we added. For these new meanings, an ID that corresponded to the different editions of the dictionaries were created. For example, if a new word was added to the first version, it has the ID starting with "TUR01-01...". The first "01" indicates the edition number and the second "01" the first letter of the added word. That is, if a new word starting with the fifth letter "d" was added in the third edition, the ID started with "TUR03-05".

Next, we took only the entries marked with "1" and sorted them alphabetically. If there were accidental additions of the same rows, they were deleted. Once we had the full list, we created the new version of the WordNet. At this stage, the words with the same IDs are combined. To further check our WordNet, we got a new list with potential mistakes. For example, if two meanings had the same IDs but different definitions or POS tags, we corrected them. Or, if there were words with different IDs but the same definitions, we made sure that they had the same ID. After this, we combined the synsets.

When we completed the first edition, in later ones we made sure to compare and check the new version with the previous ones. In this stage, we compared the meanings and listed the versions that had more than 80% of its words matching with each other. We went through this list to see if there were cases where we could match IDs. This also helped us find cases where, for example, a meaning in the 1944 version was lost in 1955 but was found again in a later edition. There were only a few cases of this type for each dictionary. After this stage, the new version of the WordNet was completed. Only in this new version, we were able to get the statistics of the data such as how many of each POS tags or how many examples of usage there were.

To prepare examples of usage, we made use of the previous versions of the WordNets. We pasted the sentences of previous synsets onto the new words that we added. These sentences were taken from previous versions of WordNets as close in time as possible for historical considerations. However, we still needed to check them for mistakes. We first morphologically analyzed them. Then, we deleted the words that did not appear in the relevant dictionaries. After this step, we had words that were compatible with their dictionaries in terms of spelling rules. If there was a new meaning added for a word, we compared this new meaning with those in the other versions to see if the new meaning was actually distinct from the others. Overall, the number of these kinds of mistakes was around 100, which is very small in comparison to our comprehensive WordNets. Lastly, we morphologically analyzed the words in the definitions to correct any mistakes.

In our process to create new versions of our WordNets, we also matched the meanings of synonymous words in the dictionaries. Moreover, for the 1974 edition, we checked the examples of usage of words with more than one meaning. We did this to make sure that the sentences exemplified the correct meanings. Finally, we had examples of usage for the synsets. However, since these sentences were automatically pasted, as it was stated previously, we had to adjust them for each word in the synset. If there were words that did not appear in the dictionaries, we did not paste those sentences.

5. Challenges and Interesting Cases

During the creation of our WordNets, we encountered many interesting cases and challenges. These include some issues with how the dictionaries were constructed and some cases pertaining to the historical conditions in the time of the editions. We had to overcome these challenges to make sure that our WordNets were consistent but also accurately reflected these dictionaries.

First of all, in all of the dictionaries we made use of the multiple entries of verbs with passive and causative voice such as *yapılmak* "to be made" and *yaptırmak* "to have it made" . Following (Bakay et al., 2021), the passive and causative forms of verbs were excluded from our WordNets.

In some cases, dictionaries had the noun versions of verbs such as *cay-ma* "act of giving up" and *caymak* "to give up". The definitions of these noun versions were always given as *caymak eylemi* "act of giving up". (Böler, 2006) reports that there are multiple entries of this type in the dictionary, but these noun versions have not gained different meanings from their verb meanings. These cases of the Turkish Dictionary have also been noted as problematic by (Uzun, 2003). Thus, we only entered verbs and excluded their noun forms.

Additionally, we did not include parentheses in the definitions. We deleted the phrase inside the parentheses when it conflicted the POS of the entry. In the fourth example in Table 1, the definition lacks the word in parenthesis that was present in the original dictionary. The original entry was "Zorla para alan (kimse)/(Someone) who takes money by force". However, keeping "kimse" would cause the definition to be that of a noun whereas deleting it makes it the definition of an adjective.

There were also a couple of cases with mistakes regarding the POS of an entry which we corrected in our WordNet. For example, the word *fırlatmak* "to throw" was categorized as noun in the 1944 version but we coded it as verb.

One of the most frequent problems we faced was that dictionaries lacked the entries of some words that were given as synonyms or used in the definitions of other entries. Even though there were many meanings with only one single word explanations, those meanings did not have their corresponding entries. For example, the entry for *ıstırap* "anguish" had the meaning "acıştırmak" in the 1944 dictionary which did not have its own entry in the same dictionary. Same was also true for some synonyms given in the definitions of some words. This meant that we were not able to group such words into our synsets. Moreover, for some words, dictionaries would not define the word itself, but rather only mention the idiom that it is used in as the definition of those words. Such words seemed to not have a meaning on their own, rather they were a part of the phrase. One such entry is given below:

küldür: Paldır küldür deyiminde geçer.
mell: It is used in the phrase "pell-mell".

With regards to the POS tags of words, there were a lot of differences between especially the older editions and KeNet. POS tags of profession words were one prominent example. While words denoting professions with the derivational "-cI" suffix -today, this suffix derives nouns from nouns- were given as adjectives in the 1944 edition, in later versions and KeNet they were tagged as nouns. For example, *gazeteci* "journalist" and *gemici* "sailor" were categorized as adjectives in 1944 but as nouns in other versions. Another interesting example is that some words were given with two POS tags. In 1983 dictionary, the word *cahilane* "ignorant" is both an adjective and an adverb, which is reflected in the definition as well.

cahilane: Cahilce, cahile yakışır (biçimde)
ignorant: Ignorantly, befittingly of an ignorant.

In the definition above, *biçimde* "befittingly" is given inside a parenthesis because it gives the meaning of the adverb, without it the definition describes an adjective. For such cases, if KeNet included only one version but not the other, we added it with a new ID. For example, KeNet only had the adverb version, so we added the adjective version of *cahilane*. Here, one thing we made sure was that the definition would correspond to the adjective meaning of the word. This meant that we excluded the word in parenthesis above.

There also were discrepancies between the POS tags of synonyms within the dictionaries. For instance, in the 1944 edition the entry for *firari* "escapee" has the synonym *kaçak*, yet the first one is categorized as a noun whereas the latter as an adjective. In such cases, we tagged them with the appropriate POS tag and wrote "NO DEFINITION".

One interesting thing to note was that the dictionaries were quite influenced by the political tendencies and other sociological factors of their time. For example, in the 1944 edition, a very long and detailed definition of *Güneş - Dil teorisi* "Sun Language Theory" is given. This theory suggests that all languages originated from the so-called proto-Turkish, the first language that humans ever spoke. This can be correlated with the nationalistic ideas that were popular at that time. Other examples include *şeriatçı* "follower of sharia", *kürt* "kurd", *şapka* "hat" where their definitions might be reflecting the political discourse of the time. One other intriguing example is the idiom *kızını dövmeyen dizini döver* "spare the rod and spoil the child". If it is translated literally, this idiom says "someone who does not beat their daughter beats their knees". However, in older versions, this idiom is given as *evladını dövmeyen dizini döver* which means, translated literally, "someone who does not beat their child beats their knees". Throughout the years, the idiom seems to have changed and gained a more "sexist" meaning.

Within the definitions, especially in the 1944 edition, there were multiple examples of the relative clauses with the complementizer "ki", which is borrowed from Persian. However, "ki" is not a very common way of relativization among Turkish speakers today. Also, looking through the dictionaries, the effects that other languages had on Turkish and the efforts to find Turkish counterparts for foreign words can be seen as well. All the dictionaries that we used were prepared after the Turkish Language Association was established. This association was expected to clear the "yoke of the foreign tongues" (Tachau, 1964). One clear example is words borrowed from Arabic. To introduce the Turkish counterparts of these words, sometimes both the Arabic version and the Turkish version of a word are given. In addition, borrowed words from Arabic that were plural were given with their plural meanings such as *dost-lar* "budd-ies", the plural form of *dost*, for *ahibba*. Also, in older versions of the Turkish dictionary, there were a lot of cases of "-î" which is the nisba suffix borrowed from Arabic. This letter was later changed to "-i".

Regarding spelling, foreign words are spelled in accordance with the phonological structure of Turkish. For example, both "Fransızca" and "Fıransızca" is present in the dictionary where in the latter "ı" is inserted in between two consonants as Turkish does not allow initial consonant clusters. Another ortographic case was that of the suffix *-ile* "with". In older versions, this suffix did not undergo vowel harmony when attached to stems with the third person possesive suffix as in *araba-s-iyle* "car-3SG.POSS-with" whereas in other forms it does as in *araba-yla* "car-with". Today, both in spelling and articulation the suffix *-ile* always undergoes vowel harmony. Similarly, in older editions, vowels before suffixes that start with the "y" consonant were spelled as close vowels, "ı/i";, as in *olm**ı**yan,* or *gösterilm**i**yen*. However, today these vowels are not necessarily spelled as close vowels as in *olm**a**yan* or *gösterilm**e**yen*. All these cases in addition to others are presented in the spelling dictionaries of the related years and an overview of those can be found in (Demirtürk, 2019).

6. Results

In this section, we show and explain the various statistical results that we got from these WordNets and their comparison with KeNet. These statistics can show the changes through the editions in different years while highlighting some interesting cases.

6.1. Synsets

First of all, Table 2 shows the total number of synsets for each WordNet. In this and the following tables, we refer to KeNet as the WordNet of 2020 since it was created in this year based on two different editions. It is not surprising that there has been an increase in the number of synsets over the years.

WordNet	# of Synsets
1944	31,762
1955	34,438
1959	35,802
1966	36,353
1969	37,327
1974	42,876
1983	55,161
1988	57,902
1998	67,347
2020	78,311

Table 2: Number of synsets in each WordNet

However, it should be noted that there are differences between the growth rates of two consequent years. The least amount of increase occurred between the 1959 and 1966 WordNets by 1.5%. This is surprising because the two dictionaries that these WordNets are based on have 7 years apart which is not the least number of years between any two consequent WordNets. For example, 1966 and 1969 WordNets are the closest to each other since they have only 3 years apart, but there is a 2,7% increase in the number of synsets, which is still a bit more than the 1959 and 1966 editions. The

WordNet	Literals	Distinct Literals	% Increase
1944	41,855	31,427	
1955	44,813	34,220	%9
1959	46,591	35,670	%4
1966	47,103	36,005	%1
1969	47,439	36,051	%0
1974	54,798	41,610	%15
1983	72,456	51,684	%24
1988	75,786	53,957	%4
1998	87,550	63,053	%17
2020	110,236	82,135	%30

Table 3: Number of literals in each WordNet

Year	Number of Words			
	1	2	3	4
1944	24,466	5,831	814	248
1955	24,502	7,528	1,317	518
1959	25,552	7,816	1,376	577
1966	25,628	8,016	1,401	601
1969	25,729	7,952	1,411	599
1974	28,557	10,272	1,735	658
1983	33,667	14,599	2,218	765
1988	33,643	16,454	2,463	853
1998	37,048	21,647	2,806	939
2020	48,704	28,417	3,556	910

Table 4: Number of words in literals in each WordNet

largest two increases are between the 1969 and 1974, and the 1974 and 1983 editions. The increase for these two comparisons are 14,8% and 28,6%, respectively.

6.2. Literals

Secondly, we have the results from the total number of literals in the WordNets, as given in Table 3. These numbers include all the different definitions that a word has. That is, if a word has 10 meanings, all of them are included in the number of literal. If we divide these numbers by the total numbers of synsets of the related WordNets, we get the average number of literals in a synset. This operation gives similar results for each WordNet, which is somewhere around 1.3 - 1.4. Table 3 also shows the number of distinct literals in each WordNet. Here, the numbers do not include the different definitions a word has; rather, even if a word has 10 meanings, the number of its distinct literals is 1. With respect to the distinct literals, while there is little change between the years of 1944, 1955, 1959, 1966 and 1969, there are larger increases in the following years, 1974, 1998 and 2020.

Table 4 shows the number of literals containing 1, 2, 3 and 4 words. There are literals containing up to 11 words. It is expected that 1-word literals are the most common ones in all WordNets and as the number of words goes up, the number of literals goes down. Literals with 2 and more words are usually idioms. 2-word literals are the second most common ones and they may also contain compound words since they were sometimes written as two separate words or sometimes as one single word. There is very little increase in the number of 1-word literals up until the 1974 WordNet. Between 1969 and 1974, there is an 11% increase and between 1974 and 1983 the increase is 18%. It seems that these more recent WordNets have more increase in the overall results. There is a 30% increase between the 1998 and 2020 WordNets, which could have been higher since there is a large gap in years between the two dictionaries. With respect to 2-word literals, there seems to be a high rise in their number between the first two WordNets. However, in the following ones until 1969, there is not a notable change in numbers. There is even a slight drop in the 1969 WordNet. While in 1969 the number of 2-word literals was 7952, in 1974 WordNet this number increased to 10,272 with a 29% increase. Moreover, there is even a larger change in the following WordNets; an increase of 42% between the 1974 and 1983 WordNets, and a 33% increase from the year of 1998 to 2020. It seems that the number of 3 and 4-word literals grew substantially between the first two WordNets, the 1944 and 1955 ones. Especially the 4-word ones increased almost by 100%. There are also increases larger than 10% between the WordNets of 1955 and 1959, those of 1969 and 1974, and those of 1974 and 1983. As it was stated before, these 3 - 4 or more worded literals are comprised of idioms. This means that especially after the 1944 dictionary idioms were more commonly entered into the dictionaries. However, KeNet has less 4-word literals than the previous WordNet, 1983, which shows that the recent dictionaries may not include longer idioms as much as the 1983 version, but still a close number to the WordNets of the years between 1959 and 1974. However, the total number of the 3- and 4-word literals within each WordNet seem to increase by each WordNet although the ratios between these two groups of literals may vary. Since these literals are usually idiom entries, it shows that by each new dictionary the number of idioms has increased.

6.3. Part of Speech Tags

When it comes to the POS tags, it can be clearly seen from Table 5 that NOUN, VERB and ADJECTIVE tags were the three most common ones in all the WordNets. Within these three categories, there was not much difference between the numbers up until the 1974 WordNet. To exemplify, in the NOUN tags, from the 1969 WordNet to the 1974 one, there has been a 13% increase and from 1974 to 1983 there is an increase of 27%. The VERB and ADJECTIVE tags in these same WordNets have similar percentages of increase; 22% in VERBS and 29% in ADJECTIVES in the former, 11% in VERBS and 35% in ADJECTIVES in the latter. Similar changes occur with the ADVERB tag; it seems to stay close in number until the 1974 when it

Pos	1944	1955	1959	1966	1969	1974	1983	1988	1998	2020
NOUN	17,022	18,224	19,017	19,256	20,013	22,700	28,794	30,110	36,151	43,869
VERB	7,359	7,993	8,157	8,291	8,583	10,469	13,526	14,188	15,947	17,772
ADJECTIVE	5,729	5,800	6,051	6,163	6,123	6,787	9,194	9,696	10,835	12,410
ADVERB	. 978	1,072	1,147	1,165	1,145	1,390	1,864	1,952	2,349	2,549
INTERJECTION	526	1,174	1,244	1,287	1,263	1,322	1,576	1,751	1,848	1,552
CONJUNCTION	74	83	69	70	70	72	81	79	79.	61
PRONOUN.	36	43	46	50	59	62	66	68	77	68
PREPOSITION	. 38	49	71	71	71	74	60	58	61	30

Table 5: Part of Speech Distribution in the Synsets

increases by 23% and in the next WordNet by 32%. The number of INTERJECTION tagged words have different results. While there were 526 words of this tag in the 1944 WordNet, it increased to 1,174 in 1955, which is an increase larger than 100%. While almost all other tags seem to gradually increase over the years, there is a decrease for the INTERJECTION tag in the 2020 KeNet, which is 15% less than the WordNet preceding it. Lastly, there are also some differences in the numbers of CONJUNTION, PREPOSITION and PRONOUN tags, but these are small differences compared to those in the other tags. These three tags also occur the least in all the WordNets. These are expected especially because PREPOSITION and PRONOUN tags are the ones with functional words.

6.4. Examples of usage

Table 6 shows the number of synsets with examples of usage. However, in interpreting this table, it is important to refer back to the steps that we took in the creation of WordNets. In each WordNet, while we put sentences from the respective dictionaries into our WordNets, we also added the examples of usage from 2020 into the relevant synsets. However, we kept only the sentences containing words that appeared in the relevant dictionary to make sure that the WordNets were historically accurate. Thus, these numbers include sentences from the dictionaries and the 2020 WordNet KeNet.

WordNet	# of SynSets
1944	10,505
1955	11,750
1959	11,859
1966	11,958
1969	12,528
1974	14,239
1983	19,095
1988	19,806
1998	21,942
2020	23,626

Table 6: Number of synsets with examples of usage

The number of examples of usage per synset is similar across the WordNets. The ratio in each WordNet ranges from 0.28 to 0.34, with an average of 0.33. So, there was not much of a change in this respect. However, when we compare the number of examples of usage between consequent WordNets, we get different results. Between the years of 1944 and 1955, the number of examples of usage per synset increased by 11%. After this increase, there does not seem to be much of a change in the WordNets of 1959, 1966 and 1969. The increase is 12% between 1969 and 1974, and 17% between 1974 and 1983. A 10% increase is observed between 1988 - 1998 and 1998 - 2020.

6.5. New Synsets

As it was stated previously, while preparing the WordNets we took the 2020 WordNet KeNet as our basis. When we encountered new words in the dictionaries that did not exist in KeNet, we added them with new IDs. The IDs with "TUR10" belonged to the words in KeNet whereas the IDs with "TUR01/02/03/04/05/06/07/08/09" belong to the new words that are added to the WordNets for the years from 1944 to 1998. Table 7 shows the number of words that are added in each WordNet.

Since we started creating the WordNets in chronological order, there are empty slots for each WordNet except the last one. It is also clear for each new WordNet that the number of synsets that were included from the previous WordNets decreases. This is because some of the meanings that were included in earlier editions are not included in later versions as they are not used by Turkish speakers anymore. For example, although with the 1944 dictionary we added 4605 new meanings, only 3658 of them occurred in the 1955 WordNet and in the following WordNets this number kept decreasing. The largest decrease occurred in the 1969 and 1983 WordNets. This may be due to the deletion of old meanings or the adding of more entries from KeNet instead of the old ones. In other words, as we come closer in time to the 2020 version, the differences between the earlier and later editions become less.

In the first four WordNets, namely those for 1944, 1955, 1959 and 1966, the addition of new meanings declined from 4,394 to 186. This is not surprising given the possibility that a meaning in the 1955 dictionary

	1944	1955	1959	1966	1969	1974	1983	1988	1998
TUR01	4,394	3,455	3,347	3,304	2,693	2,483	1,701	1,548	1,392
TUR02	-	1,483	1,416	1,383	1,151	1,068	733	686	623
TUR03	-	-	450	431	348	326	214	200	193
TUR04	-	-	-	186	154	146	114	100	94
TUR05	-	-	-	-	742	652	512	479	442
TUR06	-	-	-	-	-	1,055	676	601	556
TUR07	-	-	-	-	-	-	1,505	1,288	1,192
TUR08	-	-	-	-	-	-	-	567	518
TUR09	-	-	-	-	-	-	-	-	1,214
TUR10	27,363	29,498	30,588	31,048	32,239	37,146	49,706	52,433	61,123

Table 7: Distribution of new and old synsets in each WordNet

may have been already added during the annotation of the 1944 WordNet. However, there is an increase in the number of new synsets between the 1966 and 1969 WordNets. This is interesting given that there are only three years in between these two dictionaries. Moreover, the 1974 and 1983 WordNets also added more new meanings than their previous years. One thing that stayed the same through the WordNets is the increase in the number of new definitions from KeNet. Here, again, the largest increase occurred in the 1974 and 1983 WordNets.

7. Discussion

In this section, we summarize the process that we followed in the creation of our WordNets for Modern Turkish based on dictionaries from different years and discuss the potential uses of those WordNets. Our study overall showed that what has been done with KeNet can be extended to the new WordNets as well. Since our WordNets represent various times in the history of Modern Turkish, they have the potential to exhibit interesting historical facts about it.

In this paper, we presented our WordNets for Modern Turkish that we created with the first 9 editions of the Turkish Dictionary. These new historical WordNets were prepared by making use of the comprehensive Turkish WordNet KeNet (Bakay et al., 2021; Ehsani et al., 2018). Throughout the creation process of our WordNets, we tried to eliminate mistakes as much as possible. Also, we tried to make sure that our WordNets reflected the relevant dictionaries. To do this, we, for example, used the same spelling rules as those used in the dictionaries. We also added examples of usage for some literals from both the 2020 WordNet KeNet and the dictionaries themselves. We also reported statistical results from these WordNets. These statistics showed some changes between the WordNets in terms of the number of synsets, literals, distinct literals, number of words in the literals, POS tags, synsets with examples of usage and the number of new added words to the WordNets. Overall, these comparisons revealed that WordNets that are based on later editions are comprehensive than those that are created with earlier editions, as predicted.

In the process, we also faced some challenges. Some of them were related to the problems in the dictionaries. For example, some words that were used in the definitions or examples were not present in the dictionaries as separate entries, there were more than one POS tag for a single entry or different morphological forms of the same word were included. Other challenges were expected given the changes in the language over time. Those challenges were mostly related to the changes in orthographic rules for Turkish or the policies in using borrowed words or forms in Turkish.

Lastly, these WordNets can be used in future studies. Previously, multiple different studies and projects have been done bu using KeNet. For example, in 2020 a new version of Turkish PropBank, TRopBank, has been created (Kara et al., 2020). A PropBank (Bonial et al., 2014; Kingsbury and Palmer, 2002; Kingsbury and Palmer, 2003; Palmer et al., 2005) brings syntax and semantics together by annotating the argument structures of predicates. With TRopBank this annotation process in which both the arguments and adjuncts of verbs were included was completed on Turkish. This semantic resource can be extended to our new WordNets as well, which could be useful for future works on the historical analyses of Modern Turkish. Another semantic resource that our WordNets could be useful for is FrameNet (Baker et al., 1998; Fillmore and Atkins, 1998; Johnson et al., 2001; Lowe, 1997). This is another tool for coding semantic information of predicates. A FrameNet for Turkish has been done previously by (Marşan et al., 2021). This work can be extended to our WordNets. Moreover, these WordNets may enable us to conduct new studies on the Turkish language that investigate the historical change of the language. Overall, such studies and projects could help to demonstrate different semantic and typological features and interesting historical facts about Modern Turkish.

8. Bibliographical References

Bakay, Ö., Ergelen, Ö., and Yıldız, O. T. (2019). Integrating Turkish WordNet KeNet to Princeton Word-

Net: The case of one-to-many correspondences. In *2019 Innovations in Intelligent Systems and Applications Conference (ASYU)*, pages 1–5.

Bakay, Ö., Ergelen, Ö., Sarmış, E., Yıldırım, S., Arıcan, B. N., Kocabalcıoğlu, A., Özçelik, M., Sanıyar, E., Kuyrukçu, O., Avar, B., and Yıldız, O. T. (2021). Turkish WordNet KeNet. In *Proceedings of the 11th Global Wordnet Conference*, pages 166–174, University of South Africa (UNISA), January. Global Wordnet Association.

Baker, C. F., Fillmore, C. J., and Lowe, J. B. (1998). The Berkeley FrameNet project. In *36th Annual Meeting of the Association for Computational Linguistics and 17th International Conference on Computational Linguistics, Volume 1*, pages 86–90, Montreal, Quebec, Canada, August. Association for Computational Linguistics.

Bilgin, O., Cetinoglu, O., and Oflazer, K. (2004). Building a wordnet for Turkish. *Romanian Journal of Information Science*, 7:163–172.

Böler, T. (2006). Türkçe sözlük (tdk) ile örnekleriyle Türkçe sözlük'ü (meb) karşılaştırma denemesi. *Sosyal Bilimler Araştırmaları Dergisi*, 1:101–118.

Bonial, C., Bonn, J., Conger, K., Hwang, J. D., and Palmer, M. (2014). PropBank: Semantics of new predicate types. In *Proceedings of the Ninth International Conference on Language Resources and Evaluation (LREC'14)*, pages 3013–3019, Reykjavik, Iceland, May. European Language Resources Association (ELRA).

Demirtürk, C. (2019). Türkçe yazım kılavuzlarının gelişimi Üzerine bir İnceleme.

Derwojedowa, M., Piasecki, M., Szpakowicz, S., Zawisławska, M., and Broda, B. (2008). Words, Concepts and Relations in the Construction of Polish WordNet. In *Proceedings of GWC 2008*, pages 162–177.

Ehsani, R., Solak, E., and Yildiz, O. (2018). Constructing a WordNet for Turkish Using Manual and Automatic Annotation. *ACM Transactions on Asian and Low-Resource Language Information Processing (TALLIP)*, 17(3).

ElKateb, S., Black, W., Rodríguez, H., Alkhalifa, M., Vossen, P., Pease, A., and Fellbaum, C. D. (2006). Building a wordnet for Arabic. In *LREC*.

Fillmore, C. J. and Atkins, B. T. (1998). Framenet and lexicographic reference. In *First International Conference on language resources & evaluation: Granada, Spain, 28-30 May 1998*, pages 417–426. European Language Resources Association.

Fjeld, R. V. and Nygaard, L. (2009). Nornet - a monolingual wordnet of modern Norwegian. In *NODALIDA 2009 workshop: WordNets and other Lexical Semantic Resources - between Lexical Semantics, Lexicography, Terminology and Formal Ontologies*, pages 13–16.

Göksel, A. and Kerslake, C. (2005). *Turkish: A Comprehensive Grammar*. Routledge, New York, USA.

Isahara, H., Bond, F., Uchimoto, K., Utiyama, M., and Kanzaki, K. (2008). Development of the japanese wordnet. 01.

Johnson, C. R., Fillmore, C. J., Wood, B. M., Ruppenhofer, J., Urban, M., Petruck, M. R. L., and Baker, C. F. (2001). The framenet project: tools for lexicon building.

Kara, N., Aslan, D. B., Marşan, B., Bakay, Ö., Ak, K., and Yıldız, O. T. (2020). TRopBank: Turkish PropBank v2.0. In *Proceedings of the 12th Language Resources and Evaluation Conference*, pages 2763–2772, Marseille, France, May. European Language Resources Association.

Kingsbury, P. and Palmer, M. (2002). From treebank to propbank. In *LREC*. European Language Resources Association.

Kingsbury, P. and Palmer, M. (2003). Propbank: The next level of treebank. In *Proceedings of Treebanks and Lexical Theories*, Växjö, Sweden.

Linden, K. and Carlson, L. (2010). Construction of a FinnWordNet. *Nordic Journal of Lexicography*, 17:119 - 140.

Lowe, J. B. (1997). A frame-semantic approach to semantic annotation.

Marşan, B., Kara, N., Özçelik, M., Arıcan, B. N., Cesur, N., Kuzgun, A., Sanıyar, E., Kuyrukçu, O., and Yildiz, O. T. (2021). Building the Turkish FrameNet. In *Proceedings of the 11th Global Wordnet Conference*, pages 118–125, University of South Africa (UNISA), January. Global Wordnet Association.

Miller, G. A. (1995). Wordnet: A lexical database for english. *Commun. ACM*, 38(11):39–41, nov.

Palmer, M., Gildea, D., and Kingsbury, P. (2005). The proposition bank: An annotated corpus of semantic roles. *Comput. Linguist.*, 31(1):71–106, March.

Pedersen, B. S., Nimb, S., Asmussen, J., Sørensen, N. H., Trap-Jensen, L., and Lorentzen, H. (2009). Dannet: the challenge of compiling a wordnet for Danish by reusing a monolingual dictionary. *Language Resources and Evaluation*, 43:269–299.

Pianta, E., Bentivogli, L., and Girardi, C. (2002). Multiwordnet: developing an aligned multilingual database. In *Proceedings of the First International Conference on Global WordNet*, January.

Sagot, B. and Fiser, D. (2008). Building a free French wordnet from multilingual resources. 05.

Tachau, F. (1964). Language and politics: Turkish language reform. *The Review of Politics*, 26(2):191–204.

Tufis, D., Cristeau, D., and Stamou, S. (2004). Balkanet: Aims, methods, results and perspectives – a general overview. *Romanian Journal of Information Science and Technology Special Issue*, 7:9–43, 01.

Türk Dil Kurumu Yayınları. (1944). *Türkçe Sözlük (1st ed.)*. Türk Dil Kurumu, Ankara, Turkey.

Türk Dil Kurumu Yayınları. (1955). *Türkçe Sözlük (2nd ed.)*. Türk Dil Kurumu, Ankara, Turkey.

Türk Dil Kurumu Yayınları. (1959). *Türkçe Sözlük (3rd ed.)*. Türk Dil Kurumu, Ankara, Turkey.

Türk Dil Kurumu Yayınları. (1966). *Türkçe Sözlük (4th ed.)*. Türk Dil Kurumu, Ankara, Turkey.

Türk Dil Kurumu Yayınları. (1969). *Türkçe Sözlük (5th ed.)*. Türk Dil Kurumu, Ankara, Turkey.

Türk Dil Kurumu Yayınları. (1974). *Türkçe Sözlük (6th ed.)*. Türk Dil Kurumu, Ankara, Turkey.

Türk Dil Kurumu Yayınları. (1983). *Türkçe Sözlük (7th ed.)*. Türk Dil Kurumu, Ankara, Turkey.

Türk Dil Kurumu Yayınları. (1988). *Türkçe Sözlük (8th ed.)*. Türk Dil Kurumu, Ankara, Turkey.

Türk Dil Kurumu Yayınları. (1998). *Türkçe Sözlük (9th ed.)*. Türk Dil Kurumu, Ankara, Turkey.

Türk Dil Kurumu Yayınları. (2005). *Türkçe Sözlük (10th ed.)*. Türk Dil Kurumu, Ankara, Turkey.

Türk Dil Kurumu Yayınları. (2011). *Türkçe Sözlük (11th ed.)*. Türk Dil Kurumu, Ankara, Turkey.

Uzun, N. E. (2003). Modern dilbilim bulguları ışığında türkçe sözlüğe bir bakış. In *Dil ve Edebiyatı Araştırmaları Sempozyumu 2003, Mustafa Canpolat Armağanı*, pages 281–293.

Vossen, P. (2007). EuroWordNet: A multilingual database for information retrieval. In *DELOS workshop on Cross-Language Information Retrieval*.

Proceedings of the Globalex Workshop on Linked Lexicography @LREC2022, pages 85–89
Marseille, 20 June 2022

WordNet and Wikipedia Connection in Turkish WordNet KeNet

Merve Doğan♡, Ceren Oksal♡, Arife Betül Yenice♡
Fatih Beyhan♠, Reyyan Yeniterzi♠
Olcay Taner Yıldız♢
Starlang Yazılım Danışmanlık♡, Sabancı University♠, Özyeğin University♢
Istanbul, Turkey
{merve, ceren, arife}@starlangyazilim.com, olcay.yildiz@ozyegin.edu.tr

Abstract

This paper aims to present WordNet and Wikipedia connection by linking synsets from Turkish WordNet KeNet with Wikipedia and thus, provide a better machine-readable dictionary to create an NLP model with rich data. For this purpose, manual mapping between two resources is realized and 11,478 synsets are linked to Wikipedia. In addition to this, automatic linking approaches are utilized to analyze possible connection suggestions. Baseline Approach and ElasticSearch Based Approach help identify the potential human annotation errors and analyze the effectiveness of these approaches in linking. Adopting both manual and automatic mapping provides us with an encompassing resource of WordNet and Wikipedia connections.

Keywords: Wikipedia, WordNet, Turkish

1. Introduction

Words as the building blocks of any length and type of text, play a very important role in any Natural Language Processing task. These context dependent units can have different meanings and different types of relations between each other, which makes NLP tasks challenging. WordNet as a lexical database of these relations plays an important role in solving these linguistic challenges. WordNet consists of synonyms of synset members, making it a highly comprehensive dictionary that stores lexicographic information. In addition, semantic relations such as hypernyms and antonyms are captured by mapping through synsets.

In previous literature (Navigli and Ponzetto, 2012; Fernando and Stevenson, 2012; McCrae, 2018), one common way to enrich a WordNet is to connect it to another very detailed data resource which is Wikipedia. Wikipedia is a web-based encyclopedia which provides multilingual lexical knowledge by presenting specific concepts and named entities. Compared to WordNet which contains descriptions of words and some example usages, Wikipedia may contain much more detail regarding the corresponding concept. Combining the lexicographic knowledge of WordNet with the rich encyclopedic knowledge within Wikipedia will enable more comprehensive representation of words and therefore create a much more useful resource for the challenging NLP tasks.

This paper proposes to create this connection between Wikipedia and WordNet for the first time for Turkish language. KeNet (Bakay et al., 2021), which is WordNet for Turkish, has been mapped to Turkish Wikipedia. KeNet stores 76,757 synsets, which makes it the most comprehensive WordNet for Turkish. Not only does it have intralingual relations such as hypernym, derivational relatedness, and domain topic but it is also linked to Princeton WordNet (PWN) through interlingual relations. Turkish Wikipedia has almost 463,808 articles to date, and it is the 31st largest Wikipedia edition. Combining these two resources will be a significant contribution to Turkish NLP research.

In order to perform this important and yet challenging task, we initially started with manual annotations. After manually connecting more than 11000 synsets, we also applied some retrieval based approaches to analyze the effectiveness of these automatic approaches for future extentions and to help decreasing possible human annotation errors.

2. Literature Review

The previous studies have been shown to use automatic mapping between WordNet and Wikipedia. In this regard, one of the most important studies has been on BabelNet (Navigli and Ponzetto, 2012). In this study, a word-sense disambiguation algorithm has been used for the mapping. In this algorithm, they have used surrounding synsets and the article texts and thus, different contexts have been created for both WordNet and Wikipedia. The endeavor of mapping Wikipedia to WordNet via an automatic mapping has resulted in an F-measure of 82.7% with 81.2% Precision and this can be claimed to be a high-quality resource. Another important study (Fernando and Stevenson, 2012) has been conducted by the use of semantic similarity methods and the result has been an F-measure of 84.1%. However, the scale of this study has been small as it has involved only 200 words.

Although the common strategy has been using automatic mapping to connect Wikipedia and WordNet, there is also a study in which manual mapping is adopted. With the aim of providing a gold standard for link discovery and creating richer, more usable resources for NLP, McCrae (McCrae, 2018) came

KeNet ID	Synset	Semantics	Wikipedia URL
TUR01-0301390	gentleman	A well-mannered man who can be a good friend	https://tr.wikipedia.org/wiki/Centilmen
TUR05-0800820	smiling	Slight laugh, smile	https://tr.wikipedia.org/wiki/Tebessüm
TUR03-2700020	green crescent society	Non-drinkers' association	https://tr.wikipedia.org/wiki/Yeşilay
TUR02-2200110	orient	East	https://tr.wikipedia.org/wiki/Doğu
TUR10-0256160	equilateral triangle	A triangle with three sides equal to each other	https://tr.wikipedia.org/wiki/Eşkenar_üçgen

Table 1: Example KeNet synsets with their unique IDs, semantic descriptions and connected Wikipedia links. Synset and Semantics are translated into English for convenience. Turkish correspondance of Synset column is as follows; *centilmen, gülümseme, yeşilay derneği, şark and eşkenar üçgen*, respectively.

up with mapping 7,742 instances between Princeton WordNet (PWN) and Wikipedia manually. These synsets in PWN are the instance hypernyms of 946 synsets in which it links a synset to an instance of a concept. The instance hypernyms of synsets that have been marked are named entities in the world. McCrae adopts the strategy to match the lemmas of WordNet entries to the titles of Wikipedia articles if it matches the title regardless of case before the first comma or parentheses or any page redirecting to this article. However, this results in significant ambiguity with approximately 21.6 candidates for each synset. Taking this into consideration, McCrae resorts to category mappings to determine the differences. Following this mapping, the links have been categorized as exact, broad, narrow, related and unnamed. This research stands out as the largest gold standard mapping for link discovery and an essential resource for NLP tasks.

In creating the connections between KeNet and Turkish Wikipedia, we use a combination of manual annotation with possible connection suggestions retrieved from automatic approaches.

3. KeNet and Turkish Wikipedia Linking

In this study, the initial connections have been created manually and then ElasticSearch[1] tool has been deployed to both analyze the effectiveness of automatic approaches and also to debug the manual annotations for any possible errors.

3.1. Manual Annotation

For the manual link creation process 47,169 synsets (all Nouns) from KeNet have been used. Linguistically informed human annotators manually iterated over these instances one by one and checked whether there is any Wikipedia page which describes the same concept. During this process, the meaning has been taken into consideration as semantics has been the focus.

The main focus has been on matching the article titles of Wikipedia with synsets and in addition to this, the content of Wikipedia has been checked to see whether it can be linked on the semantics level as well. The synsets of KeNet have been matched to the Wikipedia article if their meanings and the Wikipedia definitions correspond to each other. If the synset has been the subtitle of another Wikipedia article or when synset meaning has been given on that sub-title page, those synsets have not been linked. Therefore, one-to-one correspondence between KeNet and Wikipedia page has been paid attention and, in this respect, meaning component has been a crucial indicator.

Based on these manual mappings, 11,478 instances between KeNet and Wikipedia have been linked. Several example mappings are presented in Table 1. Each row in Table 1 corresponds to a synset with its unique KeNet ID and semantics as well as the manually mapped Wikipedia URL.

Almost 25% of the synsets have been mapped with this manual approach. Other synsets have not been matched due to a number of reasons. Firstly, many of these do not have any corresponding Wikipedia article. In this category, the metaphorical meanings of the synsets are quite common. For example, the synset "*ekmek parası*" which can be translated literally as "money for the bread" meaning "bread and butter" can not be found on Wikipedia and thus, there is no mapping.

Secondly, some of them appear as subtitles but we are only after the ones which are main titles. This has been done to get one-to-one correspondence between a KeNet entry and a Wikipedia main page, and with this in mind the subtitle matching have been ignored. For instance, the synset "*ağ*" which means "the web of a spider" is found as a subtitle of the main page "*örümcek*" (spider) and as a result, the mapping between these two cannot be realized.

Lastly, the content of the article does not match with the semantics of the synset. This has been encountered mostly with the words that have more than one synset and Wikipedia is able to provide generally one or two synsets for these types of words. As an example, there are two synsets for the word "*avcı*". One of the meanings is the animal who feeds on other animals by hunting and the other one is the name given to soldiers when they spread to combat. In the mapping process, the first synset is mapped to Wikipedia. On the other hand, the latter one cannot be mapped because there is not any correspondence on Wikipedia for this synset.

[1] https://github.com/elastic/elasticsearch

3.2. Automatic Approaches

In addition to the manual annotations, we also explored automatic approaches for both analyzing their effectiveness in linking and to double check for possible mistakes in manual annotations. In this paper we start our analysis with some classical ad-hoc retrieval and ranking approaches and leave the recent neural network based approaches for future work. Furthermore we use an exact match of the synset with the Wikipedia URL approach as our simple baseline.

In both of these approaches, the latest (1st of Jan 2022) Turkish Wikipedia dump [2], which consists of 463,808 Turkish wikipedia pages, is used.

3.2.1. Baseline Approach

Wikipedia websites have a URL base (*https://tr.wikipedia.org/wiki/*) which is followed by a unique page specific term or terms (similar to examples shown in Table 1). As a very simple baseline approach this base URL is concatenated with the synset from KeNet and checked whether there exists such an URL. If there is, then that Wikipedia link is connected to the corresponding synset. For example, for the word "*centilmen*" (gentleman) our baseline algorithm would suggest the page *https://tr.wikipedia.org/wiki/Centilmen*.

A portion of the synset entries has multiple terms and in these cases, the spaces between words are replaced with an underscore sign, as Wikipedia does. An example to such case is provided in Table 1 with "*eşkenar üçgen*" (equilateral triangle).

3.2.2. ElasticSearch based Approaches

In addition to the simple baseline, we approached the task as a search problem and utilized ElasticSearch (ES) to identify the possible connections.

463,808 Turkish Wikipedia articles were indexed. Unlike the simple baseline which only uses the URL, in here other more detailed parts of the Wikipedia pages are explored as well. The following two fields were created during indexing.

- *title*: Just the title of the Wikipedia page
- *all_text*: This is a concatenation of all the text in the title, text content, interwikies[3] and categories[4] of the Wikipedia page.

[2] https://dumps.wikimedia.org/trwiki/20220101/

[3] Interwikies are the links to other Wikipedia pages. For instance, Wikipedia pages of Germany, France and Spain is in the interwikies section of the European Union's Wikipedia page, since they are mentioned within the contect of that page.

[4] Categories section of a Wikipedia page is used in order to gather articles under the common topics. For instance, Wikipedia pages of Germany, France and Spain have *Countries in Europe* category in their categories section.

In addition to different fields of index, different retrieval mechanism were used as well. The *match* operator of the ElasticSearch retrieves documents with exact matches to at least one query term as its default behaviour (works like an OR operator). Additionally, the match operator can be used with an *AND* operator and in that case, it will retrieve only the pages which contain all the query terms. A more restricted version of this is the *match_phrase* operator which looks for documents with the exact query terms all in the same order (like a phrase) they were given in the query. These different exact match operators were analyzed.

Unlike *match* and *match_phrase*, the *fuzzy* search operator provides more flexibility in search by allowing retrieval of documents with possible typos or small variations of the query terms. Since the resources we are using are formal and well curated datasets, one may wonder whether *fuzzy* search is necessary at all. However, since the Turkish language has its own special characters such as *ü, ö, ğ, ç, ı*, fuzzy search may be useful in some cases.

Addition to aforementioned operators, we utilized the *bool* and *should* operators in order to create compound queries as well. The *bool* search with *should* inside, acts as an OR operator for a given set of queries being searched in different index fields.

While formulating the queries synset (SYN) field from the KeNet was used together with described query operators over described fields of index. The following experiments were conducted:

- **Exp1:** Using *match_phrase* query to search SYN in the *title* field
- **Exp2:** Using *match* query to search for SYN in the *title* field with the *AND* operator
- **Exp3:** Using *match* query to search for SYN in the *title* field with the *OR* operator
- **Exp4:** Using *fuzzy* query to search SYN in the *title* field
- **Exp5:** Using *match_phrase* query to search SYN in the *all_text* field
- **Exp6:** Using *match* query to search for SYN in the *all_text* field with the *AND* operator
- **Exp7:** Using *match* query to search for SYN in the *all_text* field with the *OR* operator
- **Exp8:** Using *fuzzy* query to search SYN in the *all_text* field
- **Exp9:** Using *bool* & *should* query operators to perform Exp2 and Exp6 together
- **Exp10:** Using *bool* & *should* query operators to perform Exp3 and Exp7 together
- **Exp11:** Using *bool* & *should* query operators to perform Exp3, Exp4, Exp7 and Exp8 altogether

<table>
<tr><th>Experiment</th><th>Compound</th><th>IndexField</th><th>ESQueryType</th><th>S@1</th><th>S@5</th><th>S@10</th><th>Ave. # Pages</th></tr>
<tr><td>Baseline</td><td>-</td><td>-</td><td>-</td><td>47.60</td><td>-</td><td>-</td><td>-</td></tr>
<tr><td>Exp1</td><td rowspan="4">No</td><td rowspan="4">title</td><td>match_phrase</td><td>46.28</td><td>50.47</td><td>51.65</td><td>3.28</td></tr>
<tr><td>Exp2</td><td>match (AND)</td><td>46.70</td><td>51.02</td><td>52.20</td><td>3.33</td></tr>
<tr><td>Exp3</td><td>match (OR)</td><td>63.30</td><td>78.67</td><td>81.42</td><td>7.35</td></tr>
<tr><td>Exp4</td><td>fuzzy</td><td>35.88</td><td>41.96</td><td>43.61</td><td>4.56</td></tr>
<tr><td>Exp5</td><td rowspan="4">No</td><td rowspan="4">all_text</td><td>match_phrase</td><td>17.96</td><td>34.84</td><td>40.63</td><td>6.08</td></tr>
<tr><td>Exp6</td><td>match (AND)</td><td>23.17</td><td>42.93</td><td>49.03</td><td>7.03</td></tr>
<tr><td>Exp7</td><td>match (OR)</td><td>29.94</td><td>57.53</td><td>66.47</td><td>9.59</td></tr>
<tr><td>Exp8</td><td>fuzzy</td><td>11.69</td><td>23.38</td><td>28.32</td><td>5.14</td></tr>
<tr><td>Exp9</td><td>Yes</td><td>title
all_text</td><td>match (AND)</td><td>51.25</td><td>60.65</td><td>63.05</td><td>7.07</td></tr>
<tr><td>Exp10</td><td>Yes</td><td>title
all_text</td><td>match (OR)</td><td>68.11</td><td>83.10</td><td>86.51</td><td>9.62</td></tr>
<tr><td rowspan="2">Exp11</td><td rowspan="2">Yes</td><td>title</td><td>match (OR)
fuzzy</td><td rowspan="2">66.37</td><td rowspan="2">85.15</td><td rowspan="2">88.79</td><td rowspan="2">9.87</td></tr>
<tr><td>all_text</td><td>match (OR)
fuzzy</td></tr>
</table>

Table 2: Evaluation results of simple baseline and ElasticSearch with different experiments. *Bool* and *should* query operators were used in order to build the compound queries.

3.2.3. Evaluation and Results

The trec_eval[5], the standard evaluation tool of the TREC community, was used to evaluate the automatically generated candidates. Unlike other ad-hoc retrieval tasks, our dataset is designed to have a single relevant page (the Wikipedia page) rather than a list of possible relevant pages. Hence, instead of precision or recall, we used *Success@1* (S@1), *Success@5* (S@5) and *Success@10* (S@10) evaluation metrics. Given a list of candidate pages ordered based on their retrieval scores, S@N evaluation metric would return 1 in case the correct page is in the top N candidate pages.

The results of all the experiments are presented in Table 2. The first column displays the experiment ID and the next three columns detail whether the query is a compound query, the Wikipedia field used for indexing and the ElasticSearch query type in order. In addition to the Success@N scores, the average number of retrieved pages are shown in the last column. This number is specifically important because these retrieved pages are manually checked that will affect the size of the pool of pages to be assessed.

According to Table 2, our simple *baseline* is not so bad at all. It correctly identified almost half of the connected pages. The *Exp1* and *Exp2* are the most similar experiments to this *baseline* as these also searched for the whole synset in the title of the page. Overall these restricted queries return approximately 3-4 Wikipedia pages which is really efficient but with cost of missing relevant pages.

Match with the *OR* operator (*Exp3*) performed much better across all S@N metrics. In our analysis we observed that in some nominal compounds the second element which is possessed noun may be missing in Wikipedia or in the synset. For example, we have "*yeşilay derneği*" as one of our synsets and there is only "*yeşilay*" entry on Wikipedia. So, this case which had been missed with previous experiments was caught with *Exp3*. Of course this more relaxed search comes with a larger pool of around 7-8 pages per query.

Using *fuzzy* query (*Exp3*) did not help at all and returned the lowest scores so far. Also using all text within the Wikipedia (*Exp4-Exp8*) instead of the title did not provide any improvement in any aspects, as we got lower S@N scores and higher average number of retrieved pages.

In addition to simple one field searching queries, more complicated compound queries are tried as well to see the effects of combining information from different fields. Both *Exp9* and *Exp10* returned improvements over the individual experiments *Exp2* and *Exp3* respectively. With *Exp9* the average number of retrieved pages increased more than twice compared to *Exp2*. At this point *Exp3* is still better than *Exp9* with a slightly larger pool. Therefore we did not continue working on *match* with *AND* operators. Instead we continued with *Exp10* and tried extending it with *fuzzy* cases as well. Even though adding *fuzzy* (in *Exp11*) lowered the S@1 scores, it still returned the highest S@5 and S@10 scores so far. The correct Wikipedia page is retrieved within top 5 documents 85% of the time.

4. Evolving Datasets

Both KeNet and Wikipedia are evolving resources. As time passes new synsets are introduced to KeNet. Similarly new Wikipedia pages can be created or the existing ones can be updated (a change in the title also affects the URL of the page) or even deleted. Therefore keeping track of these resources and updating the

[5]https://github.com/usnistgov/trec_eval

connections between them is necessary. This continuous update or extension process will be easier to handle with the help of these automatic tools. With these tools this time consuming manual process becomes both efficient and user-friendly. The aforementioned potential updates occurred even in the creation phase of this dataset. Initially we started the annotation phase with the latest Wikipedia dump of that time. Later on as we moved to the automatic linking approaches, we started working with another version (again latest of that time; 1st of Jan 2022) of Wikipedia dump. Between these different dumps of Wikipedia we have seen that around 100 Wikipedia URLs, which were assigned as labels to our synsets, were not in the Wikipedia dump that we started using recently. However, when we tried to open these links, Wikipedia redirected us to new pages which are the updated version of the requested pages. For instance, the Wikipedia page for *Mersingiller*, which is a type of a flower family, were labelled as *https://tr.wikipedia.org/wiki/Mersingiller*, however the updated version of the same page has *https://tr.wikipedia.org/wiki/Myrtaceae* as its URL. Overall the automatic retrieval process helped the annotators to catch these changes and update the connections accordingly.

In addition to helping with the updates, the automatic approaches even help with finding the missing connections and therefore extending the connections lists. After manually mapping almost 25% of the synsets, there were 35583 synsets which were not mapped to any Wikipedia page, yet. Even our simple baseline experiments showed that almost half of our dataset was mapped correctly only with concatenation of the synset and the Wikipedia URL base. We utilized our simple baseline to create candidate URLs for the unlinked 35583 synsets. Among the candidate URLs which were generated by the baseline algorithm, there were only 2961 URLs that existed in the Wikipedia dump. An annotator manually checked these 2961 URLs to validate whether there are any missed connections. 83 URLs were identified as missing in the original dataset which were included in the final version of our dataset. As expected these are the results of human errors which exist in almost all annotated data collections. This error frequency being low is also a good indication that our initial manual annotations are in good quality.

5. Conclusion

In this paper, we have presented the connections between KeNet and Wikipedia for Turkish language. The fact that it is possible to find different parts of speech such as nouns, verbs, adjectives and adverbs in a WordNet, only nouns are found in Wikipedia. In this regard, the combination of two comprehensive resources bears fruitful results for future usages in NLP tasks because of their complemantary nature. By combining lexicographic knowledge of WordNet with rich encyclopedic knowledge of Wikipedia, we have been able to map synset instances between those two resources. Both manual mapping and automatic approaches of this linking have made possible to reach an exact match of synset with the Wikipedia page. While mapping manually have been great tool for matching process, automatic approaches consisting of classical ad-hoc retrieval and ranking approaches have helped to see how successful manual mapping has been and enabled us to retrieve the possible connections and thus, double-check also the synsets that haven't been matched. Thus, Wikipedia and WordNet connection that has been shown is crucial for machine-readable dictionary for future NLP tasks.

6. Bibliographical References

Bakay, Ö., Ergelen, Ö., Sarmış, E., Yıldırım, S., Arıcan, B. N., Kocabalcıoğlu, A., Özçelik, M., Sanıyar, E., Kuyrukçu, O., Avar, B., and Yıldız, O. T. (2021). Turkish WordNet KeNet. In *Proceedings of the 11th Global Wordnet Conference*, pages 166–174, University of South Africa (UNISA), January. Global Wordnet Association.

Fernando, S. and Stevenson, M. (2012). Mapping WordNet synsets to Wikipedia articles. In *Proceedings of the Eighth International Conference on Language Resources and Evaluation (LREC'12)*, pages 590–596, Istanbul, Turkey, May. European Language Resources Association (ELRA).

McCrae, J. P. (2018). Mapping wordnet instances to wikipedia. In *Proceedings of the 9th Global WordNet Conference*. Zenodo, January.

Navigli, R. and Ponzetto, S. P. (2012). Babelnet: The automatic construction, evaluation and application of a wide-coverage multilingual semantic network. *Artificial Intelligence*, 193:217–250.

Proceedings of the Globalex Workshop on Linked Lexicography @LREC2022, pages 90–98
Marseille, 20 June 2022

Homonymy Information for English WordNet

Rowan Hall Maudslay   Simone Teufel
Dept. of Computer Science and Technology
University of Cambridge
{rh635,sht25}@cam.ac.uk

Abstract

A widely acknowledged shortcoming of WordNet is that it lacks a distinction between word meanings which are systematically related (polysemy), and those which are coincidental (homonymy). Several previous works have attempted to fill this gap, by inferring this information using computational methods. We revisit this task, and exploit recent advances in language modelling to synthesise homonymy annotation for Princeton WordNet. Previous approaches treat the problem using clustering methods; by contrast, our method works by linking WordNet to the Oxford English Dictionary, which contains the information we need. To perform this alignment, we pair definitions based on their proximity in an embedding space produced by a Transformer model. Despite the simplicity of this approach, our best model attains an F1 of .97 on an evaluation set that we annotate. The outcome of our work is a high-quality homonymy annotation layer for Princeton WordNet, which we release.

Keywords: WordNet, Oxford English Dictionary, polysemy, homonymy

1. Introduction

Words have multiple meanings that are related to each other in different ways. Meanings which are systematically related are said to exhibit **polysemy**. One example of polysemy is the use of the same wordform to refer to a product or its producer (Pustejovsky, 1995):

(1) a. John spilled coffee on the *newspaper*.
    b. The *newspaper* fired its editor.

Aside from such highly productive alternation patterns, polysemy also includes semi-productive metaphorical extensions (Lakoff and Johnson, 1980):

(2) a. They *adopted* a child.
    b. The theory was rapidly *adopted*.

Polysemy exemplifies humans' ability to flexibly extend categories to cover new members, which is of significant interest to researchers in cognitive science (Lakoff, 1987). These extensions include figurative uses, like in example (2). The polysemisation of words also plays a key role in lexical evolution and semantic drift (e.g. Koch, 2016).

On the other hand, meanings of the same word which exhibit no systematic relation are described as instances of **homonymy**.[1] These associations are non-productive, and result instead from language change. Usually, this occurs when new word senses are borrowed from other languages, and can involve vowelshifts and similar transformations. For example, consider the English word *bank*:

(3) a. I need to get money out from the *bank*.
    b. Let's sit by the river on the *bank*.

The financial sense has its origin in the romance languages, and the river-edge sense comes from Old Norse. Another example of homonymy happens when acronyms become conventionalised, and are ultimately lower cased (e.g. Personal Identification Number):

(4) a. Put a *pin* in the hem of the fabric.
    b. Never share your credit card's *pin*.

Although homonymous meanings are not semantically related, their presence in a particular language is not random, and instead may serve a communicative function (Piantadosi et al., 2012).

WordNet (Miller, 1995) is a popular computational lexicon. In WordNet, concepts are represented as an equivalence class of wordforms associated with that concept, called synsets. WordNet makes no distinction between polysemy and homonymy. If it did, WordNet would have the potential to be an ideal repository for research into these phenomena.

Several researchers have acknowledged this shortcoming of WordNet, and have attempted to produce computational models to synthesise homonymy annotation for it (e.g. Utt and Padó, 2011; Veale, 2004; Freihat et al., 2013). We revisit this task using contemporary methods. By exploiting large language models, we synthesise a high-quality annotation layer for distinguishing between polysemy and homonymy in the English Princeton WordNet.

More specifically, to identify homonyms in WordNet, we align it with the Oxford English Dictionary, a historical dictionary of English. In this dictionary, as a general principle in lexicography, a lemma is defined as a wordform plus all its polysemous senses. Homonymous wordforms are associated with multiple lemmas. By aligning the senses in WordNet with corresponding senses in the Oxford English Dictionary, we can work out which lemma they belong to, and thus distinguish between senses which are related by polysemy

[1] This is sometimes called 'incidental polysemy', which is contrasted with 'systematic polysemy' (e.g. Pustejovsky, 1995).

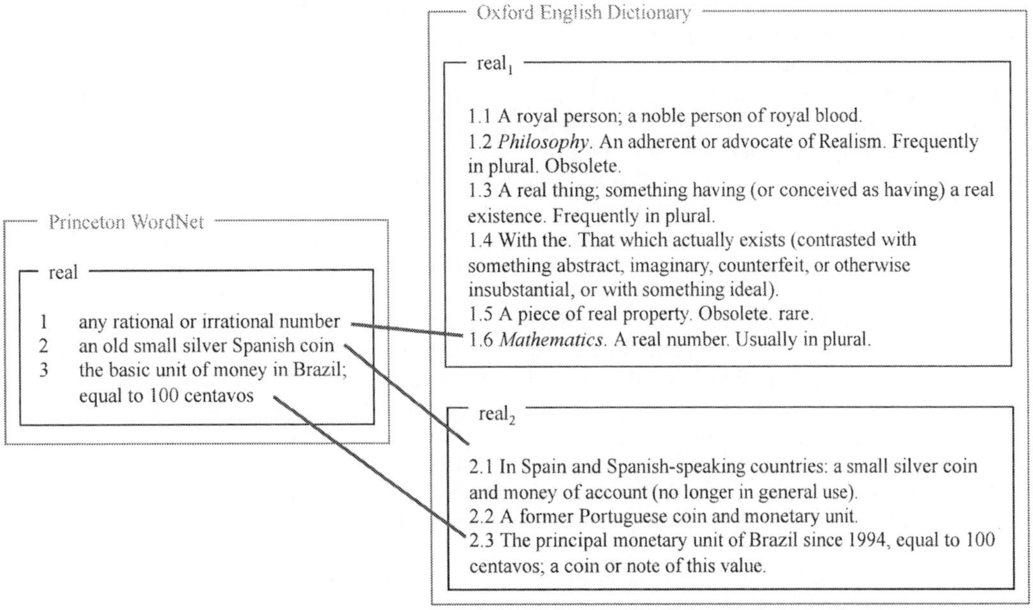

Figure 1: Noun definitions of the word *real* from the PWN (left) and the OED (right)

(same lemma), and those related by homonymy (different lemmas). Previous works that attempted to identify homonymy in WordNet did so by clustering senses. An advantage of our linking approach is that figurative senses can be correctly identified as instances of polysemy, even though their meaning might differ radically from the literal sense they extend.

To align the dictionaries, we compute the sentence embeddings of each definition using various Transformer models (Vaswani et al., 2017), and find the definition in the Oxford English Dictionary which is closest in embedding space to each WordNet definition. To evaluate the quality of the model, we annotate a small evaluation set of 196 words (554 senses). Despite the simplicity of our unsupervised method, it attains an F1-score of .97 on our evaluation set, indicating that our synthesised data is high quality.

2. Background

The **Princeton WordNet** (PWN) is an English computational lexicon, which maps wordforms to concepts, which are called synsets (Miller, 1995). Synsets are associated with a definition and often some example sentences, and are also linked to each other in a semantic network (consisting primarily of *is a* and *has a* relations). Since its creation, several works have added additional annotation layers to the PWN (e.g. Mendes and Chaves, 2001, Puşcaşu and Mititelu, 2008, Amaro et al., 2006). In research on polysemy and homonymy, we often want to build rich representations of each sense, and the PWN is associated with useful resources for that. One set of resources links synsets with textual examples, e.g. SemCor (Miller et al., 1994) and the NTU-MC (Tan and Bond, 2011). Other resources link synsets to images depicting the synset, e.g. ImageNet (Deng et al., 2009) and BabelPic (Calabrese et al., 2020).

What the PWN lacks, however, is information which distinguishes homonymy from polysemy. Consider the word *real*, the noun senses of which are shown in Figure 1. In the PWN (left), the senses appear in a single group. In the **Oxford English Dictionary** (OED), however, the senses are divided into two separate lemmas, $real_1$ and $real_2$ (right).[2] The OED is an authoritative English historical dictionary: unlike the PWN, which is a contemporary lexicon that shows a snapshot of current English usage, the OED maps each wordform to all known senses that it has ever had. Senses in the same lemma have the same etymology and pronunciation, and are likely derived from each other, i.e. they are polysemous. Senses in different lemmas likely bare no systematic relation, i.e. they are homonymous. The word *real* exhibits homonymy, but the PWN does not encode this information.

The problem of separating homonymy from polysemy in the PWN has been recognised, and several works have attempted to address it. Because manually annotating this information for all of the PWN would be expensive, previous approaches have synthesised the data using computational methods (e.g. Utt and Padó, 2011, Veale, 2004, Freihat et al., 2013). These previous works all adopt a similarity-driven clustering ap-

[2]These are the lemmas that result following our homonymy identification procedure, which is detailed in §3.1.

proach to separate homonymy from polysemy. The problem with this approach is that some polysemous senses appear "further apart" in semantic space than homonyms. For example, two polysemous senses connected by metaphor are often extremely different on the surface (e.g. the *body* of a human v. the *body* of a guitar), and so are easily confused with homonymy even though they are related.

To ensure that instances figurative polysemy are not incorrectly labelled as homonymy, we use etymological information for the identification of homonyms. More specifically, we align WordNet with the OED (red lines in Figure 1). Our work is most similar to Navigli (2006), who also aligned the PWN with the OED to cluster PWN senses. However, while their clustering was produced for the purpose of Word Sense Disambiguation (WSD), we do so for the purpose of research into polysemy and homonymy; because of these research aims, we coarsen the OED lemmas, as outlined in §3.1.

The data synthesised by Navigli (2006), originally released for a 2007 shared task (Navigli et al., 2007), clusters WordNet 2.1 senses. Since the early time of this work, many new methodologies for dictionary alignment have emerged. Several works have aligned WordNet with other resources, for example Wiktionary and Wikipedia (Miller and Gurevych, 2014; Meyer and Gurevych, 2011; McCrae et al., 2012; Navigli et al., 2021). Recently, a shared task was held on supervised monolingual dictionary alignment (Kernerman et al., 2020); in the English subtask, models were tasked with aligning the PWN with a publicly accessible version of the Webster's dictionary from 1913 (Ahmadi et al., 2020). All models participating in the subtask use a Transformer model (Vaswani et al., 2017) in some form. Transformer models are sentence encoders, which produce embeddings for each input token. In our work, we revisit Navigli (2006), and use Transformer models to produce a high quality alignment for WordNet 3.1.

Finally, we note that while a resource called 'Etymological Wordnet' already exists (de Melo, 2014), this resource is in fact unrelated to the WordNet project (Miller, 1995): it is an automatically extracted database of wordform derivations from Wiktionary.

3. Processing the OED

In this section, we describe how we extract homonymy data from the OED (§3.1), and then how we collect data to evaluate model performance (§3.2).

3.1. Extracting Homonyms from the OED

For every wordform with multiple senses in the PWN, we retrieve the corresponding lemmas from the OED.[3] Lemmas in the OED have etymology data associated with them, in the form of the language family of origin. Depending on the records available, some lemmas are annotated with more broad family information (e.g. Italic), while others have more fine grained information (e.g. French). Some have unknown origin. Because of this, sometimes it is ambiguous as to whether two lemmas are in fact related.

In these cases, we have to make a decision. We could either divide PWN senses into the lemmas as they are presented in the OED (and risk splitting polysemous senses into different lemmas), or we could merge lemmas together (and risk putting hymonymous senses into the same lemma). We choose to do that latter, because for research in these areas it is preferable to overestimate polysemy and underestimate hymonymy: if two polysemous senses were wrongly separated into different lemmas, this would provide a wrong gold standard for any model of polysemisation.

Our procedure for merging OED lemmas is as follows. Some lemmas are marked as being derived from others; in this case, we merge them with the lemma they are derived from. If there are multiple lemmas which have the same etymological derivation, we merge them. If one lemma's derivation is a subclass of another's (as with French v. Italic), we merge them. The exception to these merges is when a derivation is labelled as being the conventionalisation of an acronym; we leave these in their own lemma. Finally, if a lemma for a particular wordform has unknown etymology, we exclude that wordform (and thus assume that all its senses are polysemous).

3.2. Annotating an Evaluation Set

Sampling Data We sample wordform–part-of-speech combinations, which meet the following criteria:

- have at least two senses in the PWN;
- have at least two lemmas in the OED (following our coarsening procedure, §3.1), and further, that at least two of these lemmas have at least two senses (to avoid severely imbalanced lemmas);
- have a maximum of 15 senses overall in the OED (to reduce the cognitive load on annotators)

Following the above procedure, we sample 100 wordform–part-of-speech combinations. These combinations had an average of 2.18 lemma options in the OED, and yielded 286 PWN senses.

Annotation Procedure We need to collect a mapping of PWN senses to OED lemmas. However, as we will see in §4, the models we study work by aligning PWN senses to OED senses. Although this is not our primary concern, it would be interesting to also evaluate how well models perform at this finer granularity of analysis. Because of this, we decide to ask annotators to assign each PWN sense to a single OED sense, from which we can trivially recover the sense-to-lemma mapping which is our main interest. More specifically, we ask annotators to go through each

[3]Content provided by OED Researcher API, 2022.

word, and assign each PWN senses to a single OED sense. If there are multiple OED senses which would work, we ask them to select the best one. If there is no OED sense to align a PWN sense to, but there is an OED sense which is more broad and would include that PWN sense, we ask them to select that OED sense. If there is still not an appropriate OED sense, annotators have a choice. If they think the PWN sense is closely related to OED senses in a particular lemma, they assign the PWN sense to that lemma. Otherwise, if they think that the PWN sense is a different lemma, not contained in the OED, they leave it unassigned.

Recovering Lemma Assignments With the fine-grained sense-to-sense alignment which our annotators produce, we can reconstruct the sense-to-lemma mapping trivially. For each PWN sense that is aligned with an OED sense, we simply take the lemma that that OED sense is contained within in the OED.

Statistics and Agreement Two native British English speakers performed our annotation task. It is however not possible to report agreement in terms of chance-corrected Inter-Annotator Agreement (IAA) for a dictionary alignment task, because the number of possible categories that an item is assigned to varies depending on the wordform; we therefore report raw agreement. Both annotators gave the same lemma assignment 97.6% of the time, and the same sense assignment 80.4% of the time. 1.0% of the time, at least one annotator judged that no lemma existed for a PWN sense. 9.1% of the time, at least one annotator judged that none of the fine-grained senses was appropriate, but that an appropriate lemma existed. For comparability to similar tasks, we follow Ahmadi et al. (2020), and also compute IAA in terms of κ. Ahmadi et al. do this by treating each possible pair of senses (one from each dictionary) as a binary datapoint, which could be labelled 0 if they were not aligned, or 1 if they were . (However, we note that this method is problematic, as it overestimates agreement. This is because computations of κ assume that each datapoint is independent, and under this formulation many of the datapoints are counted as agreement although they are simply a consequence of other decisions.) Under these conditions, we find κ=0.96 (N=909, k=2, n=2) for the lemma assignments, and κ=0.79 (N=3,396, k=2, n=2) for the sense assignments. The high agreement is in line with previous work; Navigli (2006) found $\kappa = 0.85$ for sense-level alignment between the PWN and the OED (although it is unclear how they performed this computation).

Evaluation Data Having shown that our annotation procedure yielded high agreement, one annotator continued the annotation task for more examples, and labelled 96 more wordforms which met the above criteria. This yields a final annotated set consisting of 196 wordform–part-of-speech combinations covering 544 PWN senses, which we will use to evaluate model performance, §5. In this final evaluation data, 1.3% of PWN senses are not assigned to an OED lemma.

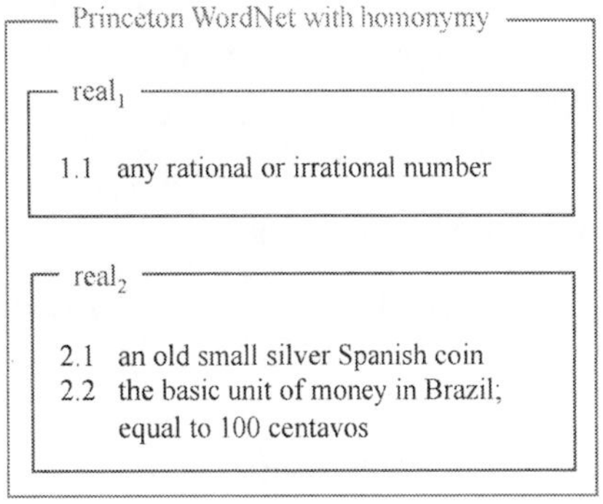

Figure 2: Our output annotation for the word *real*

4. Method

Our goal is to split homonymous PWN senses into separate lemmas (Figure 2). To achieve this, we align the PWN with the OED, in which senses are grouped according to their etymological derivation. Our method is a simple unsupervised approach, which pairs each definition from the PWN with the definition in the OED that it is closest to it in embedding space.

Let $\mathcal{S}$ be a set of all senses, which we take as string definitions. Let $\mathcal{S}^w_{\text{OED}} \subseteq \mathcal{S}$ denote the set of sense definitions associated with a wordform w in the OED, and $\mathcal{S}^w_{\text{PWN}} \subseteq \mathcal{S}$ denote its senses in the PWN. Each sense in the OED is part of a lemma, $l \in \mathcal{L}$, which can be recovered trivially; we denote the function for doing so $\text{lemma}^w_{\text{OED}} : \mathcal{S}^w_{\text{OED}} \mapsto \mathcal{L}$. Our goal is to also map each sense from the PWN to a one of these lemmas, i.e. to construct a function, $\text{lemma}^w_{\text{PWN}} : \mathcal{S}^w_{\text{PWN}} \mapsto \mathcal{L}$.

No training data for this task exists, so we experiment with simple unsupervised methods. Let sim be a function which takes a pair of definitions, one from each dictionary, and returns a measure of their similarity, $\text{sim} : \mathcal{S}^w_{\text{PWN}} \times \mathcal{S}^w_{\text{OED}} \mapsto \mathbb{R}$. For a particular PWN sense, $s \in \mathcal{S}^w_{\text{PWN}}$, these unsupervised models assign the sense to the lemma of the most similar OED sense:

$$\text{lemma}^w_{\text{PWN}}(s) = \text{lemma}^w_{\text{OED}}\left(\underset{s' \in \mathcal{S}^w_{\text{OED}}}{\text{argmax}}\, \text{sim}(s, s')\right) \quad (1)$$

Our methods vary, then, in how they define sim. We experiment with very simple approaches, which compute similarity by comparing two definition embeddings. Let emb be a function that produces a d-dimensional sentence embedding of a given definition, $\text{emb} : \mathcal{S} \mapsto \mathbb{N}^d$. Additionally, let proximity be a function which compares two definition embeddings and returns a similarity rating, $\text{proximity} : \mathbb{N}^d \times \mathbb{N}^d \mapsto \mathbb{R}$. We can then express sim in terms of these functions:

$$\text{sim}(s, s') = \text{proximity}(\text{emb}(s), \text{emb}(s')) \quad (2)$$

This formulation allows us to experiment with a variety of different implementations of each of these functions, which we detail in §5.1.

5. Evaluation

All of our models are unsupervised, and parameter-free. Each model makes a prediction for each PWN sense in the evaluation data in terms of which lemma in the OED it belongs to. In this section, we evaluate how well they do so.

5.1. Experimental Setup

Data To evaluate our models, we use the data we collected in §3.2, which consists of 196 word–part-of-speech combinations, covering 554 PWN senses. When we evaluate the lemma assignments, we analyse all 554 senses, for an accurate idea of how the model will perform on the real data (and therefore include senses which were not assigned to a lemma, which the models will necessarily label incorrectly). When we evaluate the sense assignments, however, we filter out all the senses which were not assigned to a sense, leaving 497 senses.

Models Our model formulation centres around a similarity function, eq. (2), which has two main components, emb and proximity. For emb, we experiment with four different sentence embedding models. **GloVe** (Pennington et al., 2014) is a static embedding technique, which learns to approximate a collocation matrix. **RoBERTa** (Liu et al., 2019) is a variant of BERT (Devlin et al., 2019), a Transformer model (Vaswani et al., 2017) which was trained on a masked language modelling objective. For both of these embedding spaces, the sentence embedding is taken as the mean of all the token embeddings. The next two models, **MPNet** (Song et al., 2020) and **Sentence-T5** (Ni et al., 2021), however, were designed explicitly to produce quality sentence representations. MPNet was trained on a variety of tasks for all-round performance, while Sentence-T5 was trained on sentence similarity tasks in particular. For all of these sentence embedding models, we use the implementations in the Sentence Transformers Python library (Reimers and Gurevych, 2019); where multiple versions are present, we use the largest available. The dimensionalities (d) of these model's representations are detailed in Table 1. Each of these embedding spaces might suit different similarity metrics, so for proximity, we experiment with dot product, cosine similarity, and Euclidean distance.[4] Results presented are from whichever similarity metric attained the highest results (in all cases it was dot product).

Baselines We experiment with three baselines. As a lower bound for the task, the **random** baseline assigns each sense to a random lemma for a particular word with uniform probability. Because some lemmas have more senses than others in the OED, we compute another baseline which assigns each sense to whichever lemma for the word has the **most** OED senses. Finally, following Navigli (2006), we reimplement the LESK algorithm (Lesk, 1986). The **LESK** baseline calculates the similarity between two definitions, s and s', as the fraction of the shortest definition's lemmas which are in both string definitions:

$$\mathrm{sim}(s, s') = \frac{|\,\mathrm{bow}(s) \cap \mathrm{bow}(s')|}{\min(|\,\mathrm{bow}(s)|, |\,\mathrm{bow}(s')|)} \tag{3}$$

where bow (bag-of-words) returns the set of lemmas in a given definition. This implementation of sim is used to find lemma assignments using the same algorithm as the other models, eq. (1). To tokenise the definitions and to lemmatise the tokens, we use the word tokeniser and WordNet lemmatiser from NLTK (Bird et al., 2009). We additionally filter out stop words and punctuation, also using the NLTK list for stop words.

Name	d
GloVe	300
RoBERTa	1,024
MPNet	768
Sentence-T5	768

Table 1: Sentence embedding dimensionalities

Metrics To evaluate the quality of the lemma assignments, we compute accuracy and the F1-score (macro-averaged over the lemmas). Finding the system that performs best at this level is the core interest in this paper. What is important is that a system maps each PWN sense to the correct lemma, which it can do successfully by mapping it to *any* OED sense of that lemma; even if it managed to additionally guess the finer-grained OED sense, this would only be of secondary interest to us. However, we are in a situation where we can report performance at a finer granularity because each model internally predicts a fine-grained OED sense. We therefore additionally report F1-score and accuracy of these sense assignments (macro-averaged over OED senses).

Significance Testing We use a two-tailed Monte Carlo permutation test at significance level $\alpha = 0.01$, with $r = 10{,}000$ permutations.

5.2. Results

Table 2 shows our results. Two of the baselines, random and majority, only make lemma assignments, and so we cannot evaluate them at the sense level.

The best performing model overall used the Sentence-T5 embedding space. Despite the simplicity of this approach, it attained an F1-score of 0.97 in the lemma assignment task, the main focus of this work. This was significantly better than all the baselines, and also significantly better than GloVe, the only non-Transformer

[4] Since Euclidean distance is highest for two senses which are the least similar, we take its negation.

Model	Lemma Assignments		Sense Assignments	
	Accuracy	F1-score	Accuracy	F1-Score
GloVe	.94	.93	.71	.70
MPNet	.94	.95	.76	.75
RoBERTa	.95	.95	.72	.71
Sentence-T5	**.97**	**.97**	**.84**	**.84**
LESK	.88	.88	.65	.63
most	.73	.68	N/A	N/A
random	.47	.50	N/A	N/A

Table 2: Results

embedding space. Numerically, the difference in the lemma scores was small: GloVe embeddings achieved .93 F1, only .04 less than Sentence-T5.

In the evaluation data we collected, 1.3% of senses were not assigned to a lemma (see §3.2). Our model necessarily gets all of these wrong (it has no way of leaving senses unassigned), meaning the highest accuracy it could theoretically attain would be .98—only .01 higher than it achieves. For our purposes, that it erroneously assigns these senses is not an issue: as mentioned above (§3.1), because we are interested in research into polysemy and homonymy, we opt to overestimate polysemy and underestimate homonymy, rather than vice versa. This is the effect which this will have.

The best model at predicting the sense-to-sense mapping also used the Sentence-T5 embedding space, but the quality of the mapping was not as high as its sense-to-lemma mapping, attaining an F1 of .84. This result is significantly better than not only GloVe, but also both other Transformer models. The numerical difference between the models is also more pronounced. GloVe attained .70 F1, which is .14 behind the best Transformer model, and only .07 above the LESK approach.

6. Final Annotation Layer

Having performed an evaluation of our approach on a small testset, we now present details for the entirety of the PWN. We use the highest-performing model from our evaluation, which was based on the Sentence-T5 (Ni et al., 2021) embedding space, and used the dot product to compare embeddings.

6.1. Between-POS v. Within-POS

We compute two distinct annotation layer variants, which we term between-POS and within-POS.

The OED is an etymological lexicon, and as such it can identify when two lemmas of the same wordform, but with different parts-of-speech, are derived from each other (this process is called zero-derivation). For example, as a verb, to *tango* is to perform a particular dance, and as a noun, a *tango* is that dance. In the **between-POS** homonymy annotation layer, we preserve this information, by applying our homonymy identification procedure (§3.1) to all the senses of a word at the same time, regardless of their part-of-speech.

This approach has one drawback. As mentioned above, the OED does not have complete information about all senses' etymologies. Sometimes, a sense might be labelled with less specific information than another, or might have unknown etymology. When a wordform had a sense with unknown etymology, we assumed that no homonymy was present, i.e. that all the wordform's senses were polysemous. This is to reduce the chance of erroneously labelling instances of polysemy as homonymy. However, in cases where a sense has unknown etymology, there is a chance that we incorrectly treat instances of homonymy as polysemy, an error which we would also like to minimise.

The more senses a wordform has, the more likely it is to have a sense with missing information, which may mean that it is incorrectly treated. In the **within-POS** layer, when applying our homonymy identification procedure, we treat the senses of each part-of-speech individually. This reduces the chance that a sense will be included which lacks etymology information, and so lowers the chance of missing instances of homonymy. However, this comes at the price of losing the alignment between different parts-of-speech.

In both the between-POS and within-POS variants, we exclude OED senses which were not part of the alignment. In other words, we first compute the alignment between the PWN and the OED, and then apply our homonymy identification procedure to only the OED senses which are part of the alignment. This is to minimise the unwanted effects of senses with unknown etymology as much as possible, for both variants.

6.2. Analysis

Statistics for the two variants of our annotation layer are presented in Table 3. We additionally report counts using out-of-the-box lemmas from the OED, without any of the processing in §3.1; reported as **raw**. This should give an idea of the number of exclusions resulting from our homonymy identification process.

There are a total of 21,740 words which have multiple senses in the PWN.[5] Of those, 20,169 (93%) have corresponding entries in the OED.

[5]We exclude all wordforms which are not lower case or which include spaces; this removes proper nouns and compound nouns, because these are not included in the OED.

POS	# Words in PWN	# Also in OED	# Homonymous in the OED *between-POS*	*within-POS*	*raw*	# Homonymous in the PWN *between-POS*	*within-POS*	*raw*
noun	15,019	14,228	806	849	2,830	237	244	794
verb	6,226	5,886	237	310	1,218	50	56	244
adj	6,661	6,115	75	88	303	17	17	54
adv	1,037	934	3	4	19	0	0	2
any	21,740	20,169	969	1,091	3,420	284	297	961

Table 3: Final annotation layer statistics

Using the within-POS variant, 1,091 wordforms are found to exhibit homonymy.[6] As expected, fewer were found using the between-POS variant (969, a reduction of 11%). These numbers represent the maximum number of wordforms in the PWN which our method can identify as exhibiting homonymy. Of these, with the within-POS variant we identified 297 homonymous wordforms in the PWN (27% of those in the OED), which are associated with a total of 2,139 senses in the PWN (full list of words in App. A). With the between-POS variant we identified 284 wordforms. The fact that only a fraction of homonymous wordforms in the OED were also homoynmous in the PWN is unsurprising. The OED is an an etymological dictionary, which will contain senses which are no longer used. On the other hand, the PWN is a contemporary dictionary, which will not contain archaic instances of homonymy.

Clear-cut cases of homonymy are less numerable than we might expect (279 cases; 'any' under within-POS in Table 3). These are the cases where wordforms are associated with meanings which have distinct origins and are semantically unrelated. But then again, this number represents a lower-bound for the total amount of homonymy in the PWN, as a consequence of our decision to combine lemmas in ambiguous cases. An upper-bound (i.e. an overestimation of homonymy) is represented by the raw results (961 wordforms). This indicates that between 1.5% and 4.8% of wordforms in the PWN are homonymous (estimated using the wordforms that are in both dictionaries).

6.3. Release

We release our code and both variants of our homonymy annotation layer online.[7] We additionally release a version based on the raw lemma assignments, which will be useful if overestimation of homonymy and underestimation of polysemy is preferred, but we caution that the quality of this data was not investigated in our annotation study.

[6]Note that for the within-POS variant, the 'any' part-of-speech row in Table 3 does not correspond to a simple summation of the statistics for each part-of-speech, because this would count any wordform which is homonymous in two or more different parts-of-speech multiple times.

[7]`https://github.com/rowanhm/wordnet-homonymy`

7. Conclusion

We present a new annotation layer for the Princeton WordNet, which splits senses into lemmas, making it possible to distinguish between polysemy and homonymy. We use a method which is conservative with respect to homonymy identification (we would rather erroneously label two homonymous senses as polysemous than vice versa, §3.1). Additionally, in contrast to previous work, we use an alignment-based method which will be able to correctly treat figurative polysemy. We create this annotation layer using a simple method that exploits recent advances in language modelling; although the annotation layer we produce is synthetic, the F1-score that our model attained on a small evaluation set that we produced was .97, indicating that it is of high quality.

In future work, we hope to enhance WordNet with more information. Lemmas in the OED are annotated with phonetic information; this could be used to infer homophony, which occurs which two unrelated meanings use the same phonetic form (even if they do not necessarily use the same orthographic form). An example is the word *base*, which is homophonous with the word *bass*. Additionally, if more complex models could be developed to produce a high quality sense-to-sense mapping to the OED, then we could leverage information the fine-grained senses in the OED contain about the dates of sense emergence, to make WordNet diachronic. This would be very useful in the study of language change.

Acknowledgements

We would like to thank the Oxford University Press (OUP) for giving us access to the OED research API, which made this work possible. In particular, we would like to thank Elinor Hawkes from the OUP for helping us with this.

8. Bibliographical References

Amaro, R., Chaves, R. P., Marrafa, P., and Mendes, S. (2006). Enriching WordNets with new relations and with event and argument structures. In *Proceedings of the 7th International Conference on Computational Linguistics and Intelligent Text Processing*, CICLing'06, page 28–40, Berlin, Heidelberg. Springer-Verlag.

Bird, S., Klein, E., and Loper, E. (2009). *Natural language processing with Python: Analyzing text with the natural language toolkit.* O'Reilly Media, Inc.

Devlin, J., Chang, M.-W., Lee, K., and Toutanova, K. (2019). BERT: Pre-training of deep bidirectional transformers for language understanding. In *Proceedings of the 2019 Conference of the North American Chapter of the Association for Computational Linguistics: Human Language Technologies, Volume 1 (Long and Short Papers)*, pages 4171–4186, Minneapolis, Minnesota, June. Association for Computational Linguistics.

Freihat, A. A., Giunchiglia, F., and Dutta, B. (2013). Regular polysemy in WordNet and pattern based approach. *International Journal On Advances in Intelligent Systems*, 6.

Ilan Kernerman, et al., editors. (2020). *Proceedings of the 2020 Globalex Workshop on Linked Lexicography*, Marseille, France, May. European Language Resources Association.

Koch, P. (2016). Meaning change and semantic shifts. In Päivi Juvonen et al., editors, *The Lexical Typology of Semantic Shifts*, chapter 2, pages 21–66. De Gruyter Mouton.

Lakoff, G. and Johnson, M. (1980). *Metaphors We Live By*. University of Chicago Press.

Lakoff, G. (1987). *Women, fire, and dangerous things: What categories reveal about the mind.* University of Chicago Press.

Lesk, M. (1986). Automatic sense disambiguation using machine readable dictionaries: How to tell a pine cone from an ice cream cone. In *Proceedings of the 5th Annual International Conference on Systems Documentation*, SIGDOC '86, page 24–26, New York, NY, USA. Association for Computing Machinery.

Liu, Y., Ott, M., Goyal, N., Du, J., Joshi, M., Chen, D., Levy, O., Lewis, M., Zettlemoyer, L., and Stoyanov, V. (2019). RoBERTa: A robustly optimized BERT pretraining approach. *CoRR*, abs/1907.11692.

Mendes, S. and Chaves, R. P. (2001). Enriching WordNet with qualia information. In *Proceedings of NAACL 2001 Workshop on WordNet and Other Lexical Resources*.

Navigli, R., Litkowski, K. C., and Hargraves, O. (2007). SemEval-2007 task 07: Coarse-grained English all-words task. In *Proceedings of the Fourth International Workshop on Semantic Evaluations (SemEval-2007)*, pages 30–35, Prague, Czech Republic, June. Association for Computational Linguistics.

Navigli, R. (2006). Meaningful clustering of senses helps boost word sense disambiguation performance. In *Proceedings of the 21st International Conference on Computational Linguistics and 44th Annual Meeting of the Association for Computational Linguistics*, pages 105–112, Sydney, Australia, July. Association for Computational Linguistics.

Ni, J., Ábrego, G. H., Constant, N., Ma, J., Hall, K. B., Cer, D., and Yang, Y. (2021). Sentence-T5: Scalable sentence encoders from pre-trained text-to-text models. *CoRR*, abs/2108.08877.

Pennington, J., Socher, R., and Manning, C. (2014). GloVe: Global vectors for word representation. In *Proceedings of the 2014 Conference on Empirical Methods in Natural Language Processing (EMNLP)*, pages 1532–1543, Doha, Qatar, October. Association for Computational Linguistics.

Piantadosi, S. T., Tily, H., and Gibson, E. (2012). The communicative function of ambiguity in language. *Cognition*, 122(3):280–291.

Puşcaşu, G. and Mititelu, V. B. (2008). Annotation of WordNet verbs with TimeML event classes. In *Proceedings of the Sixth International Conference on Language Resources and Evaluation (LREC'08)*, Marrakech, Morocco, May. European Language Resources Association (ELRA).

Pustejovsky, J. (1995). *The generative lexicon*. MIT Press.

Reimers, N. and Gurevych, I. (2019). Sentence-BERT: Sentence embeddings using Siamese BERT-networks. In *Proceedings of the 2019 Conference on Empirical Methods in Natural Language Processing and the 9th International Joint Conference on Natural Language Processing (EMNLP-IJCNLP)*, pages 3982–3992, Hong Kong, China, November. Association for Computational Linguistics.

Song, K., Tan, X., Qin, T., Lu, J., and Liu, T.-Y. (2020). MPNet: Masked and permuted pre-training for language understanding. In H. Larochelle, et al., editors, *Advances in Neural Information Processing Systems*, volume 33, pages 16857–16867. Curran Associates, Inc.

Utt, J. and Padó, S. (2011). Ontology-based distinction between polysemy and homonymy. In *Proceedings of the Ninth International Conference on Computational Semantics (IWCS 2011)*.

Vaswani, A., Shazeer, N., Parmar, N., Uszkoreit, J., Jones, L., Gomez, A. N., Kaiser, L. u., and Polosukhin, I. (2017). Attention is all you need. In I. Guyon, et al., editors, *Advances in Neural Information Processing Systems*, volume 30. Curran Associates, Inc.

Veale, T. (2004). Polysemy and category structure in WordNet: An evidential approach. In *Proceedings of the Fourth International Conference on Language Resources and Evaluation (LREC'04)*, Lisbon, Portugal, May. European Language Resources Association (ELRA).

9. Language Resource References

Ahmadi, S., McCrae, J. P., Nimb, S., Khan, F., Monachini, M., Pedersen, B., Declerck, T., Wissik, T., Bellandi, A., Pisani, I., Troelsgård, T., Olsen, S., Krek, S., Lipp, V., Váradi, T., Simon, L., Gyorffy, A., Tiberius, C., Schoonheim, T., Ben Moshe,

Y., Rudich, M., Abu Ahmad, R., Lonke, D., Kovalenko, K., Langemets, M., Kallas, J., Dereza, O., Fransen, T., Cillessen, D., Lindemann, D., Alonso, M., Salgado, A., Luis Sancho, J., Ureña-Ruiz, R.-J., Porta Zamorano, J., Simov, K., Osenova, P., Kancheva, Z., Radev, I., Stanković, R., Perdih, A., and Gabrovsek, D. (2020). A multilingual evaluation dataset for monolingual word sense alignment. In *Proceedings of the 12th Language Resources and Evaluation Conference*, pages 3232–3242, Marseille, France, May. European Language Resources Association.

Calabrese, A., Bevilacqua, M., and Navigli, R. (2020). Fatality killed the cat or: BabelPic, a multimodal dataset for non-concrete concepts. In *Proceedings of the 58th Annual Meeting of the Association for Computational Linguistics*, pages 4680–4686, Online, July. Association for Computational Linguistics.

de Melo, G. (2014). Etymological Wordnet: Tracing the history of words. In *Proceedings of the Ninth International Conference on Language Resources and Evaluation (LREC'14)*, pages 1148–1154, Reykjavik, Iceland, May. European Language Resources Association (ELRA).

Deng, J., Dong, W., Socher, R., Li, L.-J., Li, K., and Fei-Fei, L. (2009). ImageNet: A large-scale hierarchical image database. In *2009 IEEE Conference on Computer Vision and Pattern Recognition*, pages 248–255.

McCrae, J., Montiel-Ponsoda, E., and Cimiano, P., (2012). *Integrating WordNet and Wiktionary with lemon*, pages 25–34. Springer Berlin Heidelberg, Berlin, Heidelberg.

Meyer, C. M. and Gurevych, I. (2011). What psycholinguists know about chemistry: Aligning Wiktionary and WordNet for increased domain coverage. In *Proceedings of 5th International Joint Conference on Natural Language Processing*, pages 883–892, Chiang Mai, Thailand, November. Asian Federation of Natural Language Processing.

Miller, T. and Gurevych, I. (2014). WordNet—Wikipedia—Wiktionary: Construction of a three-way alignment. In *Proceedings of the Ninth International Conference on Language Resources and Evaluation (LREC'14)*, pages 2094–2100, Reykjavik, Iceland, May. European Language Resources Association (ELRA).

Miller, G. A., Chodorow, M., Landes, S., Leacock, C., and Thomas, R. G. (1994). Using a semantic concordance for sense identification. In *Proceedings of the Workshop on Human Language Technology*, HLT '94, page 240–243, USA. Association for Computational Linguistics.

Miller, G. A. (1995). WordNet: A lexical database for English. *Commun. ACM*, 38(11):39–41, November.

Navigli, R., Bevilacqua, M., Conia, S., Montagnini, D., and Cecconi, F. (2021). Ten years of BabelNet: A survey. In Zhi-Hua Zhou, editor, *Proceedings of the Thirtieth International Joint Conference on Artificial Intelligence, IJCAI-21*, pages 4559–4567. International Joint Conferences on Artificial Intelligence Organization, 8.

Tan, L. and Bond, F. (2011). Building and annotating the linguistically diverse NTU-MC (NTU-multilingual corpus). In *Proceedings of the 25th Pacific Asia Conference on Language, Information and Computation*, pages 362–371, Singapore, December. Institute of Digital Enhancement of Cognitive Processing, Waseda University.

A. List of Homonyms in WordNet

The list below contains the 297 wordforms which are identified as exhibiting homonymy in the PWN. The 13 wordforms which appear in the within-POS variant but not the between-POS variant are marked with an asterisk:

adder, agora, alum, angle, apostrophe, armed, ass, ball, bank, bard, bark, bar, bath, batter, bat, beat, bill, birr, boil, bole, bongo, boom, boss*, bowl, boxer, boxing, box, bracer, buffer, buff, bumble, bust, butter, bye, calf, canon, caper, carbonado, castor, cheese, chela, chess, clove, coma, compact, compound, content, con, copper, corn, corona, cosmos, courser, cover, cramp*, croup, cube, curry, dam, deuce, dick, diet, ding, distemper, dock, don, dory, down, drill*, dub, excise, fag*, fan, fawn, feller, fen, file, filicide, filing, filler, flag*, flat, flicker, flop*, flounce, forte, fossa, full, fuse, gall, game, gauntlet, genial, gill, gin, gnarl, gnome, gobbler, gobble, go, grad, grate, grave, gray, gum, gutter, gyro, ha-ha, hack, hakim, hash, hatched, hatching, hatch, hawker, hobby, homer, hood, house, hypo, impress, indent, iridic, jack, jar*, jumper, junk, key, khan, kip, kit, krona, lame, launch, laver, letter, lien, limb, lime, ling, lister, lithic, lumber, lunger, manakin, mandarin, mangle, mare, mark, match, matted, matting, mat, mean, meter, metric, mew, mil, miss, mogul, molar, mole, monstrance, mood, mould, mow, mummy, mush, must, nag, nanny, nap, net, nit, ore, paddle, pall, para, pass, patter, peewee, periwinkle, permit, phone, pile, pink, pipe, piping, pix, plantain, plash, plight, plonk, plump, poacher, poach, poise, poker, poke, poll, pom-pom, pool, pop, port, pot, psi, punch, punter, pyrene, pyrrhic, python, quack, quark, quid, quint, quiver, race, racy, rad, raft, raised, ramp, real, reef, rent, rest, retort, rip*, roach, rocket, rocky, rock, rook, root, round, router, rout, rue, rush, sack*, sake, salve, samba, sampler, sardine, scale, school, sconce, scope, scourer, scruple, scuffle, seal, seamy, secrete, set, sewer, shock, skipper, slug*, snarl, sod, sol, soma, sort, sound, spade, spanker, spell*, spike, stall*, stater, stay, stereo, still, stinger, stoop, strain, tack, talus, tanka, telluric, temple, test, tiller, timber, toot, topi, tower, tribune, tuck, tuna, unionized, verse, viola, yen, zip*

Author Index

Association for Computational Linguistics
209 N. Eighth Street
Stroudsburg, Pennsylvania 18360

ISBN 978-1-7138-6122-5

CURRAN ASSOCIATES INC.
proceedings.com